Marijuana
Home Grower's Manual

Marijuana

Home Grower's Manual

Billy McCann

Green Candy Press

Published by Green Candy Press
San Francisco, CA
www.greencandypress.com

First Published by Guerrilla Publishing in hardback 2003

Printed in Canada by Transcontinental Printing Inc.
Massively distributed by P.G.W.

This book contains information about illegal substances specifically the plant Cannabis Sativa and its derivative products. Green Candy Press would like to emphasize that cannabis is a controlled substance in North America and throughout much of the world. As such, the use and cultivation of cannabis can carry heavy penalties that may threaten an individual's liberty and livelihood.

The aim of the Publisher is to educate and entertain. Whatever the Publisher's view on the validity of current legislation, we do not in any way condone the use of prohibited substances.

ISBN 978-1-931160-56-8

This book is dedicated to my grandchildren;
let them not inherit a world of consistently poor decisions!

Also the following:
The many brave parents who cry with their children as they experience jointly the horror of drug addiction. These are the victims of street dealers and a confused government; Marijuana smokers are a far-removed and a very different breed from the users and abusers of a heavier drug regime. Hard drugs are not a natural progression from smoking cannabis. Progression is encouraged through the source of supply. Drug dealers rarely stock just one drug; they have access to many others, and are more than willing to get them for you; they make far more profit from them so why wouldn't they? Dealers depend on your dependency!

Support your National drug organizations and help get Marijuana legalized. Keep our kids away from drug dealers.

My thanks go to my very special family, who have given me their support and encouragement on days when completion of this book seemed to be a million miles away

Thanks, also to all of the contributors who have since become my friends especially Brian Bennet and POT TV and High Times for recognizing the value of this journal and introducing it to the American public. Of course there are some contributors who wish to remain anonymous for various reasons, but who are none the less important to me and the world of Marijuana.

Foreword

This is without doubt the most comprehensive, up-to-date book available for those of you who want to know more about cannabis, including material on how to grow it, its origins, its effects on society, a view on the law, its place in religion, how commerce deals with it and the culture.

For me, growing cannabis is as relaxing as smoking it. The plant responds quickly, grows almost before your eyes, and has a practical end. I have taken great pains to ensure that my book provides you with everything you'll ever need to know in the simplest terms, including enough additional information to satisfy the seasoned grower or just the plain interested.

Cannabis is the most widely used illegal drug on this planet, and one of the most intensively studied substances of all time, causing the most controversy and provoking the strongest emotions from both anti and pro groups. We see the argument for legalization creeping slowly but surely into the political agenda and according to recent polls, opinions are evenly divided between reform and prohibition, where once they were six to one against. It was recently confirmed that 16 to 30 year olds are the largest users of cannabis, although the rise in use is sharpest among older adults. This latter could be explained by the likelihood that many of these individuals may be existing or former users who have simply moved into an older age group, although first-time use among elderly citizens, particularly for medicinal reasons, is becoming more common.

By buying this book you have cast your vote for reform: **WELL DONE!** By growing cannabis you are further enforcing public opinion that the law should be changed. This will sever your need to deal with street drug dealers and the varieties of poison they peddle.

Contents

Mary Jane Puff Weed Ganja Grass Skunk Wacky Backy Dope Green Herb Skunk Gear Joint Hash Jazz Fags Pot Doobles Bush

Whatever you want to call it, you have to understand that at the time of writing this book, the growing or smoking of marijuana is still illegal in *the United States* and indeed most of the world to some degree.

Neither the author, nor the publisher condone or encourage anyone to break the law in any way. This book is for educational and reference purposes and doesn't promote illegal activity in countries where the growing or use of marijuana is illegal.

"I believe that every man, woman, and child of this earth should be allowed his or her basic human right of freedom. A freedom of choice, a freedom to indulge and a freedom to enjoy, while always maintaining a healthy respect for his fellow man.

By this gift of nature being made illegal, we are being denied our Human Right to Freedom. God gave us life, God gave us freedom and God gave us herbs to heal ourselves... Our right to life is protected... Our right to freedom is protected, but our rights to the herb have been taken from us. Who is man to deny us God's gifts"

—Author

1

Introducing Cannabis

Marijuana and Myth

1. Marijuana causes brain damage?

The most celebrated study claiming to show brain damage is the rhesus monkey study of Dr. Robert Heath, done in the late 1970s. A distinguished panel of scientists sponsored by the Institute of Medicine and the National Academy of Sciences reviewed this study. Their results were published under the title, *Marijuana and Health* in 1982. Heath's work was sharply criticized for its insufficient sample size (only four monkeys), its failure to control experimental bias, and the misidentification of normal monkey brain structure as "damaged." Actual studies of human populations of marijuana users have shown no evidence of brain damage. For example, two studies from 1977, published in the *Journal of the American Medical Association* (JAMA) showed no evidence of brain damage in heavy users of marijuana. That same year, the American Medical Association (AMA) officially came out in favor of decriminalizing marijuana. That's not the sort of thing you'd expect if the AMA thought marijuana damaged the brain.

2. Marijuana damages the reproductive system?

This claim is based chiefly on the work of Dr. Gabriel Nahas, who experimented with tissue (cells) isolated in petri dishes, and the work of researchers who dosed animals with near-lethal amounts of cannabinoids (i.e., the intoxicating part of marijuana). The scientific community has rejected Nahas's generalizations as being invalid. In the case of the animal experiments, the animals that survived their ordeal returned to normal within 30 days of the end of the experiment. Studies of actual human populations have failed to demonstrate that marijuana adversely affects the reproductive system.

1

3. Marijuana is a "gateway" drug; it leads to hard drugs?

This is one of the more persistent myths. A real-world example of what happens when marijuana is readily available can be found in Holland. The Dutch partially legalized marijuana in the 1970s. Since then, hard drug—heroin and cocaine—use has DECLINED substantially. If marijuana really were a gateway drug, one would have expected use of hard drugs to have gone up, not down. This apparent "negative gateway" effect has also been observed in the United States. Studies done in the early 1970s showed a negative correlation between the use of marijuana and use of alcohol. A 1993 Rand Corporation study that compared drug use in states that had decriminalized marijuana versus those that had not, found that where marijuana was more available—the states that had decriminalized it—hard drug abuse as measured by emergency room episodes decreased. In short, what science and actual experience tell us is that marijuana tends to substitute for the much more dangerous hard drugs like alcohol, cocaine, and heroin. If you are looking for a gateway, then first find the gatekeeper! The dealer! There's your culprit. Grow your own or go to a cannabis café and you won't have to deal with a dealer and so won't be exposed to new drugs.

4. Marijuana suppresses the immune system?

As with the studies claiming to show damage to the reproductive system, this myth is based on studies where animals were given extremely high, and in many cases, near-lethal doses of cannabinoids. These results have never been duplicated in human beings. Interestingly, two studies done in 1978 and one done in 1988 showed that hashish and marijuana may have actually stimulated the immune system in the people studied.

5. Marijuana is much more dangerous than tobacco?

Smoked marijuana contains about the same amount of carcinogens as an equivalent amount of tobacco. It should be remembered, however, that a heavy tobacco smoker consumes much more tobacco than a heavy marijuana smoker consumes marijuana. This is because smoked tobacco, with a 90% addiction rate, is the most addictive of all drugs while marijuana is less addictive than caffeine. Two other factors are important. The first is that paraphernalia laws directed against marijuana users in some countries and in some states, make it difficult to smoke safely. These laws make water pipes and bongs, which filter some of the carcinogens out of the smoke, illegal and, hence, unavailable. The second is that, if marijuana were legal, it would be more economical to have cannabis drinks like bhang (a traditional drink in the Middle East) or tea, which are totally noncarcinogenic. This is in stark contrast with "smokeless" tobacco products like snuff, which can cause cancer of the mouth and throat. When all of these facts are taken together, it can be clearly seen that the reverse is true: marijuana is much SAFER than tobacco.

6. Legal Marijuana would cause highway carnage?

Although marijuana, when used to the point of intoxication, does impair performance in a manner similar to alcohol, actual studies of the effect of marijuana on the automobile accident rate suggest that it poses less of a hazard than alcohol. When a random sample of fatal accident victims was studied, it was initially found that marijuana was associated with relatively as many accidents as alcohol. In other words, the number of accident victims intoxicated on marijuana relative to the number of marijuana users in society gave a ratio similar to that for accident victims intoxicated on alcohol relative to the total number of alcohol users. However, a closer examination of the victims revealed that around 85% of the people intoxicated on marijuana were also intoxicated on alcohol. For people only intoxicated on marijuana, the rate was much lower than for alcohol alone. This finding has been supported by other research using completely different methods. For example, an economic analysis of the effects of decriminalization on marijuana usage found that American states that had reduced penalties for marijuana possession experienced a rise in marijuana use and a decline in alcohol use, with the result that fatal highway accidents decreased. This would suggest that, far from causing carnage, legal marijuana might actually save lives.

7. Marijuana "flattens" human brainwaves?

This has since been shown to be a complete lie perpetrated by the Partnership for a Drug-Free America. A few years ago, they ran a TV ad that purported to show, first, a normal human brainwave, and second, a flat brainwave from a 14-year-old "on marijuana." When researchers called up the TV networks to complain about this commercial, the Partnership had to pull it from the air. It seems that the Partnership faked the flat "marijuana brainwave." In reality, marijuana has the effect of slightly INCREASING alpha wave activity. Alpha waves are associated with meditative and relaxed states, which are, in turn, often associated with human creativity.

8. Marijuana is more potent today than in the past?

This myth is the result of bad data. The researchers who made the claim of increased potency used as their baseline the THC content of marijuana seized by police in the early 1970s. Poor storage of this marijuana in unair-conditioned evidence rooms had caused it to deteriorate and decline in potency before any chemical assay was performed. Contemporaneous, independent assays of unseized "street" marijuana from the early 1970s showed a potency equivalent to that of modern "street" marijuana. Actually, the most potent form of this drug that was generally available was sold legally in the 1920s and 1930s by the pharmaceutical company Smith-Klein under the name American Cannabis.

9. Marijuana impairs short-term memory?

This is true but misleading. Any impairment of short-term memory disappears when one is no longer under the influence of marijuana. Often, the short-term memory effect is paired with a reference to Dr. Heath's poor rhesus monkeys to imply that the condition is permanent.

10. Marijuana lingers in the body like DDT?

This is also true but misleading. Cannabinoids are fat soluble as are innumerable nutrients and, yes, some poisons like DDT. For example, the essential nutrient, vitamin A, is fat soluble but one never hears people who favor marijuana prohibition making this comparison.

11. There're over eight-hundred chemicals in marijuana

Again, true but misleading. The August 31, 1990, issue of the magazine *Science* notes that of the 800 or more volatile chemicals present in roasted COFFEE, only 21 have actually been tested on animals and 16 of these cause cancer in rodents. Yet coffee remains legal and is generally considered fairly safe.

12. No one has ever died of a marijuana overdose?

This is true. It was put in to see if you are paying attention. Animal tests have revealed that extremely high doses of cannabinoids are needed to have lethal effect. This has led scientists to conclude that the ratio of the amount of cannabinoids necessary to get a person intoxicated (i.e., stoned) relative to the amount necessary to kill them is 1 to 40,000. In other words, to overdose, you would have to consume 40,000 times as much marijuana as you needed to get stoned. In contrast, the ratio for alcohol varies between 1 to 4 and 1 to 10. It's easy to see how upwards of 5000 people die from alcohol overdoses every year and no one EVER dies of marijuana overdoses.

Facts and Fun

1. The best way to smuggle dope into the country is to hide it up a dogs ass. That way if the sniffer dogs go to the dogs as no one will ever take any notice..it's a dogs handshake

2. Marijuana is Mexican slang for cannabis and the lyrics to "La Cucaracha" described how a Mexican soldier wouldn't go to war until he had a joint.

3. Marijuana wasn't made illegal in California until 1915

4. Jimi Hendrix sent out 3,000 joints to random addresses taken from the phone book on Valentines Day, 1967. Wonder how many went to his funeral or even sent a thank-you note?

5. In 1980 Sir Paul McCartney was jailed for ten days in Japan for cannabis possession.

6. Bill Clinton admits to smoking pot but denies inhaling. This is of course the same man who admitted to having a blowjob and said it wasn't sex! It seems he confesses to not one but two mind-altering experiences, yet didn't fully enjoy either of them. *YEAH RIGHT!*

7. Marijuana plants get more light than the dopeheads who smoke it?

8. Haile Selassie (Ras Tafari) did not smoke dope, although the herb is hailed as sacred by Rastafarians.

9. A dope smoker is more likely to overdose on Kentucky Fried Chicken and Mars Bars than on weed.

10. Watching *Big Brother* damages more brain cells than smoking marijuana.

11. Do sniffer dogs develop a drug habit?

12. A smoker ran out of weed and began to smoke curry powder mixed with shredded coconut and cream.... Police found him in a mild Korma.

13. Three great hits: "Killing Me Softly with This Bong" by the Fugees, "Smoke Gets in Your Eyes" by Brian Ferry, and "Puff the Magic Dragon" by Peter, Paul and Mary (who we've all seen at some time or other, haven't we?).

14. Cross reaction is a real problem and something you might consider as a defense. Drugs from the Ibuprofen range can cross react in the body and give the effect that you have used cannabis if you are teste. *That is to say that some "over the counter" and prescription drugs can give a test result of "positive" drug use.*

Refer to chapter 17 section 9 "False Positives" also referred to as Cross Reaction.
15. According to estimates derived from the U.S. Census Bureau and Monitoring the Future data, approximately 600,000 of the nearly 4 million U.S. high school seniors drive under the influence of marijuana. Approximately 38,000 seniors reported that they had crashed while driving under the influence of marijuana in 2001

Eleven states make it a crime to drive with any amount of illicit substance in one's system. The states with so-called zero-tolerance laws are

- Arizona
- Illinois
- Minnesota
- Utah
- Georgia
- Iowa
- Pennsylvania
- Wisconsin
- Indiana
- Michigan
- Rhode Island

Nevada has a law that sets impairment guidelines for blood and urine testing for certain drugs, including marijuana, marijuana metabolites, heroin, methamphetamine and cocaine.

The bill in Congress, which passed both the House and Senate as part of transportation packages and is now being considered in a conference committee, is modelled after the federal anti-drunken-driving laws that are widely credited with making American roads safer. The law required states to adopt the 0.08% blood-alcohol standard by 2004 or lose federal transportation money.

In 2003, 17,013 people died in alcohol-related traffic crashes, a 3% drop from 2002. In 1982, 60% of the traffic fatalities across the nation were linked to alcohol; federal studies say alcohol is a factor in 40% of the traffic fatalities today.

No simple test

But it's clear that fighting drugged driving will be considerably more complicated than the war on drunken driving:

For now, there is no widely available roadside testing device that can quickly detect drugs in a person's body, as the Breathalyzer does for alcohol.

Researchers are developing saliva and urine tests that eventually could make roadside drug tests as easy as a Breathalyzer. But the wide variety of illegal, prescription and over-the-counter drugs that can impair drivers — and the countless ways in which drugs can affect the body — make such tests a more complex challenge.

Zero-tolerance laws for drugged driving likely would spur a wave of lawsuits over individual rights.

The 20 Commandments, or Joint Etiquette

If you have seen the movie *Friday,* then you probably are familiar with Smokey's etiquette on smoking a joint: "Puff, puff, pass...puff, puff, pass..." If you have ever sat around your apartment smoking with friends, you have more than likely come up with some groundbreaking rules of etiquette of your own (as well as some pretty great stories to tell other friends who were absent). Here are some suggestions for Joint Etiquette compiled partially from websites dedicated to the right way to smoke.

1. The person who rolls the joint gets first hit, no matter whose weed it is.
2. Always compliment good joint making skills.
3. Always share your munchies.
4. Never get the joint all wet when you toke it...a wet one is disgusting!
5. Never complain someone else's weed is no good—if you don't like it, you don't have to smoke it!
6. Always smoke with the guy you buy it from—politeness counts.
7. If you spill the bong, fill it back up with water.
8. If someone gets you high, say thank you.
9. Remember if someone gets you high, it's your responsibility to get that person high sometime in the future.
10. Never pass on the roach end. Declare the joint as spent.
11. If someone who's smoked asks for a sip of your cola you must give him some. (A dry mouth is not fun.)
12. Converse of 11: If you ask for a sip, don't take a large gulp.
13. PRACTICE SAFE TOKES: Diseases like herpes can be passed on through sharing a joint. Since a condom won't fit over your head to protect you then try smoking "percies" (small personal joints).
14. Dont bogart.
15. Thou shalt not turn down a smoke. NOT EVER!
16. It is very impolite to hand someone an empty bowl, without notifying that person of its possible cashed-ness. A proper warning would be: "Here ya go...I think it might be cashed."

17. The person who fills the bowl is given the opportunity to take the first hit. It doesn't matter whose bowl it is.

18. The person who brought the weed picks the music.

19. When using a bong, DON'T blow out the ashes, unless that's what the "home-owner" does.

20. NEVER go to someone's house EXPECTING them to catch you a buzz. Of course, there are exceptions to this rule....

Resin Can Kill You!

Governments like to warn us about the supposed dangers of cannabis, most of which are downright lies, but they keep very quiet about one danger which is both very real and a direct result of anti-marijuana policies. Because it's illegal and so often supplied by profit-motivated criminal networks, street cannabis—particularly hash—is often of low quality and can contain contaminants.

In the US we suffer a particular problem with some resin or hash. A nine bar to those who buy larger amounts, on average contain ten grams (third of an ounce) of resin and up to 200g (about 7 ounces) of inert, ground-up shade leaf that has absolutely no THC or smoking value whatsoever. The remainder consists of 40g of various noxious substances. Using a scientific process known as mass spectrometry, it was found generally that the most common substances that make up your nine bar are:

• **Tranquilizers or other barbiturates** (like ketamine) **to stone you**
• **Glue**
• **Henna**
• **Dyes**
• **Carcinogenic solvents such as Toluene and Benzene** (from gasoline, turpentine or diesel)
• **Pine resin** (to mask the smell of the above)
• **Plastic** (usually coat hangers, often inserted during re-pressing bars using gasoline or diesel as the solvent)

Other ingredients found in various represses are:
• **Brick dust or sand** (this gives you your rock burns or hot rocks)
• **Wax or similar substance like shoe or car polish**

- **Condensed milk powder** (burn some and you'll recognize the smell)
- **Tar or bitumen**
- **Digested organic matter** (usually dog or cow crap, which is probably why it's sometimes know as shit, because it really is)

Whenever you buy marijuana from an unfamiliar source you run the risk of smoking unknown additives, dangerous chemicals, or insecticides, and you're definitely paying more than if you grow your own. You're basically allowing yourself to be ripped off by people who don't care about you or your health. Growing your own is the only way to guarantee your health and safety. So say no to the inferior crap and support NORML and other groups in their fight to legalize cannabis.

2

Marijuana Origins and history

Cannabis is a plant of great historical importance. Shown below is a brief timeline of its history.

Cannabis Chronology

2700 BC China: First written record of cannabis use, in the pharmacopoeia of Shen Nung, one of the fathers of Chinese medicine.

2000 BC Egypt: Made as a drink in ancient Thebes.

1000 BC India: Used as an herbal medicine.

550 BC Persia: The Persian prophet Zoroaster gives hemp first place in the sacred text, the *Zend-Avesta,* which lists over 10,000 medicinal plants.

500 BC Tibet: Considered to be an extremely holy plant.

450BC The Greek historian Herodotus describes the Scythians of central Asia throwing hemp onto heated stones under canvas: "as it burns, it smokes like incense and the smell of it makes them drunk."

200 BC Israel: Used as a medicine by the Essenes.

100 BC Chinese make paper from cannabis and mulberry.

AD 45 St. Mark establishes the Ethiopian Coptic Church. The Copts claim that marijuana as a sacrament has a lineage descending from the Jewish sect, the Essenes, who are considered to be responsible for the Dead Sea Scrolls.

70 Roman Emperor Nero's surgeon, Dioscorides, praises cannabis for making "the stoutest cords" and for it's medical properties.

400 Cannabis cultivated for the first time in England at Old Buckeham Mare.

500 First botanical drawing of cannabis appears in *Constantinopolitanus.*

600 Germans, Franks, Vikings, etc., made paper from cannabis.

700 Middle East: Brought divine revelations to Sufi priests.

800 Mohammed allows cannabis, but forbids alcohol use.

1000 The English word *hempe* first listed in a dictionary. Moslems produce hashish for medical and social use.

1150 Moslems use cannabis to start Europe's first paper mill. Most paper is made from cannabis for the next 850 years.

1200 Europe: banned as medicine by inquisition.

1484 Pope Innocent VIII singles out cannabis as an unholy sacrament of the Satanic mass.

1494 Hemp paper-making starts in England.

1545 Spanish bring cannabis cultivation to Chile.

1554 Spanish bring cannabis cultivation to Peru.

1563 Queen Elizabeth I decrees that landowners with 60 acres (0.243 km^2) or more must grow cannabis else face a £5 fine.

1564 King Philip of Spain follows lead of Queen Elizabeth and orders cannabis to be grown throughout his Empire from modern-day Argentina to Oregon.

1606 British take cannabis to Canada to be cultivated mainly for maritime uses.

1611 British start cultivating cannabis in Virginia.

1619 Virginia colony makes cannabis cultivation mandatory, followed by most other colonies. Europe pays hemp bounties.

1631 Cannabis used for bartering throughout American colonies.

1632 Pilgrims bring cannabis to New England.

1753 Cannabis Sativa classified by Linnaeus.

1776 Declaration of Independence drafted on cannabis paper.

1783 Cannabis Indica classified by Lamarck.

1791 President Washington sets duties on cannabis to encourage domestic industry. Jefferson calls cannabis "a necessity" and urges farmers to grow cannabis instead of tobacco.

1807 Napoleon signs the Treaty of Tilset with Czar Alexander of Russia, which cuts off all legal Russian trade with Britain. Britain begins to blackmail, and press-gang American sailors into illegally trading in Russian hemp.

1808 Napoleon wants to place French Troops at Russian ports to ensure the Treaty of Tilset is complied with. The Czar refuses and turns a blind eye to Britain's illegal trade in cannabis.

1812 On June 19 America declares war on Britain. June 24th Napoleon invades

Russia aiming to put an end to Britain's main supply of cannabis. By the end of the year the Russian winter and army had destroyed most of Napoleon's invading force.

1835 The Club de Hashichines, whose bohemian membership included the poet Baudelaire, is founded.

1839 Homeopathy journal *American Provers' Union* publishes first of many reports on the effects of cannabis.

1841 Dr. W.B. O'Shaughnessy of Scotland works in India then introduces cannabis to Western medicine. In the following 50 years hundreds of medical papers are written on the medical benefits of cannabis.

1845 Psychologist and "inventor" of modern psychopharmacology and psychoto-mimetic drug treatment, Jacques-Joseph Moreau de Tours documents physical and mental benefits of cannabis.

1857 *The Hasheesh Eater* by Fitz Hugh Ludlow is published. Smith Brothers of Edinburgh start to market a highly active extract of Cannabis Indica used as a basis for innumerable tinctures.

1860 First governmental commission study of Cannabis and health conducted by Ohio State Medical Society.

1870 Cannabis is listed in the U.S. Pharmacopoeia as a medicine for various ailments.

1876 Hashish served at American Centennial Exposition.

1890 Queen Victoria's personal physician, Sir Russell Reynolds, prescribes cannabis for menstrual cramps. He claims in the first issue of The Lancet, that cannabis "When pure and administered carefully, is one of the of the most valuable medicines we possess."

1895 The Indian Hemp Drug Commission concludes that cannabis has some medical uses, no addictive properties and a number of positive emotional and social benefits. This is also the time recorded as the first known use of the word *marijuana* for smoking dope by Pancho Villa's supporters in Sonora Mexico. The song "La Cucaracha" tells the story of one of Villa's men looking for his stash of "marijuana por fumar."

1910 African-American "reefer" use reported in jazz clubs of New Orleans, said to be influencing white people. Mexicans reported to be smoking cannabis in Texas. Newspaper tycoon Randolph Hearst has 800,000 acres of prime Mexican timberland seized from him by Villa and his men. Could this be the reason why his newspapers subsequently ran many stories portraying Negroes and Mexicans as frenzied beasts under the influence of marijuana?

1911 Hindus reported to be using "Gunjah" in San Francisco. South Africa starts to outlaw cannabis.

1912 The possibility of putting controls on the use of cannabis is raised at the first International Opium Conference.

1915 California outlaws cannabis.

1916 Recognizing that timber supplies are finite, USDA Bulletin 404 calls for new program of expansion of cannabis to replace uses of timber by industry.

1919 Texas outlaws cannabis.

1923 The South African delegate to the League of Nations claims mine workers are not as productive after using "dagga" (cannabis) and calls for international controls. Britain insists on further research before any controls are imposed.

1924 At the second International Opiates Conference the Egyptian delegate claims that serious problems are associated with hashish use and calls for immediate international controls. A subcommittee is formed and listens to the Egyptian and Turkish delegations while Britain abstains. The conference declares cannabis a narcotic and recommends strict international control.

1925 The "Panama Canal Zone Report" conducted due to the level of cannabis use by soldiers in the area concludes that there is no evidence that cannabis use is habit-forming or deleterious. The report recommends that no action be taken to prevent the use or sale of cannabis.

1928 September 28th: The Dangerous Drugs Act 1925 becomes law and cannabis is made illegal in Britain.

1930 Louis Armstrong is arrested in Los Angeles for possession of cannabis.

1931 The Federal Bureau of Narcotics is formed with Harry Anslinger appointed as its head.

1937 Following action by the Federal Bureau of Narcotics and a campaign by newspaper magnate William Randolph Hearst, a prohibitive tax is put on hemp in the United States, effectively destroying the industry. Anslinger testifies to congress that marijuana is the most violence-causing drug known to man. The objections by the American Medical Association (The AMA only realized that "marijuana' was in fact cannabis two days before the start of hearing) and the National Oil Seed Institute are rejected.

1938 The February edition of *Popular Mechanics* (written before the Marijuana Transfer Tax was passed) declares "Hemp—the New Billion Dollar Crop."

1941 Cannabis dropped from the American Pharmacopoeia. *Popular Mechanics* magazine reveal details of Henry Ford's plastic car made using cannabis and fueled by cannabis. Henry Ford continued to illegally grow cannabis for some years after the Federal ban, hoping to become independent of the petroleum industry.

1943 Both the U.S. and German governments urge their patriotic farmers to grow hemp for the war effort. The United States shows farmers a short film—*Hemp for Victory*—which the government later pretends never existed. The editor of *Military Journal* states that although some military personnel smoke cannabis he does not view this as a problem.

1944 New York Mayor LaGuardia's marijuana commission reports that cannabis causes no violence at all and cites other positive results. Anslinger responds by denouncing LaGuardia and threatens doctors with prison sentences if they dare carry out independent research on cannabis.

1945 *Newsweek* reports that over 100,000 Americans use cannabis.

1948 Anslinger now declares that using cannabis causes the user to become peaceful and pacifistic. He also claims that the Communists would use cannabis to weaken the Americans' will to fight.

1951 *UN Bulletin of Narcotic Drugs* estimates 200 million cannabis users worldwide.

1952 First UK cannabis bust at the Number 11 Club, Soho.

1961 Anslinger heads U.S. delegation at UN Drugs Convention. New international restrictions are placed on cannabis aiming to eliminate its use within 25 years.

1962 Anslinger is sacked by President Kennedy. Kennedy may well have smoked cannabis in the White House.

1964 The first head shop is opened by the Thelin brothers in the United States.

1966 The folk singer Donovan becomes the first celebrity hippie to fall foul of the law over marijuana.

1967 In July over 3,000 people hold a mass "smoke-in" in Hyde Park in London. The same month, *The Times* carries a pro-legalization advertisement, which declares that "the laws against marijuana are immoral in principle and unworkable in practice." The signatories include David Dimbleby, Bernard Levin, and the Beatles.

1967 The most famous bust of all, on the home of Rolling Stone Keith Richards, uncovers marijuana. Richards and Mick Jagger are sentenced to prison for respectively three months and one year. The sentences prompt an outcry that culminates in Lord Rees Mogg's famous *Times* editorial "Who breaks a butterfly on a wheel?" The convictions were quashed on appeal.

1967 In New York, on Valentine's Day, Abbie Hoffman and the Yippies mail out 3000 joints to addresses chosen at random from the phone book. They offer these people the chance to discover what all the fuss is about, but remind them that they are now criminals for possessing cannabis. The mailing was secretly funded by Jimi Hendrix, and attracts huge publicity.

1968 A Home Office select committee, chaired by Baroness Wootton, looks at the "cannabis question." Its report concludes that cannabis is no more harmful than tobacco or alcohol, and recommends that the penalties for all marijuana offences be reduced. The Campaign against Cannabis use by U.S. Troops in Vietnam commences and soldiers switch to heroin.

1969 Incoming British Labor minister Jim Callaghan rejects the Wootton recommendations and introduces a new Misuse of Drugs Act, which prescribes a maximum five years' imprisonment for possession. The Act remains in force to this day.

1970 Canadian Le Dain report claims that the debate on the nonmedical use of cannabis "has all too often been based on hearsay, myth and ill-informed opinion about the effects of the drug." Marijuana Transfer Tax is declared unconstitutional by the U.S. Supreme Court.

1971 Misuse of Drugs Act lists cannabis as a Class B drug and bans its medical use despite the recommendation of the Wootton Report that "Preparations of cannabis and its derivatives should continue to be available on prescription for purposes of medical treatment and research." President Nixon declares drugs "America's public enemy No. 1."

1972 The White House passes a $1 billion anti-drug bill and Nixon again declares drugs "America's public enemy No. 1." The U.S. Government Shafer Report voices concern at the level of spending used to stop illicit drug use. From 1969–73 the level of spending rises over 1000%.

1973 President Nixon declares "We have turned the corner on drug addiction in America." Oregon becomes the first state to take steps toward legalization.

1975 Hundreds of doctors call on U.S. government to instigate further research on cannabis. Supreme Court of Alaska declares that "right of privacy" protects cannabis possession in the home. Limit for public possession is set at one ounce.

1976 Ford Administration bans government funding of medical research on cannabis. Pharmaceutical companies are allowed to carry out research on synthetic, manmade cannabis analogues. Holland adopts policy of tolerance to cannabis users. Robert Randal becomes first American to receive cannabis from Federal supplies under an Investigational New Drug (IND) program. Ford's chief advisor on drugs, Robert Dupont, declares that cannabis is less harmful than alcohol or tobacco and urges for its decriminalization. Disturbances erupt at the end of the Notting Hill carnival. BBC News reports: "Scores of young black men roamed the streets late into the night, openly smoking marijuana joints and listening to the nonstop pounding of reggae music."

1978 New Mexico becomes first U.S. state to make cannabis available for medical use.

1983 UK convictions for cannabis possession exceed 20,000, having risen from just under 15,000 in 1980. U.S. government instructs American Universities and researchers to destroy all 1966–76 Cannabis research work.

1988 In Washington, DEA Judge Francis Young concludes at the end of a lengthy legal process that "Marijuana in its natural form is one of the safest therapeutically active substances known to man." He recommends that medical use of marijuana should be allowed, for certain life- or sense-threatening illnesses. The DEA administrator rejects the ruling. U.S. Senate adds $2.6 billion to federal anti-drug efforts.

1989 Outgoing president Reagan declares victory in War on Drugs as being a major achievement of his administration. Secretary of State James Baker reports that the global war on narcotics production "is clearly not being won."

1990 The discovery of THC receptors in the human brain is reported in *Nature*.

1991 42,209 people are convicted of cannabis offences in the UK. 19,583 escape with cautions.

1993 Hempcore becomes the first British company to obtain a license to grow cannabis as the Home Office lifts restrictions on industrial hemp cultivation.

1994 Home Secretary Michael Howard increases maximum fines for possession from £500 (US $1030) to £2,500 (US $5151). Germany becomes the first European country apart from Holland to decriminalize possession of "small quantities of cannabis for occasional use." The Liberal-Democrat conference votes for a Royal Commission; the tabloid press reports that they support legalization! Key rings with leaves taken from Hempcore's first harvest are illegally sold in such publications as *Viz*. The Home Office are aware of the situation but do not prosecute Hempcore who could have been facing 15 years and an unlimited fine. Association of Cannabis Therapeutics talks to Department Of Health about possibility of legalizing cannabis for medical use.

1995 Channel 4 dedicates eight hours of programming to cannabis on Pot Night. The BBC responds with blatant anti-cannabis propaganda on *Panorama*. Ten-millionth cannabis arrests in the United States in July. Labor shadow minister Clare

Short says the subject of decriminalization should be discussed. She is immediately denounced by other leading Labor Politicians.

1995 UK Cannabis Internet Activists form to take the campaign to reform the UK cannabis laws to the global community. Their www site is presently visited by over 2000 people from around the world each week, has been featured in the national newspaper the *Mail* on Sunday, listed in *.Net* magazine, and continues to help people take the anti-prohibition message to the press and Members of Parliament. — **www.ukcia.org.**

1997 The newspaper *The Independent on Sunday* launches a "Decriminalize cannabis" campaign. They, like us, believe that a change will come with the newly elected Labor government; they are wrong, but they do organize a big demonstration in London in March of 1998, before dropping the campaign. These large demonstrations become an annual event thereafter, although no longer organized by the newspaper.

2001 At the start of the new administration in June 2001 the police in, South London UK announce that they will no longer give anyone found in possession of cannabis a criminal record and the issue of legalization became a major issue in the campaign for the leadership of the Conservative party.

2001 October: The government sets up a Select Committee to look at drugs policy. When giving evidence the Home Secretary (David Blunkett) announces his intention to move cannabis from class B to class C, making possession a non-arrestable offence.

July 2002 The down classification of cannabis to a class C drug is confirmed to take effect in July 2003.

January 2006 The whole UK concept is still a gray area and there are talks of reversing the process.

Brief History

Hemp was so highly regarded in the East that China named their country "Land of Mulberry and Hemp." Cultivation remains intensive there. In early Taoist rituals, mystic powers, well-being, and an experience of exultation was said to be found when cannabis was added to incense burners. In common with the practice of medicine in the rest of the ancient world, the early Chinese based their doctrine, in part, on the concept of demons. In Japan, Shinto priests used a short stick with gathered hemp fibers at one end to drive away evil spirits (*gohei*).

The cannabis stem provides hemp, a strong fiber used to make nets, rope, cloth, and paper. From the weaving of fishing nets, it was discovered by the weavers that they could in fact make a durable cloth if they tightened the weave. Hemp was determined to be the base material for the oldest example of paper yet to be found, uncovered in graves of the *Shensi* province of China and detected to be around 2,000 years old. Hemp paper is prized for its resistance to tearing and has been used for rare books and historical manuscripts. Some paper money is still made from hemp fiber. Hemp clothes were worn during Japanese religious ceremonies because of its association with purity.

Zoroaster *(c. 628 BC–551 BC)*, a Persian, is the earliest prophet mentioned as being responsible for the plant's use as a sacrament. Zoroaster gave hemp first place in the sacred text, the *Zend-Avesta*, which lists over 10,000 medicinal plants. Although we use the flowers (or bud) and leaves for smoking, they're also well-recorded as being used along with the root in the preparation of numerous medicines. It's been discovered by the visual scanning of an old pharmacological book that cannabis has been used for the treatment of menstrual pains, rheumatism and malaria.

In the nineteenth century the *wonder drug* aspirin took the world of medicine's imagination and thousands of years of enjoying the flexibility of cannabis were forgotten. Today the USA is experiencing a turnaround in the laws and doctors are becoming able to prescribe marijuana in certain circumstances, as they do in Holland, Canada, Switzerland and several other countries.

Montana Approves Medical Marijuana

The 2004 elections produced the tenth state to legalize marijuana for medicinal purposes. Voters approved the Montana Medical Marijuana Act, known as I-148 on the ballot, by a margin of 62% to 38%.

The Montana initiative creates a registry system for patients with specified diseases and medical conditions. Upon recommendation by their doctors, patients can apply with the state Department of Health and Human Services for ID cards. Cardholders will not be subject to arrest if in compliance with the initiatives quantity limitations. While this portion of the new law will not go into effect until the Department of Health and Human Services drafts applications and administrative rules, the law also creates an affirmative defense to prosecution for medical marijuana patients effective immediately.

Montana becomes the second state to approve medical marijuana this year. Vermont approved it through the legislative route in January. Alaska, California,

Colorado, Hawaii, Maine, Nevada, Oregon, and Washington have workable medical marijuana laws. Arizona voters approved a similar measure in 1996 that has proved unworkable because it calls for doctors to prescribe (as opposed to recommend) marijuana, making them liable to DEA sanctions.

Tennessee April 2005

The legislature on medical marijuana has introduced a bill that would legalize marijuana for medical use in Tennessee.

Sen. Steve Cohen (D-Memphis) said one reason for him to introduce the bill at this time was to raise the public's and the legislature's awareness of a new subject.

Cohen said "Normally projects take three years to mature in the [legislature]," "The lottery took 18 years. ... I hope medical marijuana doesn't take that long."

He also admitted that legalizing marijuana for medical purposes was not ready yet for passage in the Tennessee legislature this year bu stated "I think there are a lot of medical benefits from it (marijuana)." and asked the Senate General Welfare Committee Wednesday to push the proposal to its last calendar.

Cohen intends to suggest that a study committee look at the issue over the summer and allow for public input.

Memphis Democrat, Sen. John Ford, who chairs the General Welfare Committee, said Cohen's proposal was "a piece of legislation whose time should be here now or should come very, very soon.

"We're not talking about sitting around and smoking pot," Ford said. "This is for medical purposes."

Sen. Raymond Finney (R-Maryville) requested that a summer study committee also examine the fact that the Federal Drug Administration (FDA) still outlaws the use of marijuana for medical purposes and look into how the state could overcome the issue of illegality.

The drafted legislation states that, "States are not required to enforce federal law or prosecute people for engaging in activities prohibited by federal law. Therefore, compliance with this act does not put the state of Tennessee in violation of federal law."

Ten other states — Alaska, California, Colorado, Hawaii, Maine, Montana, Nevada, Oregon, Vermont, and Washington — have passed laws to allow the consumption and cultivation of marijuana for medical use.

"Every poll that I've seen shows at least 75 percent of the public in favor of it,"

Cohen said, adding that people with health risks especially favor the legalization of marijuana for medical purposes.

"When the people are dying and they're in pain, there is nothing the government should really prohibit them," Cohen said .

November 3, 2005

Denver, known appropriately as *"The Mile High City'* became the first city in the nation to wipe out all criminal and civil penalties for adults caught possessing a small amount of marijuana.

About 54% of voters supported a ballot measure legalizing possession of less than an ounce of pot by individuals 21 and over. State laws banning pot do however still apply in Denver. Police cited most offenders under state law rather than city ordinance, for convenience.

The new ordinance is more radical than pro-marijuana measures approved over the years in San Francisco, Berkeley, Oakland and half a dozen college towns across the country. Most of those initiatives decriminalized marijuana for medical use, or replaced criminal penalties with small fines or directed police to make enforcement of marijuana laws a low priority.

Assistant city attorney David W. Broadwell, said. "Citing under state law has been a tradition here for years.... We intend to keep doing what we've been doing,"

The marijuana liberalization group SAFER ran a provocative campaign to cast the measure as vital to public safety. Although critics said it was more deceitful, than provocative. Although the Denver vote has no practical effect, advocates of relaxed drug laws said it was symbolic.

` On yard signs and billboards, campaign director Mason Tvert tried to persuade voters that marijuana was a safer alternative to alcohol arguing that street crime and domestic violence would drop if residents were legally allowed to smoke pot rather than down a six-pack of beer. College campuses too would be safer, he said, if joints replaced kegs.

In a stunt last month, Tvert dragged a mock corpse in a body bag to City Hall and surrounded it with jugs from Wynkoop Brewery owned by Denver's mayor, John W. Hickenlooper. Then he piled bags of Doritos in a heap nearby. His point:? Alcohol abuse can kill you. Marijuana gives you the munchies.

City officials accused Tvert of confusing the public by using campaign signs that read "Make Denver SAFER." (The group's acronym stands for Safer Alternative for Enjoyable Recreation.) Tvert insisted people understood his message.

Telluride, Colo., ran a more traditional campaign which failed as voters reject-ed an effort to make pot the town's lowest law enforcement priority.

Activists expect Tvert's approach to be taken up around the country particu-larly in Nevada, where pro-marijuana forces are preparing a statewide initiative to tax and regulate pot much like beer or cigarettes.

Oakland passed a similar measure last fall, but it was tabled because it con-flicted with state and federal law.

"Paul Armentano, senior policy analyst with the pro-marijuana group NORML said " Success breeds success, I think you'll see this campaign used as a model

Listed as one of the great grains of China, cannabis was used in the day-to-day diet of those ancient people. In the nineteenth century cannabis was replaced by grains considered of better taste and greater flexibility in new and old recipes. Still cultivated in Russia and several other countries, cannabis is used in animal feeds, more especially birdseed; it's also processed for its oil, which is likened to linseed oil and can be used for making paints, putty, fuel and lubricant. This strain of hemp does not provide THC in sufficient quantities to make it worth smoking; it's of a very low quality and you would have to sit in the middle of burning acreage to get the slightest buzz, unless of course you are a complete lightweight.

Once discovered by merchant seamen who took the cannabis plant from Asia and introduced it to the Western world, cannabis was cultivated all over Europe, mainly for hemp fiber to make rope, cloth or paper. Hemp fiber quite obviously became essential to the British navy for ships' rigging and colonists were paid to plant hemp, rather like the farming grants available today.

English settlers were responsible for taking hemp seed to the American colonies in the early 1600s and here the industry began to boom and hemp was in great demand. The hemp industry grew wildly efficient and eventually became the major crop of the country, second only to cotton.

Marijuana and Its Place in Religion

In India, hemp is still made into a drink that some say is the favorite beverage of the god Indra. Tradition maintains that Indra gave marijuana to the people to assist them in attaining an elevated state of consciousness and delight in worldly joys and freedom from fear. Maybe the cannabis drink that is known to have been made in ancient Thebes around 2000 BC was used in the same way. In India, c. 1000–1500 BC, cannabis was recorded in the *Atharva-Veda*, a collection of Hindu magic spells, where it was called "sacred grass" and regarded as the source of happiness, a liberator. (Shen Nung had also viewed cannabis as a "liberator.") According to Indian tradition and writings Siddhartha used and ate nothing but hemp and its seeds for six years prior to announcing his truths and becoming the Buddha in the fifth century BC. In the Tantric Buddhism of Tibet, cannabis plays a very significant role in the meditation ritual, a practice known since 500 BC, when cannabis was thought of as a most holy plant. One of the prized varieties of hash today is the potent Nepalese Temple Ball. The Copts claim that marijuana as a sacrament has a lineage descending from the Jewish sect the Essenes, authors of the Dead Sea Scrolls, with influences that go as far back as neighboring Thebes. It's the Coptic view that cannabis played an important role in early Christian and Judaic rituals as a sacrament burned in tabernacles, to commemorate such times as the communication with God on Mount Sinai by Moses, and the transfiguration of Christ. Cannabis also has links to Christianity through the Ethiopian Coptic Church, said to have been established by St. Mark in AD 45.

Evidence for the use of cannabis has been discovered in Scythian tombs. Along with the plant was found a miniature tripod-like tent over a copper censer, in which the sacred plant was burned—a tabernacle. Maybe the burning bush was just this and not a miracle at all, just a drug-enhanced interpretation of reality. Many users of cannabis in modern times describe their experiences with words such as "a oneness with God," "peace and tranquility," "reduced anxiety," "a greater understanding of life" or "a greater appreciation of music and art." Spirituality and music in particular can be arguably linked to cannabis use—from Scythian partying to soul and jazz, sixties rock 'n' roll, and the Rasta influences of today. The Sufis, Scythians, African *dagga* cults, Ethiopian Copts, Hindus, Cuna Indians of Panama, Taoists, Cora Indians of Mexico, Essenes, Buddhists, Zoroastrians and Rastafarians have all used cannabis in religious ceremonies, regarding it as part of their culture and an important sacrament. In 1895, the Indian Hemp Drug Commission published its report in seven thick volumes, concluding that cannabis has some medical uses, no addictive properties and a number of positive emotional and social benefits.

During the Middle Ages, while adopting wine as a sacrament, the Inquisition instituted by the Roman Catholic Church outlawed cannabis ingestion. Anyone found using the herb to heal others or communicate with God would be branded a witch. Pope Innocent VIII singled out cannabis as an unholy sacrament of the Satanic mass in 1484. At the very same time that European churches persecuted cannabis users, the Spanish conquistadors were diligently planting hemp around the New World to provide raw materials to produce their sails, rope and clothing.

Liberation and Evolution

"Life, liberty and the pursuit of happiness" were the words chanted by the colonists in America and hemp farming was promoted by almost every U.S. president until it was prohibited as a source of medicine and fiber. Similarly "Liberty, equality, fraternity" were the demands of the French revolutionaries, and later, in 1835 in Paris, the *Club des Hashichines* was founded, boasting members such as the poet Baudelaire, who put in verse his experience of marijuana use:

> The hallucinations begin. External objects assume monstrous forms. They reveal themselves to you in shapes never before witnessed.
>
> Then they become deformed and transformed, finally entering your being or rather you enter them. The most singular ambiguities, the most inexplicable transpositions of thought take place.
>
> The sounds are colored, the colors are heard as music. The musical notes are numbers and you solve at hair-raising speeds enormous arithmetical problems as the music unwinds in your ears.
>
> You are sitting down and smoking; you think you are sitting inside your pipe which is smoking you; you exhale self in the form of blue-tinted clouds.
>
> —from *Hashish Wine, Opium* by Theophile Gautier and Charles Baudelaire

During the period of the 1860s to the 1920s world fairs and international expositions featured Turkish hashish smoking parlors. By around 1883 parlors were open in most American cities and by the early twentieth century, there were over 500 hashish parlors in New York alone.

Marijuana and Music

In the southern United States and in South Africa, oppressive racist regimes linked the "vicious insolence" of black people with marijuana and jazz music. In

New Orleans, whites were concerned that black musicians, rumored to smoke marijuana, were spreading a powerful new voodoo music that forced even decent white women to tap their feet.

Harry Anslinger, heading the newly formed Federal Bureau of Narcotics, kept files on and assigned agents to tail virtually all jazz and swing musicians, including Count Basie, Dizzy Gillespie, Louis Armstrong and Duke Ellington. Anslinger insisted that "this Satanic music and the use of Marijuana causes white women to seek sexual relations with Negroes." This legalized racist persecution, combined with newspaper magnate William Randolph Hearst's anti-hemp campaign, tolled the death knell of legal cannabis in the United States. With the commercial sabotage of the hemp industry on his agenda, for three years Hearst's newspapers promoted the image of lazy Mexicans smoking marijuana in a yellow journalism campaign that made the American public frightened of *marijuana*—a Mexican slang word for cannabis. Few people realized that *marijuana* was the same as the hemp that had been farmed for years, or the same as cannabis, extracts of which they had been given as cure-alls since childhood. In 1937, a massive and prohibitive tax was put on hemp, effectively destroying that industry in the United States. Over the decades that followed, the various states passed increasingly draconian laws against cannabis production, supply and use.

> *If you don't think drugs have done good things for us, do me a favor, go home tonight, take all your albums, tapes and CDs and burn 'em. Cos you know what...the musicians who made that great music that has enhanced your lives throughout the years [were] real...high on drugs.*
> —Bill Hicks

Well, maybe not all of them, but just a quick flick through the average music collection will reveal a considerable number of marijuana references, from the blatant (Cypree Hill's *Hits from the Bong*) to the obscure (The Association's "Along Comes Mary"), ranging from classic English 60s psychedelic whimsy through almost any reggae album from the 70s, to current ambient chill-out favorites.

Have a Marijuana—David Peel and the Lower East Side (LP Elektra 1968, CD reissue Line Records, Germany)
　Reefer Songs—Various artists
　Viper Mad Blues—Various artists

Both U.S. import compilations available on JASS CD, 7 and 630 respectively and obtainable from Blackmail.

"Proving that appreciation of the recreational value of Marijuana was not a blinding flash that occurred sometime around 1965, these excellent compilations feature such euphemistic highpoints as "Lotus Blossom" by Julia Lee and her Boyfriends from 1947 along with the less subtle "Smoking Reefers" by Larry Adler from 1938 (author)

When "Flower Power" arrived in the 1960s, once again marijuana and music connected with the culture, this time one of peace and love. The rise in the use of cannabis was accompanied by regular media reports of pop groups smoking marijuana. In 1980, Paul McCartney spent ten days in prison in Japan for possession of cannabis. Louis Armstrong had suffered a similar fate in Los Angeles exactly 50 years before.

Cannabis only became illegal in the UK in 1925 with the adoption of the second Opium Conference in Geneva where, despite hesitation on the part of the United Kingdom, the convincing argument of an Egyptian delegate of the evils of marijuana resulted in the inclusion of cannabis in the opium laws. Several attempts to repeal the law, backed up by reports that repeat the findings of the Drug Commission Report on Indian hemp of 1895 have failed. More recently Holland refused to continue to be associated with the law.

3

Understanding the Cannabis Plant

Being a very hardy plant, cannabis can be found in the most extreme areas of the world—from near the Arctic Circle to the Equator, and from sea level to above 7,000 feet in the Himalayas. It's become the most widely grown and distributed of all cultivated plants throughout the world, a fact that's a testament to the plant's adaptability, usefulness, versatility, and economic value. Only in recent years did but the UK pick up on this asset and begin to plant fields of hemp in experimental areas all over the country as young people stumbled across fields of hemp and proceeded to flock to the area. This leaves a lot of disappointed smokers; youngsters stand around wondering why the police don't show, but they soon found out why. They would have got as much satisfaction from a standard cigarette, since the commercial hemp they puffed on was almost impotent. The USA has a similar situation with its hemp fields since experiment in commerce and pressure from the "*green*" brigade are forcing the issue of more organic and bio degradable material use in soaps, cosmetics and clothing.

Being a hardy weed, cannabis has maintained its ability to survive without human aid. Whenever ecological conditions permit, Cannabis escapes the area in which it's being cultivated and does what weeds are best at and what we expect of them, establishing wild populations.

Warmer countries are perfect for growing outside plants, and illegal growers have huge external crops. Weedy cannabis still flourishes throughout the United States, where crop seed and pollen have been distributed by wind, animals, and birds. Mostly this wild cropping is the heritage of hemp farms planted during World War II when there was a rope shortage. Some of these farms still exist today.

There's an amazing and impressive diversity within the single species of Cannabis

Sativa. Distinctive ecotypical strains have evolved and been adapted for many uses. For instance, different varieties either produce large amounts of seeds on bushy plants or give seeds rich in oil, and the taller, straight-stemmed varieties provide long fibers used for rope and cloth. Cannabis plants are hardy, can live with little water or nutrients, and develop small seeds that sprout only under the right conditions. The most important seed for readers of this book are those of the marijuana varieties Sativa and Indica. If you understand and respect the plant and its tenacity, you'll have an easy life growing and harvesting.

Marijuana plants vary in their overall sizes and yields, in the color of seeds and flowers, in flowering times, in their tastes and fragrances, and above all, in their potencies. For instance, Big Bud can yield up to one kilo of bud on its branches in the right conditions but the smoke can be mild; on the other hand, a K2 plant (a hybrid of White Widow and Northern Lights...POW!) is a fantastic smoke, but with a much smaller yield.

For the most part, potency (the strength or psychoactivity) of a given marijuana strain is a genetic factor. The potency of a plant is inherited from its mother (the seed bearer) and its father (the pollen maker). Growers should plant seeds from marijuana that they have smoked and liked, because the marijuana from these seeds will be similar in potency to the potency inherited from their parents. The marijuana grower's goal is to choose seeds from potent grass and to nurture the plants to a healthy, fully developed maturity. Nature and the plant will take care of the rest. Better still, develop clones from a good mother plant (see chapter 10) and have a smoke you can rely on as being uniform for years to come.

Understanding Cultivation

Your goal is to raise healthy, potent, and fully matured plants. Remember that marijuana is a notoriously hardy, fast growing weed that survives extreme heat, mild frosts and all sorts of abnormal growing conditions. Few diseases seriously affect marijuana, and for the most part, insects and animals have little impact on its overall growth and yield once the vulnerable seedling stage is past.

Every seed contains a certain potential for growth, overall size, and potency. Given the seed's potential, the environment then determines the actual size and potency of the plant. In an ideal environment, some marijuana varieties grow from a sprout to over 20' (6 m) tall in only 6 months, and yield up to 4.41 lbs. (2 kilos) of buds, although this may only be seen in countries with a hotter climate or a very tall

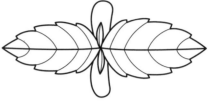

Figure 3.1: A seedling in Stage 1 of growth.   Figure 3.2: A seedling in Stage 2 of growth.

house. Seriously though, inside growth has little opportunity of producing huge plants, so we need to consider growing or developing the smallest plant with the best yield. You can, however, easily grow plants reaching 6' (1.8 m) tall that will yield around half a kilo of bud. The most commonly grown size of plant in the UK, for instance, is around 2–3' (60–90 cm), returning up to 1 to 2 oz. (50–60 g) per plant although growers are becoming increasingly aware of the benefits of using the methods adopted by the commercial grower who goes for little and often, putting a young clone into bud at just 8" (20 cm) and harvest 6 or 7 weeks later at around 14" (35 cm) with approximately 0.5 oz. (10 g) of bud per plant. Remember— these weights are an approximate average. Both smaller and larger yields have been experienced.

Marijuana is an annual plant—a single season completes a generation and the plant's future relies on the survival of the seeds, although when growing inside, you are playing God and all plants can be regenerated to produce again and again. (This will be addressed in more detail later in the book.)

The first pair of leaves that appear on a sprout of the cannabis plant are said to be entire that is they have smooth edges rather than the serrated edges we recognize as being synonymous with the celebrated seven or nine leaf Marijuana plant. The entire leaves are a part of the embryo contained within the seed. The appearance of the second pair of leaves begins the seedling stage, I which the leaves differ from the embryonic leaves by developing the more recognizable serrated margins, and being larger than their leaders. The first leaves usually have a single, spearhead shape, and the next pair usually have three blades. A basic pattern has been set: each new pair of leaves is larger and has more blades per leaf, until the leaves reach a maximum size and number of blades per leaf, usually seven but often in a perfect growing condition it's normal for them to have nine or eleven leaves, blades or fingers, although up to nineteen blades have been recorded on an eighteen-inch long leaf.

The seedling stage is completed four to six weeks into growth, followed by the vegetative stage: this is the time of maximum growth, during which time branches appear and form the plant into its distinctive shape. After another few weeks, leaf pairs that had been opposite each other (opposite phylotaxy) begin to form in a staggered position along the top of the stem (alternate phylotaxy), a sign that the plant is preparing itself for the start of sexual maturation. Marijuana is *dioecious,* which means that male and female flowers appear on separate plants although adverse conditions such as an erratic lighting program can cause plants to become hermaphrodites (with both male and female flowers appearing on the same plant), but generally each plant is considered either male or female. During the stage of preflowering, (a two-week period prior to flowering), the plant goes through a quiescent period; rapid growth slows while the plant prepares itself for the growth of flowers.

Male plants produce pollen-bearing flowers, and the females, seed-bearing flowers. Females are the preferred plant for marijuana because their flower clusters (buds) are more potent and because they yield better marijuana than the male plants. The familiar bud of commercial marijuana is a collection of hundreds of individual female flowers that form in masses generally know as bud but more professionally known as colas. The terminology generally accepted for marijuana, is that a bud is the female flower that forms an individual cluster. and the cola is a collections of buds. Once the taller male plant drops pollen and the seeds mature on the female, both plants normally die.

Marijuana grows best in fertile, well draining soil that gets plenty of water and is exposed to bright light, with a warm, airy atmosphere. Higher humidity is desirable during the vegetation stage. To reduce the complexities of the environment into factors over which a gardener can maintain some control, we may think of the environment as consisting of four basic growth factors: water, light, air, and soil. Plants live and grow by using:

- **water** from the air and soil
- **light energy** to make food and **biological energy** for growth
- **carbon dioxide** (CO_2) and oxygen from the air
- **minerals** (nutrients or fertilizers) absorbed from the soil or nutrient solution that you'll provide.

Each of these four growth factors is a link in the growth chain. The plant can grow only as fast as the weakest link will allow. Weak light limits growth no matter how abundant the water is, or how fertile the soil may be. If soil nutrients are scarce, growth is limited no matter how much light, air, or water is given.

Only after growers have watered and fertilized the plants to near excess will they recognize that low light is the reason their plants are not growing faster. I've seen growers drowning their plants or poisoning them with too much fertilizer when they've had them growing under a low wattage lightbulb and couldn't understand why they weren't ten feet tall. Growers need a general sensitivity and sense of balance toward what makes plants grow.

This book is designed to help you gain such an understanding and sensitivity. Although the best learning program is practice, we help you to avoid financial disasters and giving up in despair. A brief read through will relieve you of undue worries and misconceptions, and help persuade you to avoid events like overwatering or overfertilizing. Once you have skipped through these pages of wisdom—the result of many years of personal trial and error—common sense should be all you need to grow a healthy, potent crop.

Keep this book at hand all the time and use it often as a practical reference while you find your way through the darkness of marijuana secrets. After some time you may want to add notes that apply to your own circumstances and improve the references available to you. Keep these grow notes in you grow room and refer to plants as any flower BUT Marijuana. This way if you get a bust its either too late since they have found your plants or the notes can't be used against you as they do not refer to the offending plant.

One final thought on what constitutes common sense when it comes to plants. **Don't overdo it!** The death of many plants comes via the grower trying to force the growth process. If directions prescribe a teaspoon of fertilizer, won't three teaspoons be three times as good? **No!** Plants will do well given sensible care, so help them do what comes naturally and never try to force them.

The first crop or two is always a learning experience and even when the harvest is wonderfully successful, every grower believes that the next one will be even better, and generally you'll find that this is true until you reach optimum potential. It's a fact however that each crop gets easier to grow, because questions get answered and doubts gradually disappear, until the process of caring for your crop becomes second nature and more fun than smoking the harvest. Any experienced grower will probably say, "There's no place I'd rather be and nothing

Figure 3.3: This bud is plump and ready for harvest.

I'd rather be doing than sitting among my plants"—but remember, to get great THC (Tetrahydrocannabinol) you have to invest TLC **(Tender Loving Care).**

Where Should You Grow?

The question of where to grow and whether to use natural or electric light depends on your situation. Consider the space, time and funds you have, and the quantity of weed you want to harvest. A moderate weekend smoker could supply an adequate weed supply to satisfy his or her need with a very modest indoor setup. A small garden under an eight-foot fluorescent fixture, a sunny window or conservatory, maybe even your old granddad's greenhouse since he doesn't use it anymore! A smoker who uses more than an ounce weekly would need a single 600-watt HPS

Figure 3.4: Plants set in Rockwool and laid out in drainage troughs.

(High Pressure Sodium) lamp or a greenhouse. If you plant outside then plant out in May with some protection from late frost or winds and harvest around October.

Sunlight is free, albeit scarce in some countries, but use it whenever possible. The main problems with outside growing of course are visibility and of course odor; remember, it's called "skunk" for a reason. Window gardens or back garden plots shouldn't be visible to passersby or nosy neighbors. A greenhouse may innocently attract attention even when you use obscure plastics that transmit light but hide the greenhouse's contents. Under electric lights, growers decide when to start the plants, when the plants will begin to flower, and when they'll be ready to harvest. Controlling the basic elements of the environment is straightforward. Indoors there's no concern with the elements such as wind and rain, cold or poor soil, or whether it's springtime or the dead of winter. You make the decision by the simple flick of a switch or adjustment of the timer, creating all seasons at will. When planning your garden, you must first consider security. Growers must ensure without any doubt that gardens and lights aren't visible from outside or accessible to unexpected visitors. Be sure you do everything else in your day-to-day life in a legal manner: pay your car tax, drive

Figure 3.5: These healthy outdoor plants will benefit from a natural growth cycle.

carefully, and pay your bills: you don't want a police officer or bailiff knocking to present you with an unpaid parking fine or other bill and end up with a jail sentence for growing dope because they stumble upon your crop.

Even in countries where marijuana growing is legal, theft is a major worry. Growers must consider all the consequences before they tell anyone about their garden. No matter how proud you are of your crop or how much you want to show off to your mates, you must exercise extreme caution toward anyone who comes to visit. A fact of life is that envy, revenge, greed, or a sudden dose of morality has made thieves or informers of acquaintances and former friends.

The first and most important rule of growing is **DON'T TELL A SOUL**.

Unlike sunlight, electric lights cost money to buy and operate. First consider the minimal cost for a smaller fluorescent garden, and the expense of an HID (High Intensity Discharge lights) garden, along with the dangers of heat-seeking helicopters. Electric light gardens require more frequent care than sunlit gardens; on the other hand, they can be cared for at any time of the day because they're inside, and the lights can be on at any time that fits the gardener's schedule.

These gardens are also perfect for the grower who works for his living and more especially for those who live in a flat or studio. Using lights during the evening is best, provided no light escapes, because you are home to work in the garden usually at night, plus if you are able to benefit from cheaper night (off peak) use of electricity, you'll benefit financially. If something goes wrong with the electrics and you are there to spot it you'll save all sorts of disasters, whereby if you are at work you can't possibly. Having the lights off during the day also means that the meter isn't spinning like a maniac when the meter reader calls to read it.

You can hide electric-light gardens in closed rooms, basements, attics, closets or garages and there are even small homemade devices that fit right into your bedroom or kitchen cupboards (units) although even when hidden, large internal gardens may arouse the suspicions of the electricity company. Large metal halide lamps (MHs), or High Pressure Sodium (HPS), the main light source for many gardeners, can draw around up to 1,000 watts each, as much electricity as a 1-kw heater. If three or more lamps are used, the utility company may wonder why your electric bill has suddenly gotten so high, and may make inquiries about your electricity usage or investigate a possible short or similar problem. Growers who decide on large electric-light gardens often run their lights at night when other tenants or neighbors are asleep, so that they don't spot anything suspicious or hear ventilators buzzing. In a home situation, commercial growers limit their electrical consumption so that their usage is less obvious to the electric company. If asked, the best excuse is that you've installed electric heating. Never be stupid enough to rig your meter for free electricity. The chances are that you'll get a larger sentence for stealing electricity than you would for growing dope.

Large HID gardens may be very noisy. Ballasts may hum loudly, and light balancers (if installed) may cause considerable vibration, as would HPS lamps and ventilators. Commercial growers who are concerned about the scent of their marijuana need to make a greater financial investment and will need to carefully construct their ventilation box to deplete the extractor noise to almost nil. To eliminate odor completely, fit a carbon-filled filter on the air out line, before the extractor unit. Consider all possible problems before you set up your system, especially if it's going to be a large commercial operation. Small gardens usually need no special security precautions. Again, common sense is the key. Think it all out stage by stage and consider how any stage could give the game away—then simply eliminate any element that tells the tale.

REMEMBER: The police have more resources than you could ever afford and can draw on years of experience. There aren't many tricks they haven't seen and they're more educated in the drug world than you are because they pool their knowledge worldwide. While it remains illegal to grow marijuana, your liberty is at risk. If you share your secret with just one friend, then you have doubled your chances of getting caught. If you really don't want to get caught growing then don't grow.

Once you have read the first chapters you can decide between the two basic options within a fundamental decision: to grow or not to grow; if the choice is to grow, then you'll need to decide if you're going to grow with electric light or natural light. The rest of the information provided here is common to both situations. However you imagine that you'll be growing, you'll find useful information in all chapters.

Marijuana growing is fun, and more rewarding than you might imagine. The purpose of this book is not to encourage you to grow illegally, but to report how growing is done legally, and how it may be done when growing is legal and the law is better defined for cultivation.

As a grower since 1979 while living in Holland, I've experienced and enjoyed more harvests than I can count, and I've smoked myself into happy oblivion with homegrown bud more times than I can remember. In fact now I think about it, I can't remember growing anything...*WOW! Good stuff this weed.*

Take every opportunity to support groups that are trying to legalize cannabis, like NORML in the United States and UKCIA in the UK. Whatever country you live in, there will be an action group for you to join. I have to say my greatest personal pleasure in life, except for one other obvious activity, is to be with my plants and chill. If they never legalize growing then I will turn to growing tomatoes in my old age. *YEAH RIGHT!*

4

Let There Be Light

Lighting: An Overview

Q: So what's so important about Lighting?

A: It allows you to be God in your garden!

To budget on light is like stealing from yourself

To grow Marijuana and gain the best results it's essential that you understand the importance of the **photoperiod**. The photoperiod tells your plant what to do and when. When growing with lights, you control the environment of your plant and can effectively switch the photoperiod from summer to winter or, in other words, switch from the vegetative to the flowering period.

PHILIPS, a Dutch electrical company who supply the world with electrical equipment of all kinds have supported and designed every single aspect of lighting needs imaginable and their contribution to horticulture is barely rivaled. Philips lighting is excellent in quality and diversity for the marijuana grower. Their Website offers lots of information useful to growers in understanding light usage and availability and much of the information below comes from there. Although Philips lighting is recommended here and they have developed the listed lamps for horticulture, they did not intend their products to be used to grow cannabis and do not support illegal activities.

Daylight versus Artificial Light

The process of photosynthesis, which is usually referred to as assimilation, consumes by far the largest amount of light energy. For this reason, in this chapter, which is devoted to the relationship between the available quantity of daylight and the amount of additional artificial lighting that may be required, we will only consider assimilation lighting. We have to say in advance that the available quantity of light isn't the only factor that determines the process of assimilation. The type of plant (particularly its concentration of chlorophyll), the temperature and the CO_2 content in the air are also important factors. But it's a fact that, particularly in those areas that lie between the 40th and 80th parallels, there will be a shortfall of light during the winter months. The lower quantity of light (down to 1/10 of that during the summer) is due to the considerably shorter length of the days combined with lower light intensity caused by the low-lying sun and frequent cloud cover. Under these circumstances, light is definitely a limiting factor, and if we require unhindered growth, we have to add an extra amount of light energy. The main question is, of course, how much light do we have to add each day in order to attain the optimum quantity of light energy for the plant? In order to be able to calculate this amount, we must, know the requirements of the plant, and, on the other hand, we must know a bit more about the available quantity of daylight. The total daily quantity of radiation, which the earth receives from the sun, can be expressed as intensity (energy per area) multiplied by time. This quantity is referred to as radiation quantity, light quantity and daily quantity, and is usually expressed in joules per cm^2 (J/cm^2). In many countries, meteorological centers measure these daily quantities and publish them every day.

If the daily quantities, which are published by the meteorological centers, are compared with these average quantities, it can easily be seen whether there's a shortfall of light. This information can then be used as a starting point for drawing up a daily artificial lighting scheme.

However, if the climate in a greenhouse has to compensate very precisely for fluctuating weather conditions, then it must have its own weather station that is able to measure the local overall radiation (usually by means of a solarimeter that is set up outside). Now, first of all, the reading outside in J/cm^2 must be converted to a quantity in mW/m 2 (net radiation between 400 and 700 nm) which is useful for the plants inside the greenhouse.

First of all, we must realize that the solarimeters which are used for measuring the daily quantity, in fact, measure all radiation with a wavelength of between 300 and 3000nm However, only radiation between 400 and 700nm is effective for the process of photosynthesis. In order to calculate the useful amount of light (i.e., that with the correct wavelength), we have to multiply the overall radiation by an average factor of

0.45: 0.45 236 = **106 J/cm²** (visible radiation outside the greenhouse).

However, we have to reduce this figure still further because the radiation quantity was measured in the open air, whereas the plants are inside a greenhouse. In order to calculate the quantity of light inside the greenhouse, we have to take the following factors in to consideration: the design of the greenhouse (including the surface area and the type of glass), the location of the greenhouse, the time of day and the season and the extent to which the roofing material is old or dirty. For a modern greenhouse, we can assume a maximum light transmission of 0.70. The visible radiation inside the greenhouse can thus be expressed as:

0.70 106 = 74 J/cm²

And finally we have to perform a few more operations if we're to obtain a figure that can be used by growers. First, it's more convenient to work with m² in greenhouses. As 1 m² = 10 000cm², we now have:

10 000 74 J/cm² = 740 000 J/m²

We have now obtained a unit that refers to the quantity of energy per unit of time: this is referred to as intensity. As 1 watt is equal to 1 joule per second, Then 1W = 3600 J/hour, or 1 J/hour = 1/w/3600. Substituting this in the formula, we see that 92 500 J/hour/m² = 92 500/3600 = **25.70 W/m²** (net visible radiation between 400 and 700 nm). If we now express this figure in mW/m², then we see that the January figure of 236 J/cm² of overall radiation provides us with about 25 700 mW/m² of useful radiation for the plants in the greenhouse. We can now work with this figure because we can compare it with the unit of radiation that is usually adopted for artificial lighting. And then we shall find that the figure that we have determined, when related to the other growth factors present in the greenhouse, is not high enough to ensure that the plants in the greenhouse can grow satisfactorily. In other words, light is in this case the factor that limits growth. The direct formula for converting the quantity in J/cm² measured outside the greenhouse into a quantity in mW/m² that is available for the plants inside the greenhouse is: 1 J/cm² = 875/n mW/m², where n = the number of hours over which the daily quantity of radiation is spread. In the case of very dirty greenhouses (transmission = 0.30), this equation becomes: 1 J/cm² = 580/n n/wn².

In conclusion, we should like to say that lamp manufacturers in general make their products for illumination applications. For practical reasons therefore, such as the fact that luxmeters are in general use, it's not surprising that the unit of lighting intensity, lux (= lumens/m^2) is also used for the purposes of plant lighting.

Day-Length Reaction

One of the most remarkable mechanisms in nature is the reaction of living organisms to short and long days. In our regions the day length controls the life of nearly all organisms. The fact that trees and bushes lose their leaves in autumn is mainly caused by the shortening of days. Trees and bushes develop sleeping buds in order to survive winter. These buds only come out when the days grow longer and warmer. The migration instinct of birds is controlled by day length. Short days in autumn mean that birds feel the need to migrate. As soon as the days in spring become longer, they cannot resist the urge to return. Short-day plants originally come from the tropics. In the area between the Tropic of Cancer and the Tropic of Capricorn, the day length varies between 12 and 14 hours. Long-day plants are at home in areas north and south of the tropics. In these areas the days are longer than 14 hours in summer.

The periodic lengthening and shortening of the days is called photo periodicity (photo = light, periodicity = recurring regularly). The fact that some plants are sensitive to long and short days was discovered in 1920. In that year Garner and Alard discovered that a certain tobacco plant (Maryland Mammoth) only bloomed if it was given a few short days of light. Other plants reacted the other way around. Earlier Klebs had already discovered that he could let certain plants bloom in winter by giving them a few hours of light at night.

Qualitative, Quantitative

Species that only bloom with a specific day length are called qualitative long-day plants or quantitative short-day plants (sometimes the term "obligatory" is used instead of "qualitative"). Qualitative means that the day length is decisive for the transition from growth phase to flowering phase. The limiting value, which can be quite exact, is called critical day length. A plant such as Xantium pennsylvanicum blooms after being exposed to 8.5 hours of light during one night, but refuses to bloom after being exposed to 8 hours of light over many nights. There are also species, which, irrespective of the day length, move spontaneously from the

Figure 4.1: This is a plant in Stage 4 of growth. Notice the wispy bud formation.

growth phase to the flowering phase. It does not make much difference whether they get much light within a short period or get a bit less light over a longer period. The only thing that matters is the degree of light: exposure intensity rather than exposure period.

The quantity of light thus plays a main role regarding growth and flowering. However, a number of species in this category cherish a certain exposure period. Some plants bloom spontaneously when the days are rather short. Although they're not really short-day plants we call them quantitative short-day plants. On the other hand there are also quantitative long-day plants. They preferably bloom when the days are rather long (the term "facultative" is sometimes used and has the same meaning as "quantitative"). In practice the terms qualitative and quantitative are also used for different phases of development of plants. For example: with long-day plants the making of buds is strictly linked to a specific day length (over 14 hours). The making of buds is therefore qualitative. However, the growth of buds is often quantitative. By making the day longer or shorter we can still accelerate or restrain the blooming of plants in this phase of development.

Long-Day Plants

More detailed research showed that with many plants the day length is decisive for the time of flowering. There are species of plants that are ready to bloom as soon as the days have more than 14 hours of light. A few weeks later a choice selection of flowers and blooming shrubs embellish our parks and gardens.

Short-Day Plants

A different group of plants only bloom in autumn, when the days grow shorter. These are called short-day plants (SDP). They bloom when they have received less than 14 hours of light a day. There are also plants that start to bloom when they first go through a short-day period and then a long-day period. This situation occurs in the period of early spring when there's only 12 hours of light a day, while early summer already has 16 hours. Conversely, there are also plants that bloom after a long-day period followed by a short-day period (LDP-SDP).

Day-Neutral Plants

Last but not least, there's a large group of plants for which the day length does not influence the flowering period. When these plants have finished growing they move spontaneously from the growth phase to the flowering phase. We call them day-neutral plants (DNP).

From the point of view of illumination, as opposed to plant irradiation, the effectiveness of a lamp is determined by two factors: First, by the proportion of the electrical energy it converts into radiant energy, in the visible part of the spectrum (roughly between 400 and 700nm); and second, by the distribution of this radiant energy over the visible spectrum. In order to be able to understand this, it's necessary to realize how the eye evaluates radiant energy of different wavelengths. The average human eye has maximum sensitivity to radiation at a wavelength of 555nm (green light). This sensitivity decreases to radiation of both longer (red) and shorter (blue) wavelengths. The sensitivity curve of the human eye has its peak in the yellow-green part of the spectrum (555nm) and decreases toward both the red and blue sides.) In the case of red light (650 nm) the human eye is only 1/10 as sensitive as it is to green light (555nm). In other words, ten times more red light is required than green in order to obtain the same lighting level. The unit for luminous energy, the lumen, takes the eye sensitivity curve into account.

Photoperiod

In real terms the photoperiod is the number of hours in a day (measured by light) against the number of hours in the night (measured by darkness). In their true environment, as long as the daylight hours are long, the plants will vegetate. As autumn approaches with its longer nights, the darkness signals to the plant that winter is coming and it's time to flower so that it can develop seeds, without which there couldn't be a new generation. Marijuana plants constantly produce a hormone called phytochrome which is the hormone that initiates flowering. Hormone levels rise within the plant when the dark period is long enough to promote flowering rather than leaf growth. If phytochrome is exposed to the smallest particle of light, it could be rendered inactive. This knowledge is useful in outside growing, especially in Europe where the days are short. I will explain how you can benefit from this, depending on your location, later in the text.

If you're in living in the Northern Hemisphere, you might already know that the longest day of the year (the most hours of light) is June 21st, and the shortest day of the year (most hours of darkness) is December 21st, and that March 21st brings us the equinox, which simply means equal light (12 hours of light and 12 dark). With an electric lamp and a timer, these days no longer exist. You can be God and make as many long days as you want, similarly with the shortest days. (All dates are reversed if you are in the Southern Hemisphere)

Other conditions may exist peculiar to the area you live in that can determine daylight duration, such as cloud cover, maybe a mountain close by or even trees. Cannabis will switch to flowering when the nights shorten to around 12 hours, although there are some older females who will flower at 18 hours but will give a poor harvest. This change takes place after a period of lengthened darkness between 8 and 11 days, depending on the variety of plant that you have chosen to grow. Ask when you buy your plants for any advice on this to save you having to experiment. If there's no advice, you'll soon get to know the best times for your variety, and your loss of crop from experimenting will be negligible. Daylight hours don't affect the male plant in the same way as the female plants. Male plants can flower under days of 18 hours of light.

So now you see the influence of the photoperiod: whenever we decide we want our little ladies to bud, we just reduce the photoperiod to initiate flowering. For my own particular preferred plant, K2 Indica (White Widow x Northern Lights), I usually give 24 hours of complete darkness, followed by a twelve on and twelve off lighting regime. The 24 hours of darkness ensures that the plant goes into bud. Within 8 days I usually see evidence of flowering, although it could be as soon as 7 days and as many as 15 in some varieties, so don't panic if you don't see signs in the earliest time period.

There may be times when we want to prevent flowering, especially in greenhouse growing conditions for off-season crops. If you're growing in the greenhouse then you may be affected by the short photoperiod of winter, which will cause premature flowering, producing undersized plants with a small expected yield and extended vegetation. We can use our lights on timer to coincide with shorter days, supplementing the natural photoperiod to increase to at least 18 hours of light. Make sure the changeover in light is minimal in effect as sudden flashes or changes may flick your plants into bud, which is exactly what you're trying to delay. You must also be aware that your plant may enter a hormonal change in sex. Marijuana plants can produce hermaphrodites, that is, develop both male and female reproductive characteristics, having both stamen and pistils. A female plant may become male or hermaphrodite if she suffers light shock.

Short Glossary of Lighting Terms

Candela The unit of measure for the intensity of light at the source, roughly equal to the amount of light in any direction from the flame of a candle.

Color Rendering Index (CRI) Color rendering is the ability of a light source to produce color in objects. The CRI is expressed on a scale from 0–100, where 100 is best in producing vibrant color in objects. Relatively speaking, a source with a CRI of 80 will produce more vibrant color in the same object than a source with a CRI of 60.

Color Temperature Color temperature denotes the overall color appearance of the light itself. When referring to a source as either "warm" or "cool," the color temperature is being discussed. Color temperature is expressed in units of Kelvin. Lamps range from 2100–7500 Kelvin. Lower color temperature (3000K) represents "warm" light, higher (4100K) represents "cool" light.

Exitance The term used to describe the total light which comes off of a surface. Exitance is dependent upon the illuminance on and the reflectance off the surface.

Foot-candle The unit of measure for the density of light as it reaches a surface. One foot-candle is equal to one lumen per square foot. Measured foot-candles are sensitive to the distance from the source to the surface of measure (inverse square law) and the angle at which the light reaches the surface (cosine law).

Illuminance The density of luminous flux on a surface, measured in foot-candles (one lumen per square foot) or lux (one lumen per square meter).

Illumination The result of the use of light.

Instant Start A circuit used to start specially designed fluorescent lamps without the aid of a starter. The circuit utilizes higher open circuit voltage than is required for the same length preheat lamp, to strike the arc instantly.

This circuit is used today in slim line and cold cathode lamps. Instant start 40-watt bipin lamps are made with a short-circuiting device built into the base.

Intensity The degree of light emitted from a source. Intensity most often varies given the direction at which one views the source. Intensity does not vary with distance. A candle produces the same intensity in a given direction whether on a table in front of you or one mile away.

Kilowatt (kW) A larger unit of power, a thousand watts (1000 watts = one kilowatt).

Kilowatt Hour (kWh) The measure of electrical energy from which electricity billing is determined. For example, a 100-watt bulb operated for 1000 hours would consume 100 kilowatt hours, (100 watts x 1000 hours = 100 kWh).

Light The energy that allows us to see. Professionally, light can be expressed in four terms. They are intensity (candela), lux (lumen), luminance (candela/square ft.) and exitance (lumen/square ft.).

Lumen The unit of measure for the light energy that flows in air is known as a lumen. The total light output from electrical sources is expressed in lumens. A uniform source of one candlepower placed in a sphere emits 12.57 lumens, or mean spherical candela equals to 12.57 lumens.

Lumens Per Watt (LPW) A measure of the efficacy of a light source in terms of the light produced for the power consumed. For example, a 100-watt lamp producing 1750 lumens gives 17.5 lumens per watt.

Luminance The term used to describe the specific light which comes off a surface whether off a filament, lightbulb, lens, louver, tabletop, etc. Luminance varies with both the direction from which you view the surface and its gloss characteristics. Luminance is measured in candela per square foot.

Preheat A circuit used in fluorescent lamps wherein the electrodes are heated or warmed to a glow stage by an auxiliary switch or starter (it can be a glow switch, thermal type or a mechanical device like a push button) before the lamps are lighted. This system was used on the original fluorescent lamps and is still in use today.

Rapid Start A circuit designed to start lamps by continuously heating or preheating the electrodes. This circuit is a modern version of the trigger start system and requires lamps designed for this circuit. In the rapid start two-lamp circuit, one end of each lamp is connected to a separate starting winding. The other end of each lamp is connected to a common winding. Except for slim line lamps, all modern fixtures using 40-watt and higher lamps are equipped with rapid start ballasts.

Rated Average Life The operating life (hours) at which 50% of the lamps are still operating. Where a plus (+) is used in stating the life, survival rate is 67% at the stated time.

Trigger Start A circuit used to eliminate the starter and start the preheat lamp almost instantly. In this circuit each electrode is connected to a separate winding in the ballast so that the electrode is continuously heated. This circuit is primarily used on 20-watt and lower wattage fluorescent lamps today.

Voltage (V or E) A measurement of electromotive force or the pressure of electricity. This is analogous to the pressure in a water line; i.e., pounds per square inch. The voltage of a circuit is the electrical pressure it gives. In an incandescent lamp, "voltage" designates the supply voltage to which the lamp should be connected. In other lamp types, it may refer to "operating voltage" of a lighted arc discharge lamp.

Watt (W) Unit used to measure power consumption of lamp.

Lighting

Lighting is the main contributor to an indoor garden, so we will discuss it in some detail. It's very simple to supply indoor plants with the desired amounts of water and nutrients and it's similarly simple to provide the correct amount of lighting. The size of your garden will determine your light source, strength and electrical usage. Similarly, the amount of light you use will determine the dimension of your garden, the variety of plants you'll grow, the size of your plants and your harvest. Consider lighting very carefully. What will your electrical system **SAFELY** handle in terms of wattage? You may need to get the advice of an electrician on this matter and the best way to do this in a covert manner is to relate wattage used to a more domestic utility such as an electric heater. For instance, if you're running a single 1000-watt HPS light then relate that to a 1kW electric heater. **NEVER** run High Intensity Discharge (HID) lighting from a household electric light fitting; they need a far greater wire grade. The supply fuse in your consumer unit should be at least 30 amperes for a decent-sized garden, although if you are running just one single lamp then 15-amp fusing will be sufficient, but it's up to you to do your sums first. The full picture of what you might be drawing from the particular fused circuit requires careful consideration. Power to amp is easily worked out: add up all the items you are running from your circuit in total power and use OHMS law to measure the amperage required. OHMS law is power divided by volts equals amps. For example, 1000 watts (1kw) divided by available voltage being 110V electricity. If you are operating a large garden, you will need to run it from its own ring main. It's quite simple to run in a new one from your standard consumer unit which often has either a redundant fuse or a spare facility to add a fuse. It is not advisable to use a kitchen ring main. The dedicated electrical circuit in a kitchen is demanding and mostly cannot spare its energy, since its appliances, like the kettle and tumble drier, use a lot of energy.

MAINS VOLTAGE CAN KILL!!!

The conditions in a greenhouse or grow room are generally damp and humid. Please take extreme caution with all electrical installations. Timers, plugs, sockets and any other electrical fitting should be clear of water contact however small the risk or quantity of water. If you use a humidifier in your garden, then all fitting should be in a separate area, and a light fitting, like all other equipment, must be earthed. Use rubber matting or sheet wood material

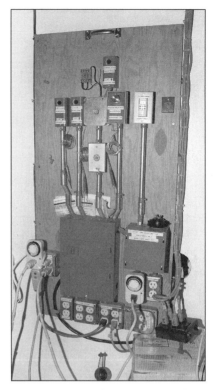

Figure 4.2: A professional mains set up for power distribution.

without nailing to floors or wear rubber-soled footwear. If you're in any doubt about wiring or other electrical matters and you feel insecure about what you're doing, then consult an electrician or use the Internet Websites that provide secure information about marijuana growing.

With the correct lighting almost any plant can be grown indoors. It's important to know the level of light a plant needs for the best crop. The most common mistake made is to provide plants with too little light, providing poor harvests, or too great a light, which will "burn" the leaves or scald buds.

High Intensity Discharge Lighting

The home gardener need look no further than the modern HID light (High Intensity Discharge). It's simple to use and will cover a large area. HID lighting has come a long way in the last few years. New developments in both lamp and reflector

Figure 4.3: Examples of metal halide (HID) and high pressure sodium (HPS) bulbs.

design have improved efficiency beyond anything imaginable five years ago (Fig. 4.3). We're in an age of the DIY enthusiast, a time when Mr. Average wants more than the simple device that has been made available to him in the past. Lighting is no longer the mystery of the initiated and professional or commercial grower; there are many appliances on the market now that you can buy, hang and simply plug in. I have no hesitation in declaring lighting to be the single most important purchase for the keen grower. It extends gardening to a 12-month pleasure and allows you the grower to be the creator of seasons.

Any white light encourages plant growth of course, but the lamps we're describing are designed specifically for maximizing growth and light-to-cash efficiency.

Fluorescents for Modest Growers

Fluorescent lighting units come complete with ballast, sockets, a tube and are easily hung; sometimes the fitting will come with a reflector, (don't confuse this with a diffuser). This type of fitting would be the value best to purchase. Fluorescent lighting is an inexpensive alternative to buy, cheap to run and causes no heat buildup; there are no alarm bells ringing with the electricity supply company, and it can't be spotted by the heat sensing helicopter. It also needs no special attention other than safety factors regarding installation, since its electrical demand is low. There are many types of fluorescent tubes on the market in various lengths, wattage and even color spectrum like warm white, cool white and natural day light.

Many growers who have experienced fluorescent gardens have been disappointed with the results, but then you can't have everything can you? The disappointed growers have probably been impatient, not waiting long enough for their harvest, or maybe not giving their plants enough care. Plants grown under fluorescents will take longer to mature in comparison to those grown under HID lights, but you'll have the benefit of lower-cost electricity, lower initial purchase outlay and less chance of being detected. You have to take all these factors into account before you decide to grow and decide it's worth it to put up with the extra weeks of waiting. Just be satisfied with your savings and rest easy when a knock comes on your front door.

Figure 4.4: Fluorescent lighting means slower growth but less detectable heat.

Because fluorescents generate a weaker light, the grower needs to ensure that all plant tops are kept at the same level and as close to the light as possible. It's quite easy to raise smaller plants simply by putting pieces of wood, brick or even books under the container, otherwise the final crop may be just a little bud and a lot of leaf. It's a good idea to place fluorescent lighting laterally as well as above the plants to promote side and under growth. Careful growers will manage to bring off some great yields under fluorescents providing they're patient and sensitive to the plants' needs. Fluorescents are really for the moderate smoker who can't or doesn't want to invest much money or devote time and space to a larger system. Fluorescent light makes no difference to the potency of marijuana.

For rooting and cloning, fluorescent lighting is far more successful than HID lamps since the light is softer and more caring to the young plants; it's also ideal for raising males for pollen, and starting seedlings, before transferring them to a HID system. Some commercial gardens use fluorescent lighting for shelf cultivation, and in a cloning system for rotation of the crop.

Standard fluorescents use about 10 watts per linear foot and come in lengths up to 12' (3.6 m). The most popular sizes for gardens are found to be 3' (90 cm), 4' (1.2 m), 6' (1.8 m) and 8' (2.4 m). The 3' (90 cm) and 4' (1.2 m) tube will fit into an average cupboard while the 6' (1.8 m) and 8' (2.4 m) unit will fit the average box room or garden shed, so areas that usually gather junk can now actively contribute to home income. I won't labor on the benefits of lamp length, save to say that if you can use an 8' (2.4 m) then do so, and anything under 4' (1.2 m) will give very poor lumens. Your choice, however, will be dictated by the size of space available. If you have to use a 3' (90 cm) tube then use a VHO (Very High Output). Tubes over 13' (4 m) long are clumsy, and fragile to handle or put in transit, so use is generally impractical.

Philips must have the first word in the product range since they have provided so much information for this book. First I would like to make my own opinions clear. I trust everything Dutch when it comes to growing and since Philips are right there in the heart of the growing country, where tulips, daffodils and dope come from, then I have to assume that they know all there is to know about the marketplace and market needs. The Philips range of lighting suitable for growing marijuana belongs to their horticultural range, in which you're looking for the TL product line listing TL70/80/90® . TL-D 90 de-lux comes in lengths and sizes shown in the chart below and is the main source of horticultural lighting. These are a low-mercury discharge lamp with a tubular 26-mm envelope. Having a high quali-ty fluorescent coating the TL-D 90 de-lux can be used with conventional electron-ic gear and has varying color designations.

It gives off excellent color rendering (Ra>95), achieving high efficacy with HF gear and creating atmospheres from warm white to cool daylight.

The TL70/80 comes in 4' (1.2 m), 5' (1.5 m), 5.5' (1.6 m) and 7.75' (2.4 m). The TL80® lamps achieve over 100LPW, operating on instant start electronic ballast, and TL70 and 80 meet EPACT requirements of course. Their lower wattage produces up to 40% savings over the F96TR system that used to exist. Trichomatic Phosphors provide high quality high lumen maintaining 97% at 6000 hours. The cathode guard ensures superior lumen maintenance through lamp life and reduces lamp end blackening. Their T8 HO has a high lamp efficiency of up to 95 lpw, operating on automatic ballasting; it gives 50% longer life than the T12 HO lamp with a mas-sive 18000 hours. It also has a lower system wattage providing up to 385% energy saving over the T12, The high lumen maintenance is 90 of 7200 hrs.

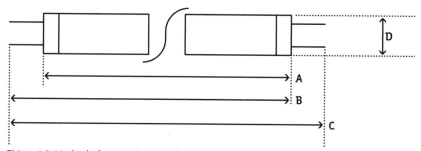

Figure 4.5: Method of measuring T2-D lamp to calculate output.

T2-D de-lux lengths and sizes

Amm	Bmm	Cmm	Dmm
589.8 max	594.9 max	604.0 max	26
1199.4 max	1206.5 max	1213.6 max	26
1500.0 max	1507.1 max	1514.2 max	26
437.4 max	444.5 max	451.6 max	26

Sylvania® / Osram® Fluorescent Lamps

Sylvania and Osram are one and the same group of companies with differing

TL-D 90 de-lux

Watts/Color	Color rendering Lumen Output (Lm)	designation index (R2)
18w/930	95	940
36w/930	95	2250
58w/930	95	3650
18w/940	95	1000
36w/940	95	2400
58w/940	95	3850
15w/950	98	680
18w/950	98	960
36w/950	98	2300
58w/950	98	3650
18w/965	98	870
36w/965	98	2100
58w/965	98	3350

product ranges available across the world, and have developed the Gro-Lux® range of fluorescent lights for horticulture, 40W, T12 rapid start fluorescent lamp, and GRO-LUX® phosphor lighting for plant growth. The average life rating for this product at 12 hours operation per start is 28,800 hours; average rated life is measured at 3 hours per start on 2-lamp, rapid start magnetic ballasts per IES recommended practice. The lamp life using single-lamp rapid start ballasts may be reduced. The life ratings of florescent lamps are based on 3-hour burning cycles under specified conditions and with ballast meeting ANSI specifications. If the burning cycle is increased, there will be a corresponding decrease in the average hour of life. Minimum starting temperature is a function of the ballast; consult the ballast manufacturer. The "RS" designation has been eliminated to simplify the ordering abbreviation. 40W Rapid Start Lamps may be used in starter operated fixtures designed for 40W preheat lamps. Life rating for preheat service is 15,000 hours average approximately.

The 40W, T12 Rapid Start fluorescent lamp, GRO-LUX ® Wide spectrum phosphor for plant growth, aquarium and meatcase applications, has 3400K color temperature, 89 CRI; average life rating at 12 hours operation per start is 28,800 hours. Average rated life is measured at 3 hours per start on 2-lamp, rapid start magnetic ballasts per IES recommended practice. Lamp life on single-lamp rapid start ballasts may be reduced. Approximate initial lumens after 100 hours operation. The life ratings of fluorescent lamps are based on 3-hour burning cycles under specified conditions and with ballast meeting ANSI specifications. If the burning cycle is increased there will be a corresponding increase in the average hours of life. Minimum starting temperature is a function of the ballast; consult the ballast manufacturer. Again the "RS" designation has been eliminated to simplify the ordering abbreviation. 40W Rapid Start lamps may be used in starter operated fixtures designed for 40W preheat lamps. Life rating for preheat service is approximately 15,000 hours average.

Most manufacturers sell a line of watt-saving fluorescents, which give about 10% less light and use about 20% less electricity. There are fluorescents tubes called power twists: these tubes, which have more surface area, give out 15% more light per watt consumed. Most manufacturers offer tubes in efficient use, and higher output versions, but you'll often have to go to a specialist retailer who deals in lighting only rather than your local DIY (do-it-yourself) store.

White light contains all the colors of the spectrum, giving out some red and blue light from any white light source. Plants use light of all colors to some degree, except for green. There are purple-looking Gro-tubes designed and marketed to emit primarily red and blue light, however it's claimed that these lamps provide little or no assistance or real benefits to growing marijuana, so save your money and buy a standard light. In practice, as long as the lamp produces sufficient red and blue light you're rocking.

Daylight, Warm White and Cool White are names given to varying degrees of white lighting. Daylight, for instance, gives more blue light than red. If you mix a blue lamp and a red one you'll create a similar growth situation to the HID balancer system although of course nowhere near as effective. For four-tube gardens use one blue to three red tubes and so on.

Tubes Strong in Blue Light	*Tubes Stronger in Red Light*
Cool White	Warm white
Daylight Soft	White
Blue Fluorescent	Merchandiser White
	Red Fluorescent

Higher-Output Fluorescents

Higher wattage fluorescent lamps are available in VHO (Very High Output) and HO (High Output). The VHO runs at 27 watts per foot and the HO runs at 14 watts per foot. VHO lamps give twice the light and use three times the power of standard lamps and have to be fitted with a special fitting and ballast. One advantage of fluorescent tubes is that they may conform to an odd space with limited head room such as a shelf, closet, loft or basement, and take up less vertical space for gardening than HIDs.

HID Lamps

HID lamps consist of High Pressure Sodium (recommended for budding) with its red/orange spectrum light, and Metal Halide (recommended for vegetation) with its blue/white spectrum of light. Just to confuse you however, modern research indicates that the most modern sodium lamps have enhanced blue/white light and are more than adequate light sources for every stage of growth. Sodium lamps are the choice of the professionals in all areas of commercial growing. They do it for the money, so they can't be wrong. Sodiums are also far more powerful and efficient than halides and they're improving all the time. In recommending an HPS lamp I would have to say go for 600 watts, changing the lamp yearly.

Recommended Lamp Combinations

Single lamp:	high pressure sodium (HPS)
Two lamps:	one metal halide (MH) and one HPS
More than two lamps:	ne MH to every three HPS lamps
Special attention to vegetative growth:	metal halide
Special attention to flowering/budding:	high pressure sodium

The above chart provides the perfect balance, but to the average smoker who wants to maximize, I can own up to having first-class results by using only HPS lamps and know very few growers who mix their lighting. So if you still don't know what to do, stick to HPS.

HID lights may be purchased with remote ballasts or as a combined or integrated unit. Most growers prefer the remote ballast because they can be mounted outside the garden area or placed on a shelf leaving only a lightweight lamp to hang, making an easier job for raising up and down as the plants require. It's also safer, since major electrical parts can be isolated from the watered areas.

HID: Metal Halide (MH) and High Pressure Sodium Vapor (HPS)

High Intensity Discharge lamps (HIDs) are the most efficient electric light source available indoors. HID lighting illuminates a larger area than other lights, give a greater intensity, and penetrate leaves. More often than not, if you see a picture of horticultural lighting in a Dutch grow room or greenhouse, it's usually a PL Horizontal Reflector. The PL reflectors were developed by Hortilux Schreder Labs. The reflectors are manufactured using high quality aluminum (99.8% pure), then polished and anodized, resulting in a microscopically faceted surface. This creates a highly efficient, uniformly diffused light pattern. Light intensity will decrease with an increase in distance from the light source. It's because of this law of nature that a smaller reflector will reflect more light than a larger one, due to less distance between the light source and the reflective surface. P.L. reflector systems are some of the most efficient reflectors available to the hobby grower. These reflectors will reflect more light with an even distribution to your plants when compared to other reflectors.

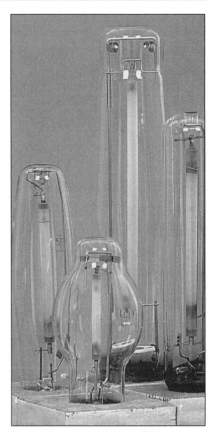

Figure 4.6: Variant of clear metal halide and high pressure sodium lamps.

Figure 4.7: Remote ballast for high pressure sodium lights.

Figure 4.8: Ovulated tubes are fitted to coolers (extractors) in order to lower heat.

FOR PERSISTING HEAT PROBLEMS CONSIDER AN
AIR-COOLED HOOD FOR YOUR LAMP OR AN AIR-CONDITIONING UNIT.

Add an Air-Cooled Housing option that comes in place of the standard socket assembly and cord set. Your chosen reflectors can easily be mounted in this air-cooled housing. Adding this option is an effective way of dealing directly with bulb heat. Having tested the prototype, I found that it out-performed all other air-cooled reflectors offered. This is an excellent choice when using CO_2. If you currently have a lighting system, you can upgrade with a P.L Conversion Reflector and that can also be upgraded with the air-cooled housing.

Both MH and HPS lamps come in several sizes: the halides range up to 1000 watts and beyond, sodium vapor bulbs go up to 1500. For most vegetating situations I recommend 250-watt lamps in small areas or for bringing on mother plants and rooted clones. In larger grow rooms I use one 600-watt lamp per square meter. The use of 1000-watt bulbs may not be the most efficient nor is it necessarily the most productive to use in smaller situations. One thousand watts of lighting is more suited to commercial cultivation or the experienced grower. Remember the higher the wattage you use, the more heat is given off and so the more efficient your air control will need to be to keep the room around 70°F.

The smallest lamp versions come in self-contained units with the ballast built into the fixture. In an area three to five feet square, mini-horizontals are a simple, moderate, yet very effective source of lighting for a personal mini-garden. The most efficient, modest setup you can buy is a 600-watt HPS with a horizontal reflector; this produces an astonishing 92,000 lumens (light output). Your reflector is equally as important as the lamp wattage and the Super Nova reflector certainly gets my recommendation. It's easy to work out that any lamp of, say, 400-watts will take the same energy or money as any other 400-watt lamp but reflectors can add to efficiency and the Super Nova is said to add 30% to light efficiency. A 600-watt lamp doesn't add much to your electric bill, and the bulb lasts for about two years. If you buy your lamps as individual components, then remember that they have to have their own particular ballast, which should be purchased along with the HPS bulb or at a later date from the same manufacturer. When you buy a lamp, go for the best you can afford and make sure that all of your equipment is manufactured to Underwriters Lab recommendations in the US. There are many cheap versions made for the lower market that really don't save you money in the long run. There's only one way to grow and that is the safe, efficient way.

The SuperNova® works on a double parabola that deflects light and heat away from the lamp itself and maximizes light deflection onto the plants and also improves lamp life. The extra light produced by a good reflector costs you no more on electricity and just a few dollars extra to purchase; the extra light efficiency is free once the lamp is paid for.

Philips has prepared its own high pressure sodium lamps for use in horticulture with a GES base. These are within the SON range. First there's the **SON-T PIA AGRO®**, a high quality 400-watt, high pressure sodium vapor lamp with PIA (Philips Integrated Antenna) technology. This lamp features a sintered aluminum oxide discharge tube enclosed in a vacuum clear soda-lime or hard-glass outer tube. The discharge tube is filled with sodium mercury amalgam and xenon starting gas. A clear tubular outer bulb, this is specifically designed for plant irradiation. The color temperature (k) reaches 2050 color rendering, (Ra) is 25, and lumen output rated at 55,000. This lamp can hang and run in any position with a lamp efficacy of 130. A second specific lamp made by **Philips®** is the **SON-T PIA PLUS®**. This high quality product is a high pressure sodium lamp with PIA (Philips Integrated Antenna) technology, sintered aluminum oxide discharge tubes with integrated antenna, enclosed in a vacuum soda-lime or hard-glass outer bulb. The discharge tube is filled with sodium mercury amalgam and xenon, completely lead free lamps (lead free cap mounting). Outer bulb is clear tubular. The benefits the SON-T PIA PLUS® is the PIA technology for increased reliability and lower early failure rate with reliable ignition throughout its lifetime.

The SON-T lamp technical specifications

Watts	Color Temp	Color Rend	Lumen Output	Lamp efficacy	Burning position	Product number
150	1950	23	16500	110	ANY	192295
250	1950	23	32000	128	ANY	179876
400	1950	23	55000	138	ANY	179883
600	1950	23	90000	150	ANY	197429

Osram/Sylvania

The **PLANTASTAR®** is the grow bulb from Sylvania/Osram and it comes in 400-watt and 600-watt versions for our application. The Plantastar® has been developed to meet demand and the requirements of growth technology. This lamp has a low failure rate and is therefore low maintenance, and has a constant luminous flux during the first 10,000 burning hours; after this time, about every two years it's advisable to change the lamp. Solid, high-impact construction with its patented shock absorber makes this lamp very usable in the average garden where space is short and bumps are often, so fewer breakages happen through accidents. A great feature is that the lamp has a moving antenna so there's no chance of the antenna breaking away from its anchor

Plant specific parameters of the 400 and 600-watt lamps:

Photosynthesis W/m^2	1.58
PAR-Wert W/m^2	2.4
u-Einstein 400-700 nm at 1k Lux	12.00
u-Einstein 350-500 nm at 1k Lux	0.8
u-Einstein 600-700 nm at 1k Lux	0.6
SPF	0.5

Technical Specifications of the 400 and 600-watt lamps

Plantastar ®	400 W	600 W
System wattage	450	645
Lamp wattage	400	600
Supply voltage	230	230
Lamp voltage	100	110
Staring voltage	4/5	4/5
Mains current compensated	2.5	3.3
Lamp current	4.5	6.06
Color temperature	2000	2000
Luminous flux klm	55	87
Lamp luminous efficacy sd/cm"	138	145
Average luminance cd/cm"	750	770
Operating position	ANY	ANY
EAN Code 4050300	620084	620107

Light Balancers (Movers)

Light balancers come in two configurations, linear or circular. Linear balancers move backwards and forwards along a linear track, and are best suited to a rectangular garden. Circular balancers either rotate the lights 360°, or move them 180° in two equal movements, making sure the full circle is covered. MH or HPS bulbs hang on mechanical arms and movement is created by a small electrical motor repeating a cycle. Light balancers save on electrical costs, considering the

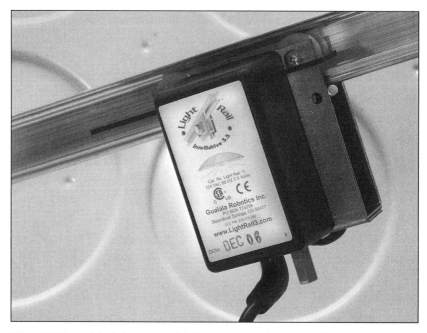

Figure 4.9: Linear light balancer on rail helps to save on electricity and lessen heat output.

extended area that they illuminate against their running costs.

The most efficient way to use an HID lamp, which should be considered by every grower, is provided by the Light Rail 3. Technology has come to the small grower's rescue. The fantastic Light Rail 3 is a simple, effective device based on a six-foot track with a precision engineered carrier that quietly moves the light back and forth over the growing area. The sun moves, so why not your light?

A light mover allows you to use less lighting to cover a vast area, gives uniform growth, saves moving lights up and down, allows your lights to be much closer to the plant while still avoiding burning of foliage, and eliminates shading problems. Using fewer lights in the room also means less heat is generated and so it's easier to achieve the desired temperature. The Light Rail 3 uses just 5-watts of electricity and costs around $1.50 a year to run. It's a readily available, worldwide sales product and has been extensively tested and developed in actual growing conditions. The Light Rail 3 carries an unconditional guarantee. The circular carrier has a plus in that if you use only two lamps and two movers, then one can be a Metal Halide and one can be a High Pressure Sodium, giving a perfect light balance, minimal costs and maximum harvest.

The supplemental lights described here are best used when the grower wishes to supplement or add more light to an existing light system or to a natural light garden. For extending the photoperiod any lamp will do.

Low-Pressure Sodium Lamps

Low-Pressure Sodium Lamps (LPS) are only mentioned in my book because they're offered by a few distributors that advertise in marijuana publications. I believe they're virtually useless in the garden, although they perform well as supplemental lighting. They're monochrome, give off too much heat, explode if splashed with water and cause plants to elongate when growing. They must have a place somewhere in horticulture but I have yet to find it when it comes to marijuana.

Light Spectrum

White light is made up of all the colors of the rainbow, and differs only in the amount of light radiated by each color band, which gives them their own identity by the degrees of whiteness. An incandescent bulb generates mostly red, orange and yellow light and little blue light. White fluorescents have a balanced spectrum, so they appear white. Looking at a metal halide (MH) you'll notice that the blue spectrum reflects in the blue/white color. High Pressure Sodium vapor lamps (HPS's) appear orange because of their red, orange and yellow light spectrum.

Photosynthesis and chlorosynthesis, the two life processes that plants use to transform light energy into biochemical energy for growth, use light energy primarily in the blue and red regions. For normal growth a plant needs the correct amount of radiant energy in both regions of the spectrum.

Metal Halides versus High Pressure Sodium Lamps

HPS lamps give the best return for overall costs, even though they have a strange light spectrum. They're also safer then MH lamps. HPS lamps are your best buy and are your best performers except for starting seedlings and rooting clones. HPS bulbs are better in areas of possible insect invasions. The yellow-orange color of an HPS does not attract night insects, which are drawn more to white lights such as MH. Growers using several HID bulbs often balance the light spectrum by mixing HPS lamps and MH lamps, or by using HPS lamps only for flowering in rotating gardens. British scientists support the mixture of lighting as offering a well-balanced use of the lighting spectrum

Rated wattage is power consumed by the bulb alone. When using a ballast, add 10% more watts usage. Metal halides (MH) are manufactured to be positioned either in the vertical or horizontal usually + or -15°, and they operate safely and last longest only in their intended positions. High pressure sodium lamps, however, may be mounted horizontally, vertically, base up, base down, or universally, meaning in any mounting position. Horizontal lighting is available in MH form depending on the manufacturer recommendations. When used with an appropriate horizontal reflector, MH lamps direct much more light to the plants than vertically suspended lamps, and have comparable lifetimes. Make sure that the bulb offered to you was manufactured for horizontal positioning.

A bulb's useful lifetime is based on 10 hours or more per start. The lifetime of fluorescents, MHs, and HPS bulbs decreases each time the bulb is turned on, and they last longer if continuously lit. Since the lumen output decreases with age, most growers use old bulbs for seedlings and new bulbs for general growth and flowering. Experienced growers replace bulbs every nine months. In general, replace MHs for flowering every year. Replace HPS lamps used for flowering every two years maximum, or 13,000 hours of use for a 24,000-hour-rated lifetime. I personally replace all of my HPS lamps every 12 months to maximize on yield, and sell the old lamps back to the grow shop for them to sell as secondhand. That works quite nicely for me, the supplier and anyone who wants to start up in the HID world of lighting but can't afford new equipment yet. A lumen is a unit used for measuring light and a mean lumen is the midpoint of lumens produced in a bulb's lifetime. Initial lumen is the light expectancy of a new bulb. Mean lumen demonstrates the average amount of lumens a bulb delivers during its useful lifetime. Initial lumens is the figure distributors use to advertise their bulb. Mean lumens are about 75% percent of the initial lumens.

I haven't labored on light spectrum and wavelength charts or charts comparing the spectrum of bulbs to photosynthesis and chlorosynthesis curves. I don't want you as a grower to become obsessed with TDS, (technical distress syndrome), and forget that your original intent was to grow good dope. Instead I thought I would just deal with small differences throughout the book so that they make sense and take on a true perspective as most intensive lighting information available makes little difference to the crop.

MH bulbs emit dangerous levels of UV and particle radiation if the bulb cracks in the outer protective sleeve. A broken bulb may continue to operate without the grower realizing that there's a problem. Exposure to a damaged bulb may cause serious eye and skin damage. Some bulbs have safety features that will make the bulb burn out if the protective sleeve becomes damaged. Although their output is less than ordinary MHs, this is a small price to pay for an extremely important safety feature.

Some of the experienced HID gardeners may think I'm being overly cautious, but read what Sylvania says about their Super Metalarc MH, one of the most popular bulbs that hang naked above many marijuana gardens: "Operate in fixtures which are enclosed in tempered glass or other suitable materials that are capable of withstanding the discharge of hot quartz arc tube particles." Sylvania warns that "all MH bulbs marked M, MS and MM, **MUST** be encased in tempered glass fixtures". The hot quartz particles pose a danger of injury and of fire.

MH and HPS Bulbs and Fixtures

The best place to look for distributors of complete systems with bulb, ballast, and reflector is in one of the regular marijuana publications.

These systems are put together with the idea that you're probably growing marijuana and so they are constructed with this in mind. Most systems include the bulb, ballast, a reflector, and enough extension cable so that the ballast can be placed outside the grow area and the cable can reach the bulb hanging from the ceiling. Distributors sell just about anything else a grower could possibly want, including light balancers, pH meters, moisture meters, Co_2 emitters, soil test kits, hydroponic systems, and much, much, more. Always buy bulbs and ballasts at the same time, they're not all interchangeable.

Reflected Light

Proper attention to reflectivity can increase the amount of available light by up to 30%. It's important that the plants are surrounded as closely as possible by reflective surfaces. This can easily be achieved by placing the lamp in a corner of the room and constructing two lightweight, mobile walls of reflective material, which can be moved out as the plants grow bigger. Walls can easily be painted with flat white paint, which is an excellent reflector. If it's not possible to paint the walls they can be hung with black/white plastic film, which can also be used for the floor. Polystyrene foam sheeting can be used in many different ways; it's a superbly reflective material and highly recommended. The ultimate reflective floor covering is brilliant white vinyl, which is tough and hardwearing. The most reflective material of all is MYLAR, a space-age material, which is like a flexible mirror and can reflect 92% of light back onto the plants.

Reflectivity Levels

Material Reflectivity			
Black	Less than 10%	Flat white paint	80%
Aluminum foil	75 %	Polystyrene sheeting	80%
Semi-gloss white paint	70%	Mylar sheeting	92%
White/black film	85%		

Aluminum foil, believe it or not, does not provide a good reflective surface even when it's flat. When it becomes crinkled, which it inevitably does, it'll become even less effective. A far better reflective surface can be achieved with a couple of coats of flat white paint. I use a white/black plastic film that can be bought off the roll, which is also excellent for putting over windows and does not allow light to shine through it. It's wipe-clean and very cheap, it also makes an excellent reflective floor covering.

Be careful when you choose your paint. The paint to use is water-based, flat, white paint that contains no varnish substance (matte emulsion); these are known to absorb certain colors in the spectral waveband. Glossy paint should never be used as it lends itself to bright spots and glare. In a temporary situation where you may not wish to use paint, we would strongly recommend polystyrene foam sheeting. These sheets can be attached to the wall with blue tack and removed at the end of the crop. It's always good to have a few spare sheets on hand as it can be used in many different ways to maximize the light around your plants; it also insulates your floor to offer some protection from electrical shocks. White/black/white plastic sheeting (which can be bought also as black/white), is another excellent material that has helped to make indoor gardening possible. As its name implies, this tough sheeting is white on each side with a black layer sandwiched in between; the white/black explains has black on one side and white on the other. Tis product comes on a roll, and performs an important dual function of excluding unwanted light on the one hand and reflecting desirable light on the other. Provided that it's carefully placed, the plastic sheeting can be used to make a room completely light tight.

In the first place, it can be used to cover windows when constructing your grow room. This is extremely important if you're using grow lights, as an uncovered window will tend to light up large areas of the neighborhood, which can attract attention and possibly invite burglary or vandalism. In the second place, the exclusion of all natural light will allow you to have total control over your plants' light source.

Controlling the source of light means that flowering can be induced by reducing the light hours. This is a commercial technique favored by flower producers such as chrysanthemum growers. White/black/white plastic film can also be used as a floor covering, helping to protect carpets from water or nutrient solution which can easily be spilt or splashed. A combination of white paint, polystyrene sheeting and white/black film will allow you to build a grow room in which all the visible surfaces are white. This will ensure the maximum use of the light that you're providing.

Figure 4.10: Black/White polythene is used white side out to reflect light.

Timers

The use of an efficient timer is absolutely essential for the indoor or greenhouse grower. Timers are used to automatically turn your lighting system on and off. Indoor gardens run on 10 to 18 hour cycles generally and it's essential that timers be reliable. A failed timer could mean that lights remain on which will have a big impact on your power

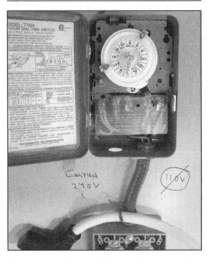

Figure 4.11: Timer unit is used to control the garden's light cycle.

bill and could also completely disrupt the flowering cycle by confusing the plants and possibly putting them back into vegetation. On the other hand if the lights remain off then your vegetating plants can be kicked into bud or even worse the erratic lighting can cause your little ladies to become hermaphrodite and cause a subsequent complete loss of the crop.

Ordinary plug-in timers can be bought cheaply enough at your local DIY store but they're not suitable for more than one or two lights and can be prone to failure. For complete peace of mind, a timer of industrial quality is recommended. Better still, use a complete garden control system, which has a multi-function timer, 2 ventilation motor outlets with heat sensor automation, a water pump outlet with as many as 4 lighting outlets that will run up to 8 lamps complete with its own relay, a further relay for additional uses and a spare 240-volt outlet. If you use a plug-in timer then you must use a relay; it'll divert the power load away from the timer. The timer switches on the relay which in turn sends power to the light ballast whose job it is to ignite the lamp.

Power Consumption

The amount of electricity needed to grow plants indoors can be surprisingly small and it should never be seen as a reason not to go ahead. The beginner is strongly advised to work out power consumption before starting, to ensure that the operation will be cost effective. A few figures have been included here as guidance but you'll need to check your local rates to see if they apply to you. If off-peak power is available then take advantage of it where possible.

Factory-produced timer units are neat, efficient and simple to use by mounting on a suitable wall with screws; plug them into a normal outlet, your ballasts then plug into the unit. There are other devices available for multi-outlet use including timers for commercial and industrial use.

5

Setting Up
Your Grow Area

By now you should have decided where to locate your garden, how much you want to spend on it and therefore how big it'll be. Now let's design the place of your dream, fix up the walls, decide how to water and get the girls growing. We have already talked about lighting in its most complex use applicable to the growing of marijuana.

This book is designed to get the new grower up and running and support those existing growers who are looking for something a little better than they already have, to whet the appetite and satisfy your needs. Now that you understand the lighting systems available, setting up a garden can be as straightforward or as complex as you want it to get. From now on you're in control of the time you put in and the harvest you get out. The larger the garden designed, the more preparation is needed. Small fluorescent gardens may need no more than a simple light fitting over the plants; maybe instead you want to convert an unused cupboard area, which would easily accommodate a single 400-watt or even 600-watt HPS providing you use a heat exhaust system. A simple electrical bathroom extractor will often suffice. You may want to include light balancers to use less lighting and electricity in a box room, basement or loft area, or you may even want to make your life easier still by installing a mechanical watering system and getting really elaborate with a CO_2 dispenser. Let's talk about some ideas and see where it all takes you. After all it's your bank balance we're breaking into, isn't it?

Indoor Grow Rooms

Let's draw a plan together. Having decided on the area in which you intend to grow, look at that area and consider all of the security aspects that must be attended to first, to avoid detection by unwanted visitors. Don't forget, even in countries where it's legal to grow dope there are people in your circle of friends who will talk about your venture to outsiders, which in turn may lead to thieves making a visit to your garden and stealing your crop. There are three main telltale areas to deal with: light, heat and odor. Let's talk about these in order. **Light**: If you're using a box room, can the light be seen through the window of that room by passersby? An HID lighting system is so obvious since the glow of orange light and its intensity is easily detectible to the suspicious passerby, educated would-be thief, or local police officer. The second consideration is **heat**: if a heat detector is aimed at your grow area then it'll light up like a Christmas tree. We have to disperse this heat, spread it evenly or lose it all together. As to **odor**: your plants are going to smell, we all know that, more especially when they're in bud.

The last thing we want is for the neighbors to complain or if it's in a bedroom of a shared household, like your parents' house for instance, then we don't want them getting inquisitive or annoyed, do we? If you're venting to an outside area, will the smell be wafted along the street? Similarly if you're venting to another room the odor will be detected. Are you using a spare room in your own house that visitors may stumble across when they're looking for the bathroom, is it an area that a tradesman might have to access to service an appliance or gain access to a service meter? One last consideration is electricity, although this is more of a safety issue in my book because an inadequate supply will lead to fires, or may overload and blow the supply fuse. Since it's a safety issue that may cause a visit from a professional outside agent like the service providers or at worst the fire department, then it must be considered a security factor also. All tradesmen are bound by law to alert the authorities of any suspicious activity. Let's consider these security issues one by one and talk about some of the alternatives we might consider to deal with them.

Light

This is easily dealt with by using the white/black/white or the white/black film described in chapter 4. The best way to do this is by neatly fixing the existing curtains inside the window opening. Make sure there's a little wrinkle in the curtains to give a natural effect. Then prepare a sheet of plywood or other compilation sheet wood material cut to approximately 4" (10 cm) larger than your window area and designed to sit on top of the windowsill; if there's no protruding sill board then all the better. The board can either be fixed to the wall with rawl plugs and screws, using screws at least 1.6" (4 cm) longer than the thickness of the wood, or with an adhesive product such as Nonails or a good brand of High/Low Mod Silicone, lay two thick lines of the adhesive to the edges of the board and press firmly to the wall. The downfall of using the adhesive method is that you'll have to support the board under pressure until the adhesive cures. Remember to remove all wallpaper so that you're fixing the adhesive to the plaster finish, otherwise the weight of the board could tear the wall paper and fall. The plus of using adhesive is that there'll be no drill holes in the wall and no drilling noise for anyone who shares the house with you to hear. Once the board has been secured to the wall, cover the whole wall, floor to ceiling and wall to wall with the white/black film leaving the white side facing into the room and providing a good reflective coating.

Heat

This one is more complex and will be dealt with more thoroughly later in the book with information on using electrically controlled heat sensors, heaters and air conditioners. For now we'll deal with the first basic means of heat control, the mechanical exhaust motor. You'll need to purchase two silent running ventilation motors. The size of the ventilator will be determined by the size of the room. Measure the room height by the width by the length to get the cubic area. If it's 10' (3 m) long and 6' 6" (2 m) wide you just now multiply the two numbers together to give you 65 ft^2 (6 m^2), then multiply that number by the height of the room to give you the cubic capacity. Assume the height of the room is 8' (2.5 m), we multiply the 65 ft^2 x 8', which equals 520 ft^3 (6 x 2.5 = 15 m^3). Now multiply the cubic capacity by 20 giving you a required air change of 10,400 ft^2 (300 m^3) every three minutes.

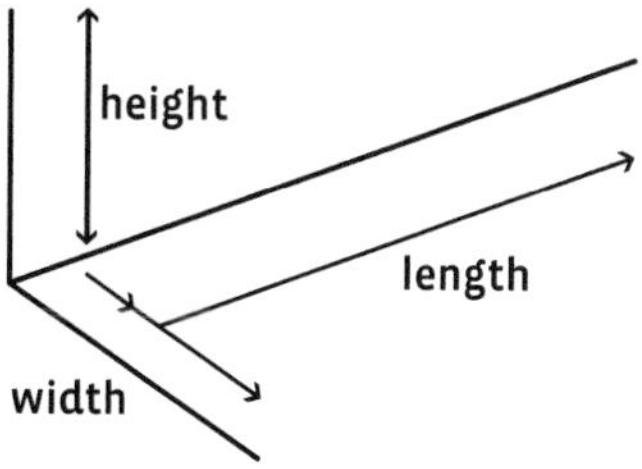

Length	10 feet (3 m)
Width	6.5 feet (2 m) x
Sq Meters	65 feet^2 (6 m^2)
Height	8 feet (2.5 m) x
Cubic ft.	49 x 66 feet (15m x 20m)
(cubic m)	= 3234 feet^3 (300 m^3)

Figure 5.1

Figure 5.2: A suspended ventilation unit is used to control heat and oxygen quality.

You'll need a second unit to pull cool air into the room. This unit will be slightly smaller in capacity than your exhaust unit. The exhaust will go either through an outside wall, a window, or the ceiling into the loft space. It can be taken from the room through flexible tubes that you can buy from your grow equipment supplier or some better equipped gardening stores and join them to a plastic pipe similar to that used for drainage that can be bought from your local DIY superstore or building supply merchant. During winter months it's a good idea for the unit that pulls air into the room to be fitted into an inside door or inside wall of the house so that you're pulling in slightly pre-warmed air from other rooms to help maintain the temperature rather than cold air from the outside, this may create a problem of overheating on occasions when the outside heat is greater than the inside heat but is an asset during colder weather You can use a series of pipe adapters and vents to carry the air into the room through a ceiling vent also which is out sight mainly. It's possible to introduce manual valves to driect flow from a pipe that has a dual source of air and useful for shutting off outside air in the winter asnd inside air for the summer. it may all sound complicated but, believe me it's quite easy and catered for by supply companies of growing materials.

A great way of fooling any heat detector is for the hot air vent to be placed in the ceiling of your grow room, pulling the hot air up and into the roof void or loft.

That way, should a heat detector be aimed at your house, the whole house will glow at the same heat rather than one room glowing like a hot coal. Another alternative is to take the vent pipe into a branch of your toilet waste vent pipe so that the hot air comes out of the top of the pipe, which could easily fool otheres into believing it may be hot water from your bath waste. The vent motor inward can be fitted at floor level or ceiling level inside a box stuffed with rockwool or some similar material, packed tightly around the motor to keep the unit running quietly so there's no vibration or sound to annoy or alert neighbors.

Figure 5.3: Individual branches of weed hanging out to dry.

Make three holes in a box, one on the side where the air blows out of the box at the same size of the vent and two at the end where the air comes into the vent; these holes will be the size of plastic foul or sewer pipe supplied by your local DIY store, usually 4" (110 mm) diameter. One will go through into the house area and one will go to the outside, then you can control which pipe you'll use for incoming air, cold or warmed, and you now have your own air conditioning unit. Both pipes must be fitted with an old stocking or pair of panty hose stretched out over it to stop sucking in unwanted insects, etc. The easiest way to do this is to put the tights over a pipe end before two pipes are pushed together.

Warm household air will be sucked in at low level at one end of the room, maybe through an internal wall—or you could fit the vent unit above the door—and through the wall then down inside low via the flexible hosing available from your grow shop or the supplier of the vent unit. Since hot air rises, then we take the hot air out at high level through an outside wall or ceiling. The room should be maintained at 26° for best growth and budding.

The vent into the loft area should also be fitted in a box to silence it and eliminate vibration made in the same way as the air-in unit except that this box will have just two holes corresponding with the motor mounted inside, one on the bottom to suck air in and one on the top to blow air out. To mount the box in the loft area rather than hang it in the room would be ideal, so that it'll then be adequately supported and take less installation. You can make the job very neat by fixing a vent over the hole so it isn't just gaping, but as it's only you who are going to see it then it doesn't really matter unless you're a fussy person and obsessed with neatness.

The boxes can be made of ply wood sheets, or any other sheet wood material, maybe you have some old wardrobe doors lying around that are going spare. Always use scrounged items if you can with the exception of electrical material. Boxes only need be constructed in 6.5" (12 mm)-thick materials. All you need in the way of tools is a jigsaw and a screwdriver. Place screws every 4" (10 cm), and glue all round contact edges for sound job or use. The top of the box must have a removable panel so that you can access the electrics or the removable homemade insect filter at Figure 5.5. A further major plus to the air ventilation system is that you'll gain free oxygen from the atmosphere, which the plants require to thrive.

If you are sucking air into the room, especially from outside, there will be airborne objects such as insects that aren't welcome. The best way to deal with this is by fitting a filter as previously described by sliding panty hose over the 4" (10 cm) pipe or make a filter. To make an insect filter that is removable, all you need is an old metal coat hanger, bent square, then slide the leg of a stocking or one leg of an old pair of panty hose over the top of it. This makes a nice removable filter that will stop all unwanted insects in the room, especially in the summer when gnats are looking to lay their eggs in your water system. Their larvae cause irreparable damage to your root system. Finally, treat yourself to a heat sensor unit with vent controllers.

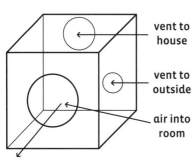
Vent in box. Two 0.5" (110mm) holes in one end accomodates plastic vent pipes.

vent to house

vent to outside

air into room

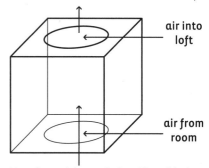
Vent box with two holes. Size of hole corresponds with size of vent outlets.

air into loft

air from room

Figure 5.4: How to design ventilation distribution boxes for optimum heat dispersal.

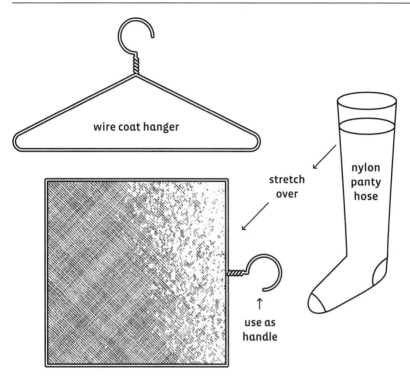

Figure 5.5: Construct your own effective air filter to stop insect infestation.

Both ventilation units plug into the regulator box, which has a heat sensor coming from it. The sensor hangs in the middle of the room so that when the temperature gets to that which has been set, the unit shuts down either on the in or on the out motor. This saves electricity and keeps the room at a steady ambient heat. Reasonable to good quality controllers cost from $100 - $200 although there are many variations and special offers around.

Odor

Odor is the most simply dealt with security threat, but it'll cost you. There are negative-ion generators available on the market; they're another draw on your electricity supply although it's only 5–20 watts of power. There are several available, including hanging ones that reduce grime collected on surfaces close by and can also eliminate the possibility of shocks or damage that may occur on contact with water. Negative-ion generators are OK when it comes to ridding yourself of odor in your house and are quite effective in small situations, but they are no replacement

Figure 5.6: In-line carbon filter works with air changer to eliminate odor.

for carbon filters. Carbon filters can be an integral part of a ventilation unit or purchased as individual units to attach and can even be fixed directly to the vent motor either in line with a spigot or with flexible tubing such as Isoflex. The tube comes in white or silver, and of course the silver is preferable for reflective value. The flexible tubing comes in varying sizes to suit the motor and filter and some are lined with an insulation material to dampen sound.

6

Grow Rooms and Wacky Ideas

We have already discussed the kinds of lighting available; now let's apply that knowledge to the space you have decided to grow in. Generally speaking a height of 6' (1.8 m) is required if you're growing with 1000-watt lamps, although I suggest you stick to 400 or 600-watts, in which case 4' (1.2 m) height is adequate for Sea of Green method of growth which is described in more detail later. The size of planting pot you use and the height to which you grow your plant is a secondary deciding factor when considering room height. Let's say that you're growing what is known as a Sea of Green: this is where we put 25 plants, each in a 1 gal. (5 L) square pot under one 400-watt lamp. If you have a normal room height of 8' (2.4 m) then you could double tier, as the height you'll need per layer is only 4' (1.2 m). So in a full height cupboard of 3' (1 m) that might stand in the corner of your room you could be growing as many as 50 plants under two lamps. The cheapest way to do this would be to build the cupboard into the corner of your designated room against an outside wall. Make vent holes on the bottom of the side panel adjacent to the wall and fit.

You would of course have to vent any constructed area to take away the heat, using a 4" (110 mm) diameter plastic foul or vent pipe bought from a builders' or DIY store (you could ask a friendly builder or plumber if they have any off-cut pipe that would suit you—again, always scrounge materials where you can; you may even have a friend who has a piece of pipe lying in his garden, garage or shed). The vent pipe needs to be taken to the outside of the house either by a flexible pipe or straight through an existing ventilation area that may have been built into the house from new. Look for the louver vent in your bedroom or kitchen, the one that you keep blocking off with newspaper to stop the draft coming in! The cheaper

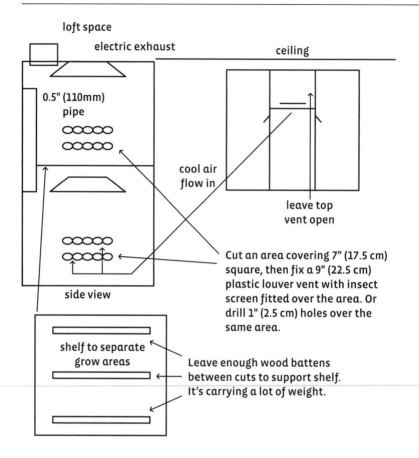

loft space

electric exhaust

ceiling

0.5" (110mm)
pipe

cool air
flow in

leave top
vent open

side view

Cut an area covering 7" (17.5 cm)
square, then fix a 9" (22.5 cm)
plastic louver vent with insect
screen fitted over the area. Or
drill 1" (2.5 cm) holes over the
same area.

shelf to separate
grow areas

Leave enough wood battens
between cuts to support shelf.
It's carrying a lot of weight.

Figure 6.1: An easy-to-build square grow cupboard using plywood or other sheet material.

but less effective alternative is to fit a louver vent on the inside wall of the cupboard and suck air through it, leaving a small window open in the grow room to allow cool air to enter the room from outside. This cheaper alternative, although not as efficient, is more security conscious. At the top of the inside of the cupboard you'll have to fit a vent motor to suck out the hot air and draw the cool air through the lower vent. The best place to put the vent out is in the ceiling, blowing the hot air up into your loft space. This plan is going to give you 50 plants growing in a meter square space of your bedroom—how cool is that?

It's essential that the dividing shelf be watertight, otherwise water may spill when you feed your plants on the top shelf and find its way into the electrics of the lower shelf causing an electrical fire or other disaster.

To draw heat from the lower grow area into the top and out, use another section of the 4" (110 mm) vent pipe, making sure that the pipe extends below lamp area to ensure heat is drawn away. The hot air will eventually be blown out into your loft space. If there's a problem with the warm air being blown into the attic space, for instance maybe the area is shared or open to your neighbor's property, and so the odor has to be contained. Take a normal 4" (110 mm) plastic pipe or a 100mm hose similar to that used for tumble dryer vent pipe from the mechanical vent and through an outside wall or up through the roof so that it looks like a stench pipe or central heating vent. A mechanical vent for 1 sq. yd. (1 m²) by 8' (2.4 m) high cupboard must be capable of moving 88 sq. yd. (45 m³), three times per minute. The cupboard should of course be lined with Mylar, white/black film or painted with a matte white emulsion for maximum reflection.

Loft Conversion

Attic or loft conversions can be difficult when space is limited. Again, we need a maximum of 4' (1.2 m) in height if we're using HID lamps, or 30" (45 cm) if you're using fluorescent lights. I am making the assumption that you'll want to maximize growth and shorten harvest time, so I am going to describe HID usage here. The first thing to do is measure the height to maximize on the floor area. Let's look at an example.

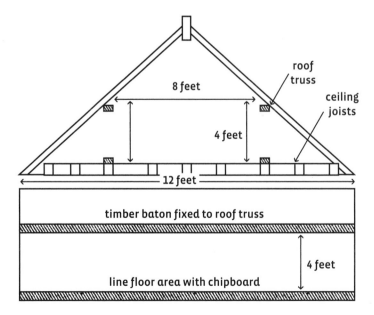

Figure 6.2: First stage of loft conversion for a grow room area.

Take the lefthand side of the roof pitch first. Get a tape measure and measure up from the top of the ceiling joists to a height of 4' (1.2 m) where you reach the bottom of a roof truss and mark with chalk, then use the same measuring technique with the right pitch. Measure between the two points laterally; that will give you the usable floor area. Lay 0.7" (18 mm) chipboard to ceiling joists with 1.4" (35 mm screws); never nail timber to roof trusses or ceiling joists as this may loosen the roof tiles or ceiling boards respectively. You'll need a couple of lengths of roofing baton (also known as lathe), which can be purchased from a DIY superstore or builder/roofing merchant. This is the timber used to fix tiles to your roof. It's very cheap and usually pressure-treated so it won't rot.

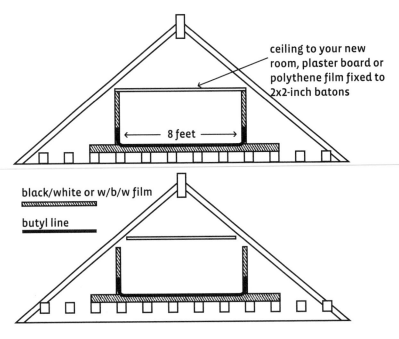

ceiling to your new room, plaster board or polythene film fixed to 2x2-inch batons

8 feet

black/white or w/b/w film

butyl line

Figure 6.3: Second stage of loft conversion for grow room area.

If you can't purchase the baton then buy ordinary 1.5" (37 mm) square sawn timber. Screw the baton to the chipboard at the desired width, in this case 8' (2.4 m), then screw the same type of baton to the roof trusses as shown in drawing above. These four timbers are set to take the upright supports to be fixed at 2' (60 cm) centers, then 0.5" (12 mm) chipboard or wood similar to the uprights by using screws and so forming side walls. Once you fill in the ends with another chipboard panel using the same method, we have created a small room. Cut a door opening into the front section (unless the attic hatch is inside the room you have just built). The cheap alternative would be to fix white/black/white film to the roof joists and let it fall down the sides at the edge of the floor section. You must have a floor section that is well-supported as the new area will be taking a lot of weight. The floor has to be lined with butyl pond liner; this will take any water spillage and stop leaks going through your ceiling or spoiling the timber floor.

Simply staple the film to the roof truss timbers and let it fall down onto the floor area. Fix a baton under the film to take the weight off the staples and let it drop toward the floor. The floor still requires a butyl liner to hold water spillage.

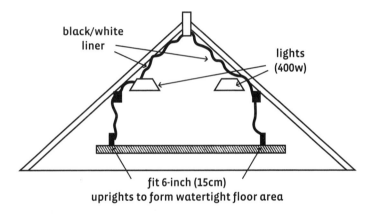

black/white liner

lights (400w)

fit 6-inch (15cm) uprights to form watertight floor area

Figure 6.4: A low-cost loft conversion alternative for budget growers.

Lighting can now be fixed inside. Fitting is as described within the lighting section in Chapter 4. In a room of the size shown in our example you'll have a square meter of plants each side with an open section through the middle to access plants for maintenance. Watering may be done manually or designed to have a pump fitted on a timer (watering will be dealt with fully in chapter 11). Two inlets, (one internal and one external) with one exhaust via mechanical ventilation will deal with temperature control. The sizes of units are determined by using our calculation described earlier. The inlet will be taken from outside and through the roof with an alternative inlet from the house area that will be taken through a ceiling vent and cut out at a position you'll decide upon during your planning stage. The exhaust emits through the roof area or straight into the roof void (attic space).

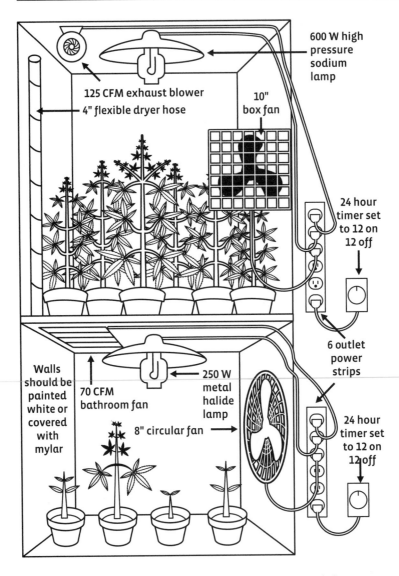

125 CFM exhaust blower
4" flexible dryer hose

600 W high pressure sodium lamp

10" box fan

24 hour timer set to 12 on 12 off

6 outlet power strips

Walls should be painted white or covered with mylar

70 CFM bathroom fan

250 W metal halide lamp

8" circular fan

24 hour timer set to 12 on 12 off

Figure 6.5: Small area grow cupboard incorporating a nursery area below.

Cupboard Gardens

If you have a landing cupboard or bedroom cupboard that is not being used, or is underused then this can be useful to you as a grow area. A cupboard of say 2'6" (75 cm) wide and 3' (90 cm) deep will take up to 6 good sized plants or as a Sea of Green around twenty 1.8 gal. (5 L pots). You have to decide on the best harvesting for you: either go for as many crops as possible, maximizing on the year or go for immediate weight, depending on your patience and outlook.

Cupboard gardens like the one shown in 6.5 are capable of housing 15 plants in 2 gal. (7 L) pots. This cupboard is 2' (60 cm) deep by 18" (175 cm) wide and lit by one 600-watt, HPS lamp with an exhaust at ceiling level. On the floor of the cupboard there are two propagators, one heated and one standard. This is the "nursery," used to keep a constant supply of plants growing to feed the garden above.

Staircases

Staircases can offer fantastic spaces underneath that will be useless to most people and usually hoard all the old rubbish that could be thrown away. Get in there and have a clear out, find homes (or a bin) for the things you have lurking in the darkness, and fit it out as a great little garden area. You have the opportunity to convert this space into your personal "Stairway to Heaven."

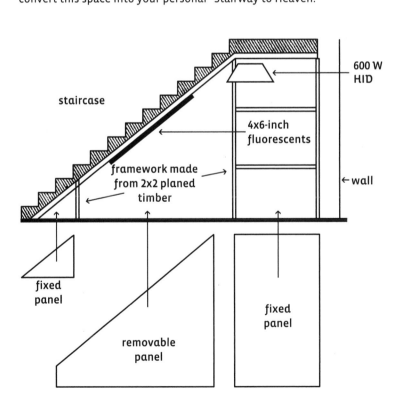

Figure 6.6: How to construct a grow room under the stairs of your home.

The area available is generally just under a 3' (1 m) wide and about 6.5' (2 m) long so as a Sea of Green you're looking at around 40 plants, allowing for some movement for maintenance. Here we can use a cross between fluorescents and miniature HID. Your largest problem in this situation is going to be maintenance so I would recommend a Sea of Green with an automatic watering system. One immediate situation that you may have to deal with in an understairs situation is that the utility service meters may be fitted in there. This can be overcome by asking your service provider to move them to an outside wall or lobby. There's generally a charge for this but if you tell them you're working all the time and their meter reader can't get access until late evening, then they may waive their charges for their own benefit.

I've shown you how to design a fill-in panel under the stairs where no infill exists. Form a frame of 20" (50 cm) planed timber and fit the two fixed panels as shown. Make a further panel for the center portion. The center portion can be lifted in and out of place and fixed with simple suitcase latches, screws, bolts or push-in pegs.

Two bathroom-type air vents, one in and one out, can deal with ventilation. Use a negative ionizer in the room to take away the smell. If the smell gets to be too noticeable you can burn incense sticks or take the vent through a wall into the next room. If a little extra money is available then put in a carbon filter and use a better exhaust unit; you can always sell your first harvest to pay for new equipment, providing you're in a country that allows such sales to take place legally. Maybe you can even do a swap.

Wacky Ideas

A neat idea for the bedroom, suitable for just one or maybe two plants, is the speaker cabinet idea (Figure 6.7). This is a simple, effective, cabinet using any sheet wood material like plywood or chipboard to form a dummy speaker cabinet. The cabinet can stand in your bedroom or lounge and look every bit the part, (you could even make it a working speaker). The design is a simple oblong box that can be as tall as you like and fitted with fluorescent tubes to grow your plants. Because we're using fluorescents, we can grow from a tiny clone up to the largest plant that will fit your cabinet. There's far less heat from a fluorescent so foliage won't burn. Plants can even touch the lamp if required. In this instance you may only be growing one or two plants, so we will use a method referred to later in the book where we pinch out the top growth to give around four tops or colas to your plant rather than just the one.

The speaker cabinet can be as big as you like, but for this example I am going to make it 3' (90 cm) high by 2' (60 cm) square. So you need to cut four pieces at 3' (90 cm) by 2' (60 cm) for the sides and 2 pieces at 2' (60 cm) square, one for the top and one for the bottom. To each corner of the cabinet you'll need to fix one piece of 2" (5 cm) wooden angle fillet running from top to bottom; this can be bought from any timber yard or building supply store and is usually used for connecting flat roofs to a house wall. Fix the fillet with screws and suitable adhesive. Start by fixing the fillet to the side panels of the cabinet as below. Having fixed the four pieces of fillet, you can now fix a fluorescent fitting to each corner with the electrical connections at the top of the fitting.

Lay one blank panel to the floor, apply adhesive to the top face edge of the panel in two strips and press the left panel fitted with angle onto the blank panel Now do the same with the righthand panel Then fit the final blank panel to the top by the same method. Now we have the sides ready. When the adhesive is set stand the whole thing up. Place the panel cut for the bottom on the floor and put one track of adhesive around the edge. Now stand the whole cabinet on top, fixing square to the bottom of the speaker cabinet. The final top piece will be made

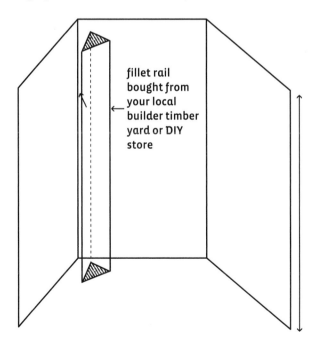

fillet rail bought from your local builder timber yard or DIY store

Figure 6.7: Design and build speaker systems to house a single plant.

as a removable panel for you to access and maintain your plants. This can just as easily be a side panel if you find it easier, just adapt the construction. Paint inside of all panels with flat white emulsion before fitting together.

Now that you have your cabinet it can be "authenticated" by buying stick-on speaker covers from your local car radio store, Tandy, or perhaps someone is throwing away some old speakers and you can take the covers from those! You'll always find old speakers at the garbage dump if you want to make the journey. You can if you wish be a little more authentic and adventurous by actually cutting out holes in your cabinet and fitting them with real speakers so that the things work. Drill holes in the sides or back at a low level and again at the top back to create cool air flow or your plants will just die from heat exhaustion. Fix a small fan from an old computer to keep the air moving inside and keep it all cool; a new one is only a few dollars and will do the trick. A small bathroom fan can be fitted to the top rear of the box to draw out hot air. You could even fit flashing lights to the unit. Make sure the lid fits light-tight and that all holes to the rear have light traps in them made out of cardboard or metal. A simple maze design will work fine. Use your imagination. Remember, my suggestions are just that, suggestions, and can be improved upon for authenticity or how the grow boxes can best fit into your room and look like a piece of furniture.

Maybe you have a bunk bed with an action area under it. This is a perfect grow area for you to use. Consider this if you have the space. Look at your bed, take out all of the fittings except the top bunk of course; the bottom bunk goes, cupboards plus any shelving. Start your conversion by lining the undersection

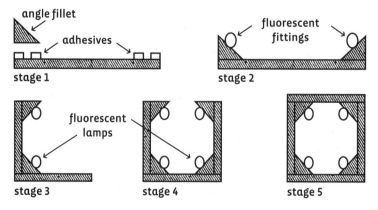

Figure 6.8: Construction of speaker cabinet showing lighting system.

The next generation of clones sits waiting to be transplanted.

These freshly rooted clones have been recently transplanted into 4 inch rockwool cubes.

Transplant clones into at least a 4 inch pot to allow adequate room for rooting.

Blocking light from contacting the rockwool cubes discourages algae growth.

This beauty exhibits a large cola and sizeable lateral buds.

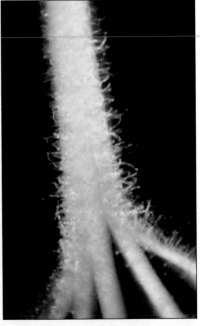

A close-up view shows the individual THC gland stalks and heads.

This plant is a nice size to induce flowering for sea of green.

Large flowering plants drink rapidly. This one needs a watering.

Don't rely on your memory. Label plants to keep things straight.

Expanded clay pellets block light from reaching the roots and support bigger larger root mass.

Keep plants from resting on top of flood/drain holes.

This spaghetti tubing is used to drip water individual plants.

After initial vegetative growth these plants will need to be separated for more growing space.

Green, healthy clones should transplant well and take off right away.

Big buds are a product of a well tuned room and the right genetics.

Numerous lights are required to cover this abundantly packed room.

Light movers maximize wattage and the amount of space being used by spreading the light to reach all parts of the garden.

These plants needed to be braced to support the weight of the ever increasing buds.

Only the Rockwool is garbage; everything else can be reused.

Cleaning the expanded clay pellets to use for the next crop is relatively easy and saves money.

A disinfectant will kill any algae or mold that may be growing on the pellets And slightly watered down bleach works well.

Lightly rubbing the pellets will also remove old root matter.

Once the pellets are disinfected they are removed from the table.

The clay powder and other residue is then rinsed away.

A wet/dry shop vac helps speed up the cleaning process.

The screen keeps the vacuum from getting clogged.

The screen also helps accelerate the drying process in this large scale grow op.

This reflector offers better light distribution but is somewhat cumbersome.

An economical yet effective reflector.

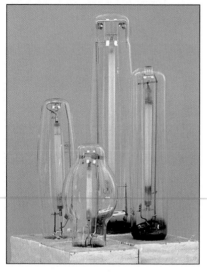

Metal Halide bulbs are easily differentiated from high pressure sodium bulbs by their distinctive football shape.

The box around this ballast greatly reduces noise and keeps wires organized.

Even a flashlight at night can alter flowering cycles but you never know when you may need it.

Controller boxes help to automate the room. This unit is for a ventilation system.

Air conditioners lower humidity as well as temperature.

Ventilation is key. Make sure to use quality fans with enough CFM for the size of the room.

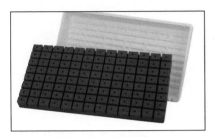

Oasis cubes are an excellent medium for rooting clones.

Keeping the clones at the correct temperature will decrease rooting time.

A watering can should come with every soil garden.

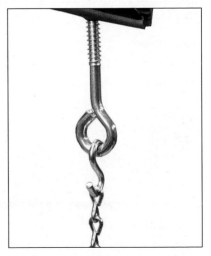

Eyelet hooks are perfect for hanging lights from.

A vigorously growing male's flowers are ready to drop their pollen on the garden.

This single male will be enough to pollinate the entire room if a seed crop is desired.

Fresh seeds like this should be dried before storing.

Ripe seeds release easily from the calyx that holds them.

A mature and fertile seeds should be brown and not crush too easily.

This unit regulates airflow to individual air stones.

Aerating the water aids root and plant growth while hindering algae from establishing itself in the reservoir.

Activated carbon filters are the tool of choice for drastically reduces odor problems from stinky strains.

A well organized control centre keeps everything in one place.

This vigorously growing garden's large top buds and dense plant structure will provide for a heavy yield.

Zip ties are very handy for training and supporting plants.

Mango 49
Ice 42
Mazar 34
TOTAL 125

Making notes to compare with future gardens will accelerate your learning.

Product Mixing and Reference Chart
Measurements in Milliliters Per Gallon

	PLANT STAGE	LIGHT HOURS	DURATION	MICRO	BLOOM	GROW	PLANT AMP	UNCLE JOHN'S	pH	EC	PPM	
Progressive	MIXTURE		Recirculating Systems ~ Using Coco Coir, Rock Wool, Hydro Rock, etc									**Cutting Edge Solutions**
	Cuttings Rooted	18 Hours	Customer Preference	5 ml	5 ml	10 ml	10 ml	10 ml	4.0~6.5	1~2.5	550~1150	
	Vegetative Mix	18 Hours	1-2 Weeks	8 ml	5 ml	15 ml	10 ml	10 ml	4.0~6.5	3~4	1200-1950	
	Transition Mix	12 Hours	1-2 Weeks	8 ml	15 ml	5 ml	10 ml	10 ml	4.0~6.5	1.7~3.5	890-1680	
	Bloom Mix	12 Hours	4-8 Weeks	8 ml	20 ml	0 ml	10 ml	10 ml	4.0~6.5	2.5~3.2	1400~1580	
	Optional Flush	12 Hours	5-10 Days	4 ml	10 ml	0 ml	10 ml	10 ml	4.0~6.5	1.5~2.5	830~1080	
Conservative	MIXTURE		Drain to Waste Systems ~ Using Coco Coir, Rock Wool, Hydro Rock or 100% Soil									
	Cuttings Rooted	12 Hours	Customer Preference	5 ml	5 ml	10 ml	10 ml	10 ml	4.0~6.5	1~2.5	550~1150	
	Vegetative Mix	12 Hours	1-2 Weeks	5 ml	5 ml	10 ml	10 ml	10 ml	4.0~6.5	1~2.5	550~1150	
	Transition Mix	12 Hours	1-2 Weeks	5 ml	10 ml	5 ml	10 ml	10 ml	4.0~6.5	1.3~2.3	700~1090	
	Bloom Mix	12 Hours	4-8 Weeks	5 ml	15 ml	0 ml	10 ml	10 ml	4.0~6.5	1.2~2.2	640~1050	
	Optional Flush	12 Hours	5-10 Days	2 ml	5 ml	0 ml	10 ml	10 ml	4.0~6.5	0.5~1.2	230~580	

NOTE PLANT AMP™ CONTAINS ORGANIC ACIDS WHICH CAUSE A TEMPORARY LOW pH READING. DO NOT ADJUST pH. THE pH WILL RISE NATURALLY AS THE PLANT UPTAKES THE CHELATED CALCIUM IN ONE OR TWO DAYS.

True to its name, this is a reference chart and is not written in stone. Each strain and garden will require slightly different levels of nutrient.

The bright fuchsia pistils on this plant are a characteristic of the particular strain not the growing method.

With only a few pistils having receded thus far, this bud could use a few more weeks before being harvested.

This marvelous looking nug is almost ripe for the picking.

of the top bunk with plywood, MDF or chipboard. To the back wall, fix a 1" (2.5) x 2" (5 cm) planed and square edged wooden baton and panel that out with a similar timber to the rest. Hang curtains on the front and you're set. Fit out the area under the bed with shelving if you wish to grow under fluorescents. You can adapt this idea to include any lighting technique you prefer.

A single size bed is usually 6' 6" (2 m) long and about 3' (1 m) wide so it provides huge potential. Put 2 shelves under the bed so that using the floor space also you'll have at least 13' (4 m) of grow area, in 2 rows of 6' 6" (2 m). All you have to do now is fix your lighting.

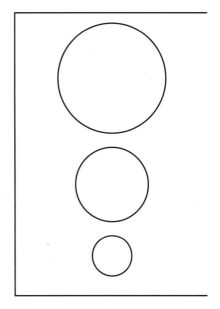

Figure 6.9: Finished cabinet with dummy gauzed speaker openings.

You won't need mechanical ventilation to remove heat since there will be very little; just leave a window slightly open in the room. Make sure you don't let the neighbors' kids stay over or any old friends, as they can get nosy or stumble across your secret.

Friends sleeping over may not be amused at your ingenuity if they find your garden. Mind you I can't think of any better way to spend the night than lying on a bed of good skunk—if you can't sleep, try counting buds instead of sheep. And if you still can't sleep, smoke some bud, you'll soon doze off (note: weed bud works better than sheep).

Now I guess you have thought of some more obvious alternatives like converting the garden shed or even the garage but you may have no out buildings available; indeed you may have no spare rooms either, so here are some alternatives. Buy a cheap box van: these make great grow rooms, parked up at the side or rear of the house, and no one takes any notice. These vans can be bought for less than $100. Often you can get a vehicle with a broken or no engine from someone who is just pleased to see the back of it. You may be lucky enough to get hold of a van that is already boarded out, but if you don't then you can do it quite easily yourself.

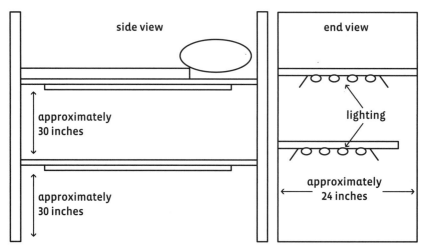

Figure 6.10: Bunk beds converted to include two grow areas (sweet dreams).

Get some polystyrene slabs from your DIY store and spray them with adhesive, stick the pads to the roof and sides of the van. Alternatively, you can form a frame up the sides and across the roof in 1 sq. in. (25 mm) timber, then fix 0.3" (8 mm) in plywood or hardboard to it either with suitable adhesive or staples. Fit out the inside of your van like any other growing room. The cheapest alternative is to buy some of the white / black plastic sheet liner htat we spoke of before, spray it with adhesive, and stick it to the sides and roof of the van. Run an adequately rated extension lead to the van from your house and always make sure the whole reel is unwound, never leave it partially wound, as this is likely to cause a fire.

Another great alternative to the van is to buy a cheap old towing trailer like you would use for weekend vacations, strip everything from inside with the exception of the fused power unit and the heater and water system if they exist; these facilities will be very useful to you later on. Line the sides of the van with black/white film, hanging curtain or drape like as this stops light leaks through the windows and nosy neighbors looking in. Take care also that you cover the roof vent. Form another curtain of black/white film across the width of the trailer sealing any end kitchen area from the grow area. Fit out the grow room as you would any other, except that the mechanical air ventilation system will be taken through the floor, just as you will with the van conversion. This is by far the best way since no visible outlets exist, although the vents may allow light to show. This problem can be dealt with by forming a shield or staggered outlet similar to the speaker box outlet; this will be fitted underneath the trailer floor on the outside.

Here's one more great little idea that was passed on to me by Keith Wilson. It takes very little money, a little longer in grow time than HID, but has superb effects.

Requirements

All you'll need is an end cut off of a roll of welded mesh such as that used for aviary wire, 4' x 3' wide (120 cm x 90 cm); the gauge is not important, let's say 1" (2.5 cm) by 0.5" (13 mm holes)(12 mm) .You'll also need:

1. 2 gal. (10 L) plastic pot (although any size will do, but you'll also have to change the width of the mesh to suit);

2. Plywood disc the same size as the pot;

3. 2 x 3' (90 cm) fluorescent fittings complete;

4. 10' (3 m) length of 2"x 2" (5 cm x 5 cm) plained and square edged timber that you need to cut into 2 pieces at 4' (1.2 m) and 2 pieces at 2' (60 cm);

5. A length of lighting flex and a plug with suitable amperage fusing incorporated (around 13 amp)

Take the two 4' (120 cm) pieces of timber and fix them securely to the timber disc at opposite sides with equal spacing by glue and screw fixing. Then fix the two smaller pieces of timber to the bottom of the lengths of wood forming what looks like little feet. Fix complete fluorescent fittings to the inside of each 4' (120 cm) length of timber. Don't fit the tubes until the mesh is in place, in case they break. Now take your mesh and roll it round the plywood disc, pinning as you go with staples. Once you have rolled the mesh neatly around the disc, then join along the edges where the two ends of the mesh meet, also fix the mesh to the other upright timber, again with staples.

Now with the timber joined together and the mesh neatly fixed, you'll have to insert the fluorescent tubes carefully in place up the inside of the mesh tube. The flex would have been fitted earlier and the two fittings linked together. You can use two plugs although one is adequate. Plant your clone or seed-grown plant into the 2 gal. (10 L) pot and place the lighting unit you have just made over the plant, taking great care not to damage your "little lady' as she sits waiting patiently to be fed by light.

The plant will grow up inside your mesh tube and caress the glowing fluorescent fitting. **Take great care when watering the plant, making sure water is clear of the electrical fittings.** As the plant grows it'll cling to the fluorescent tube and grow inside the mesh giving a full bud growth over its full length. There should be very little leaf and a good harvest as the light is equal all round the plant. There will be no burning because of the low heat output of fluorescent lights.

Play with these ideas for now and by the time my next book is released you'll be ready to move on to bigger and better things. I guess the absolute smallest cost you can expect for setting up a small garden that would suit a modest smoker—not counting your clone, which you may be able to talk a friend into giving you—would cost no more than $54 and use only about 150 watts of power.

If you set up a fluorescent system always use the longest tube possible in every instance. Never use two 4' (1.2 m) tubes when you can use one single 8' (2.4 m) tube. A single fixture produces more light and is cheaper to buy than two, easier to set up, and easier to raise and lower for plant height adjustment. An inexpensive system is a unit consisting of four fluorescent tubes that will consume approximately 320 watts of power covering 11/2 sq. yd. (5 m²), as shown in the converted bunk bed system. It would be a good idea to include a cloning area within your garden system or somewhere else to keep a regular supply. For the cloning system you would use three or four 4ft fluorescent fittings.

Two regular smokers would set up a larger system but still spend very little compared to street prices and get quality weed. Four 8' (2.4 m) fluorescents could return from 5–15 oz. (142–426 g) of weed every four to five months plus of course there are the leaves and clippings to boost that to at least twice the weight.

For a garden of one 600-watt HPS lamp, a fan, and an extractor with a small but adequate heater and timer you would only draw off around 1 kilowatt. All this could run from a 13-amp outlet quite safely and return you around just over 1 pound (454 g) of weed every 16 weeks using 3 kilowatts as our maximum usage. Not bad for such a small investment in both money and time. For best results, a minimum of 20 watts per square foot (30 square centimeters) is desired; to work out the wattage required in your room, just multiply length by the width to give the square footage and then again by 20 to give the total watts required.

The more light you give your plants the greater the production and the quicker the growth so don't by shy to put in the power. Most growers use a calculation of around 60 watts per 0.35 yd. (0.3 m).

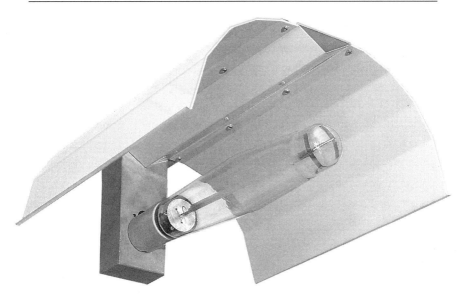

Figure 6.11: HPS lamp and reflector complete with built-in resistor.

Reflectors and Light Balancers

Always buy a good reflector when you purchase HID lighting. Most makes have their own design but consider what I have already said in the lighting section. If you have decided to mount vertical lamps, then broad-cone, deep-cone, and parabolic reflectors are all designs to consider when buying an HID. If you're not using a light mover then stick to parabolic reflectors since they concentrate the light by around 20% more than the alternatives and increase plant growth.

Horizontally mounted reflectors can produce 20% more light than vertical HID parabolic reflectors, while HPS lamps mount in any position. You must purchase the correct bulb for MH, although the use of MH is fairly scarce now, and you may never even have to consider this. The only good application for a cone reflector is when you're using MH with HPS lamps in multiple-bulb gardens, trying to achieve a perfect light spectrum.

When using a light balancer, position the lights closer to the plant tops. The broad-cone system illuminates the whole garden with a mix of light spectrum continuously since the light radiates to a broader area. Make sure that the garden's perimeter is surrounded with reflective surfaces such as Mylar or matte white paint. Because the light moves constantly, you can position lamps closer to the tops of the plants without burning them. The constantly moving light eliminates the pyramid effects found under stationary lights, where growth concentrates under the center of the bulb while growth on the periphery of the garden lags behind. Light movers distribute the light source more evenly and illuminate all parts of the garden.

You'll be looking for light movers that take from 40 to 50 minutes to complete one rotation or one back-and-forth movement. Whirly-gig, which moves back and forth 180 degrees, covers a 8' (2.4 m) wide circle or a 10' (3 m) circle with extenders. The Sun rotates in a complete circle every 40 minutes. Two lights illuminate a 10ft-diameter circle. Extension arms and another bulb increase the effectively illuminated area to cover a 15' (15 m) wide circle. Linear balancers such as the Solar Shuttle cover a room 8' (2.4 m) wide by 10' (3 m) and up to 18' (5.5 m) long with extenders. One advantage of rotating light movers is that they evenly mix the light spectrum using HPS and MH lamps in conjunction. If you have a problem with availability or consumption of electricity, install a light balancer instead of another HID bulb. Light balancers usually draw low-wattage watts, so the dimensions and yield of your garden increase without any noticeable difference in power consumption. Light balancers have from one to four "arms," each of which holds one MH or HPS bulb and reflector/fixture. If vibrations from your light balancers are a problem, use foam-rubber strips between the ceiling hardware on which you mount the mover and the mover itself to help dampen vibrations.

Figure 6.12: Umbrella shade designed for better distribution of light from a single lamp.

Figure 6.13: Radial arm lighting carries four lamps on one rotating unit for even distribution.

Hanging Your Light System

The most common setups to raise and lower lights is to hang the fixture with chains or rope from hooks attached to the ceiling, beams, studs in the wall, or via a frame mounting your lamps. The frame or individual lamp can be raised at will to maintain the appropriate distance from the plant tops as the plants grow. Photographs on page 92 show two separate pulleys that attach to each end of a piece of chipboard with lights fitted on it so that dual height plants can be grown and lights adjusted accordingly.

A less common setup has the lights fixed in place with a supporting bed below that carries the plants. This method is used mainly in greenhouses or where a skylight is used, generally when electrical lighting is nonexistent and the grower relies on natural light.

The bed or "flat" is lowered from the light source as the plants grow taller; they may also be used with HID lamps that are fixed in place on light balancers, or with fluorescent shelf gardens, where it's more convenient to lower a bed rather than to raise a fixture. When using the flat bed system, which would be made of strip

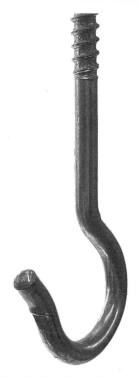

Figure 6.14: Pulley for raising and lowering your lighting system.

Figure 6.15: Hook on which the pulley connects to ceiling of grow area.

wood, plywood, or any otherh sheet wood material. Place plants on blocks of some kind to keep the tops level so that all the plants get the same light and keep them close to the light source; you mustn't have them cramped against any form of lighting. It would be much more practical to use hydroponic mediums rather than earth or Cocos to avoid the lifting or maneuvering of dead weight. You may not need to raise the fixture at all for HID gardens if you grow a fast-turnover crop where the plants are less than three feet tall when harvested. This is common when the crop is matured under HIDs on light balancers after being started under a smaller fluorescent system.

Make sure that raising or lowering the fixture or platform is easy—you're going to have to make adjustments a few times during the plants' lives. A heavy system will cause you problems that may lead to you breaking a plant stem, or losing a branch or top if you drop it. If you hang the light system from the ceiling, locate a ceiling joist, and screw strong hooks directly into the timber. Joists are located above the ceiling board and are usually spaced at 16" (40 cm) centers. The easy way to find the center measurements is to go to the room above or attic space and measure the distance between nails fixing the floor covering to the joists underneath; this visual inspection will also tell you which way the joists run across the room.

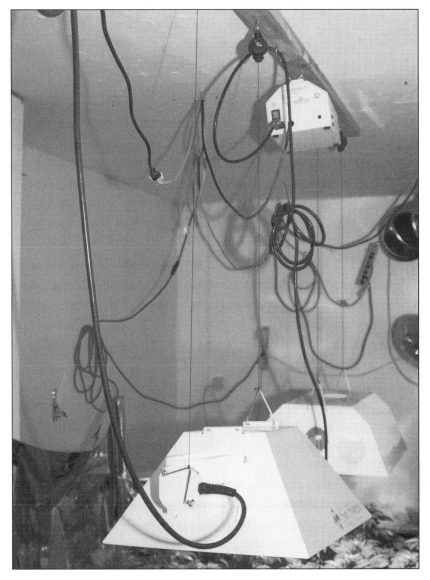

Figure 6.16: Hang ballasts high in the room away from wet floor areas.

Plaster is too weak to support heavy fixtures, so if you're fixing to walls make sure you drill to a good depth, finding brick or block giving at least a 2" (5 cm) deep fixing hole. Use plastic wall plugs or expanding bolts to fix your tie hook. If a wall is particularly weak then fix a full timber length to it and then fix your hook to that. Suspend the fixture from a hook at the ends of the wooden strip. Clothes hooks or shelves in closets should be sturdy enough to support a light fitting. Anchor gardens under bunk beds to the bed's supporting frame or into the bed's mattress platform.

For MH and HPS lamps you could use a pulley, but all you really need is a strong hook imbedded overhead (in the ceiling) over which you run strong cord attached to the lamp fixture. At the other end, mount a boat cleat, a piece of timber, or two strong nails spaced about six inches apart for securing or tying off the cord. By wrapping the line several times around the cleat or two nails, you can secure the line much more easily than if you try to make a knot around a single anchoring nail or hook while holding the weight of the fixture. Always use a rope or chain for support. Never use the electrical feed wire to hang a fixture, allow the electrical wire to hang free—and off the floor! Leave at least a 6" (15 cm) space between the ceiling and any HID because the fixture will get very hot.

Several holes for mounting are predrilled in the top surface of all fluorescent fixtures and often, HID reflectors. The easiest procedure for raising fluorescents is to slide S-shaped hooks through the holes. Make two loops of rope, about 6" (15 cm) long, and attach them to the S hook at each end of the fixture. To each loop, attach another S hook connected to a chain that's secured above each end of the fixture. When raising the lights, simply move the top S hook to a higher link on a chain. Raising the fixture is then easy, and the nonconducting rope loop breaks electrical conductivity between the fixture and you. This helps prevent possible shocks if you raise the fixture when the lights are on. It also stops you from burning yourself when you want to lift the lamp since you won't be touching any hot surface.

Fluorescent Setups

You can buy ballasts and end sockets separately to make lighter, moveable rise and fall units, since ballasts make up most of the fixture's weight. Surprisingly, it's often cheaper to remove parts from a whole fixture than to buy the parts separately. Mount the ballasts permanently on a wall or on the shelf's frame, and run the wires to the sockets, which you should mount on plywood or a wooden frame. Position the ballasts on a wall or support midway between the lowest and highest positions that the fixture will be, in order to minimize the length of the wire you need to run.

Make reflectors from cardboard or sturdy paper stapled to the wood and face them with aluminum foil or white plastic, or better still make them from

Figure 6.17: Clones under fluorescent lights are ready for planting.

aluminum. Don't let the reflectors contact the ends of the tubes. Obviously of course you can buy factory-made reflectors that fit your lamps perfectly. Mount sockets on a frame of plywood. Space the sockets evenly across the width of the garden. In typical fixtures, the bulbs are centered close together, and much of the light is kept bouncing around within the reflector or between the bulbs. Spacing the tubes evenly across the width of the garden actually increases the light (by as much as 40%!) directed toward the plants. For example, a four-tube, 320-watt, 8' (2.4 m) fluorescent system covers an area about 2' (60 cm) wide. Space the tubes from 2" (5 cm) to 6" (15 cm) apart. However you mount the sockets, always provide individual reflectors for each bulb.

On Reflection

Reflective areas in all situations are important to the productivity of your harvest. Walls, ceilings and floors should be prepared to provide reflection of light. It can be done very cheaply with emulsion or paint. Floors should be covered with plastic in a house situation to seal and protect them from water spillages. In greenhouses, use white granite rock, white quartz chips, white sand, or even pallets or concrete painted white (use external quality paint). Reflective areas are even more critical in low-light and natural-light gardens.

A flat white paint produces a better reflective surface for an even, well-distributed reflected light than glossy paints or aluminum foils do. Paint all adjacent surfaces with flat white paint, or cover the surfaces with a reflective material. A first-class reflective material for any situation is Astrolon, a heavy-duty cloth/plastic material with a reflective, silvered matrix surface. Astrolon doesn't scratch or crinkle, lasts for years, and resists damage from sunlight, physical abuse, extreme temperature swings, and high winds.

Double-layered plastic, black on one side and white on the other, is another excellent reflective material; it also works very well as curtains to surround the garden. This double-layered plastic is of a heavy gauge, and is a better choice to cover and protect the floor, yet reflect light. Look through any reflective material toward the lights to see if light shows through. Any light coming through is lost so if any light comes through then try using a double thickness.

Mylar is popular in grow shops, but it's a very delicate material and can only be used once as it tears. The biggest mistake people make with Mylar is putting it up back to front. Mylar, which was developed for NASA, has a mirror finish and is very reflective, although just 12% more reflective than flat white paint so you may not want to bother with the expense. It just depends how close to perfection you want to get. Giving a first-class reflective surface, (providing you don't mess with it or disturb its surface), it could only be bettered by using mirrors. There are however two problems with Mylar: first, it's electrically conductive so it's not a good idea to hang Mylar curtains from or near a fixture since it could conduct an electric current to you; second, it can only be used once; it can't be moved because it crinkles and spoils, so it's useless in the long-term cost effective race. For reflective curtains, Astrolon or white plastics are nearly as reflective, plus plastic isn't electrically conductive, so in terms of safety, they are better choices than Mylar.

Window gardens also need reflectors; otherwise the backs of the plants get little light. You'll see the obvious increase in light once you've installed reflectors. Surround the backs of the plants with a reflective perimeter and cover the floor with white plastic. For large plants, string a strong cord from which reflective curtains may hang to surround the window garden. Ventilation is very important to the health and growth rate of the crop so open a small window close to the plants.

Reflectors should not completely encase a garden, thereby cutting off all airflow. Leave open spaces at the ends of fluorescent gardens. Check for heat buildup, and cut holes near the tops of the reflectors to vent excessive heat. For HID lighting, leave open space above the garden. Lamp reflectors are just a few dollars and it's always better to go and buy the custom product. I could describe how to make your own reflectors, which is quite simple. However I'm not going to get you into penny pinching unless it's at no loss to end-product value.

Safety

Does your prospective grow room have enough electricity to safely power your lights? For any system other than HIDs, this should never be a problem. Fluorescent systems don't take much more power than adding a TV, but for any 1,000-watt HID garden, you'll need to find out how much power (wattage) you have at your disposal and adapt your electrical system to suit. Most houses and apartments in the US are supplied with 110 volts and have adequate power available and the best fuse or circuit to pick up is the one that serves an electric stove, central heating boiler or hot water tank where the supply is no longer used. All of theses circuits usually run off a 30/32-amp fuse. You can also go to your good old DIY superstore these days and buy an up-rated fuse to fit into your consumer unit (fuse box) or even put in a new supply to serve your garden using an additional switched consumer unit. Never connect HID systems to the electric light circuit or wall lights.

Before you buy any large light system, find out how much current is available in your prospective grow room. Go to your fuse box and read the amperage off the fuses or the circuit breakers. You may need an electrician's help to set up all of your equipment, although most mail-order houses provide instructions for both 110 volt light installations. Next you need to find out which circuits power your grow room, and what other rooms are on the same circuit.

To find out which outlets are served by a particular fuse or circuit breaker, plug a lamp into an outlet, remove fuses or shut breakers one at a time, until the light goes off. When the light goes off, you know that this fuse or circuit breaker services the particular outlet that you have chosen to use. Turn all other breakers back on or put back fuses. Move the lamp from outlet to outlet until you find all the outlets that are on this circuit (it's still off, and the lamp won't light unless it's on another circuit). If you have to do it alone, use a radio: it's easier and will save you running up and down stairs or in and out of rooms to see if the light's still on. Turn the sound of the radio up so that you can hear it from the fuse box.

A large room or basement may have more than one circuit servicing its outlets. Often you find that upstairs and downstairs are on different circuits and if you're lucky the front and back may be separated also, giving you more scope. Once you find out which sockets are on the chosen circuit, determine the total wattage available and deduct the value of any item that regularly uses that circuit. This will determine exactly how much wattage remains usable. The wisest move would be to use an upstairs circuit as this is least likely to have larger domestic items regularly plugged into it. **NEVER** overload electricity units. Be **secure** in the safety of adequate fusing. To figure wattage, multiply the amperage (current) read from the fuse or circuit breaker, and multiply it by the voltage (European UK is usually 230 volts and the USA is 110 to 120 volts). Available wattage equals total amperage times volts: W = I (amps) x E (volts). Using 230 volts as an example, a 15-ampere fuse will give you 3,450 watts, providing nothing else is taken off of it. (15 amperes x 230 volts = 3,450 watts.) That is enough to run a good-size garden. In practice, always leave a safety margin of at least 20%, because some power is lost through heat and resistance of electrical runs; so the maximum power a 15-ampere circuit can provide is actually 2,760 watts. For safety reasons, calculate no more than seven 400-watt HID for each 15-amp circuit providing nothing else is on the same circuit, and less of course additional items that make the room more professional, like fans, water pumps, etc. If the room does not have enough current, have new circuits run by an electrician before you purchase any equipment. Whatever you do with electricity, if you don't understand it then get in a professional. If you understand it but can't quite work out what you want then ask a professional. Everyone will help and your supplier usually has the knowledge you need. Just tell him you're growing orchids; go to him with all of your details (leaving out the fact that you're growing dope of course) and get advice. Don't be shy; you may feel a little guilty and suspect that they know what you're doing but that's only because *you* know; they won't have a clue, so don't worry. However, never chance inviting them to your home to look and never give your right name or address.

If your garden is in an area without electricity and you have no chance of getting any to the area, then use a generator. Diesel generators are more than satisfactory, as they'll run on cheap red agricultural diesel if they operate outside. Make sure that exhaust gases (deadly carbon monoxide) are safely vented via extraction pipes. NEVER work where there's exhaust leakage or a chance of breathing in fumes. Generators, however, are very noisy and dropping the unit below ground level will help. If you're mechanically handy, adapt a car exhaust to reduce noise. Before you buy a generator, ask for a demonstration and choose the quietest. Maybe there's an auction sale that you know of that sells industrial machinery, or try looking in one of the free add papers. Propane generators are the safest inside installation; they burn cleanly when the flame is blue so the rule is, if you buy secondhand then have it serviced by a professional. The exhaust given from a gas generator is Co_2, which increases growth in the garden. You should still never be in the room when the gases are being fed in, to do so would prove *FATAL*; always use your extraction unit. Most petrol generators can be adapted to run on propane just like your car; ask your supplier if he can get you a kit or do it for you.

To reiterate: there's always a danger from electrical shocks and short circuits with electric-light gardens because water and electricity are in close proximity. You'll be in a garden where there are lights and fixtures with water in pots, a tank, or possibly on the floor, so you're always in danger as they can all conduct electricity. Buy and read a safety manual on working with electricity. The danger is greater with larger systems, such as HID lamps, which draw huge current. Danger from electrical shocks can be eliminated or at least reduced to non-dangerous proportions with the three-wire grounding system. Check all electrical equipment that you buy from mail order or grow shops because some equipment comes from countries that sometimes do not wire their products with a ground.

Always follow every possible precaution and you should never have a problem.

Turn off all electricity in the garden while watering. Use a secondary light to see what you're doing and never care for your plants when the floor is wet or moist with electricity on in the room. Few of you will shut the lights off every time you water, but at least make sure that you never touch a fixture or a reflector while you're watering or caring for your garden. Take the precaution of wearing thick rubber-soled shoes or lay wooden slatted floor panels to isolate you.

The first thing that electricians teach their apprentices is to use only one hand. That is, don't ever touch two conductors at the same time, whether fixture, floor, or reflector. Never become the bridge between a potential electrical source and ground. In a growing room this means don't touch an electrical fixture with one hand while your other hand touches a reflector if your feet are on a moist floor. You'll be placing yourself as a conductor between source current and an electrical ground.

For safe gardening, never touch the fixture unless the electricity is shut off; don't raise or lower the lights. Keep all electrical cords raised off the floor and away from water. Ballasts on a damp floor are very dangerous. If you cant mount a ballast on a wall outside the grow area then put it on a piece of thick polystyrene; something like the sections used for packing a washing machine are fine. Try to isolate all electrical connections by putting them outside of the grow room. If you have aluminum foil on the walls or some other metallic reflector, don't touch it while standing on a wet floor or handling the fixture. Don't fool around with electricity. You could be seriously burned or killed.

Don't take chances or become complacent as time goes on just because you're getting away with it. One mistake with electricity could be your last. Although electricity is in effect invisible, there are telltale signs to look out for such as

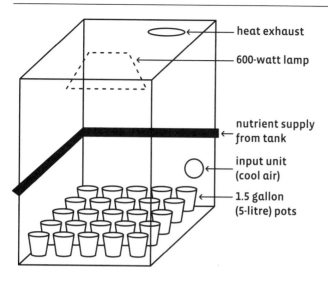

heat exhaust

600-watt lamp

nutrient supply from tank

input unit (cool air)

1.5 gallon (5-litre) pots

Figure 6.18: A complete grow room kit constructed of 2" square timber and black/white polythene.

charred or burning wires or the blackening of fittings. Touch wires when they have just gone off and see if they feel hot. Poor or lose connections can cause fires, so make sure that fixing screws are tight and there is no arcing. An electrical fire at night could be responsible for killing your family.

When you spray your plants, take a few extra necessary precautions. Sprays work best by spraying the undersides of the leaves. This means that you'll direct the spray upwards toward the lights when foliar spraying. When hot, lights will implode when they contact water. Incandescent or HID bulbs will do so forcefully when hit by a single droplet of water; obviously, the spray of glass fragments could blind you. Always turn off the lights and wait until they cool before you spray the garden. Raise the light system above the spray, and wipe bulbs dry before relighting. If an HID lamp cracks or breaks, don't look at it! Avert your eyes and pull the plug. Wait for the bulb to cool before you handle it. It's useful to have a secondary light in the room for your maintenance periods. Fluorescents might not implode, because they operate at cooler temperatures, but why take a chance?

Clean your lamps periodically as they'll collect dust from static electricity, which cuts down their usable light output. Don't just wipe the underside of the bulb; the dust settles on top so take them out and clean them properly or you'll lose reflective light. Hot bulbs may implode from pressure or from being cleaned with wet solutions so again leave them to cool to room temperatures before cleaning. You'll need to change old bulbs at some time. Always turn off the lights.

When HID lamps are turned off, they require about a 15-minute wait before they'll relight.

Wear UV screening sunglasses when working in any garden, more especially with HID lamps. Any good pair of sunglasses should screen most UV rays. The wearing of an appropriate mask, which covers the mouth and nose, is advisable for any grower who is mixing soil or soil additives and powders, or spraying with any insecticide.

Message

I know there have been several items in this chapter that are repeated from the other sections. No, I'm not smoking and having a memory loss, it's just that the repeated items are very important and I can't stress enough that there are certain keys to a successful harvest and your well-being. If I can save your life by boring you with repetitive advice then I can take your criticism. I can guarantee that I will repeat myself several times more as you read on just to hit important matters home harder, but when you have finished you'll know it all and thank me when you're enjoying your harvest.

If you aren't too good at DIY, and don't want to call in an expert or pal, then look around at what's on offer; there are units supplied absolutely complete. A 1.2 sq. yd. (1 m^2) compact unit with all the tools you'll ever need to grow up to 25 plants at one go is cheap to buy, at around $600.

7

Growing Methods

There are of course many growing methods, and I could probably fill several books just on this subject alone, so what I'm going to do is discuss the most proven and actively used methods. You'll take these methods and make them your own as time goes on, experimenting with and adapting them to suit your own personal situation, needs, and plants.

Growing with Natural Light

The things we have for free in this world are natural gifts from God—the right to light and air. Take advantage of these freebies wherever possible. Although cropping will be seasonal because you don't have the same control year round that you would have with electric light, it'll be at a nominal cost to the grower. The results can be astonishing even if you live in the coldest of climates, so don't be put off because you don't live in California or Australia. Use a skylight, porch, greenhouse, cloche, window space, your back garden or even a window box. We're just talking home grow here and not mass cultivation in fields although many of the same principals will apply.

Growing outdoors with natural light, there are two huge benefits: one is that fresh air is abundant and provides the plants with all that they need to flourish, and the other is that natural light reaches around and into your plants, feeding the lower branches as well as the upper, where electric light in an indoors electrically controlled grow room really only treats the tops of the plants. If you have previously grown electrically, you'll notice a distinct difference in the way your plants grow under natural conditions. The main difference of course is that they'll grow slower; be patient though, the results are worthwhile and it's costing you nothing after all.

Plant outside (in pots if you want a little more control) using the same earth preparation as in all other instances, whether in pots or in the ground. Growing in an outside garden means that the soil has to be well draining; marijuana doesn't like boggy situations. If your garden floods through poor drainage then plant out into a raised section so that the roots can breath. If you grow in pots, indoors or out, then it's easier to manage the plant, turning her occasionally to benefit from equal sunlight then when the time is right you'll be able to harvest her indoors with a cup of tea and your feet up. As soon as you cut your plant she will start to dehydrate and wilt, making the leaves harder to trim; by taking the whole potted plant in, it'll stay fresh and easier to harvest.

I mentioned earlier that growing with natural light is seasonal, and heard you say, "So when are the seasons?" Well, if you plant out in spring, (late April to early May), which is the preferred time for gardeners generally, after the last frost, then your harvest will be about autumn time (mid to late September). You can of course wait a little longer, and plant out in summer (around June or July) and have an early winter harvest or even have two harvest periods by staggered planting, one in spring and one in summer. If you want to use natural light for winter planting, then you'll have to use supplemental lighting, which we have covered in chapter 4. Supplemental lighting is really only valid for use in a greenhouse or window growing, not outside; although there are external use lighting units available you'll be defeating your object of using natural lighting and laying what amounts to a landing strip for the police helicopter. If you have your plants in a window space then try to keep them small so that they won't be noticed by neighbors. It's far better to keep plants small and flood them with light to get maximum yield rather than grow them large and starve them of light. The bigger the plant the more she will be noticed.

The best way to start growing from seed is to bring seeds off in the greenhouse or under a cloche, which is a bell shaped cover that can be made from glass or plastic to protect them from frost. Maybe you can bring them off indoors, then "prick out" before putting outside (that is to say take out the small plant one by one and replant with more space around them). The best way of course is to grow from clones, which will have a far better survival rate (see chapter 10). Winter weather is unfriendly and at best unpredictable, so keep some form of protection handy—a wind screen or cheap, clear covering of off the roll plastic sheeting over a frame. If you are growing a tropical variety however then they'll need much more protection, when the temperature drops are extreme plants may die.

Late start gardens are not always successful outside if we have an early winter, but a good idea is to grow your plants amongst other native plants in your garden; they'll provide some protection from high wind. A window crop started early may outgrow your window space, especially if you are growing from clones, so plan your garden well, and get to know your plant and its breeding. Some plants bush out—like Durban Poison, which I am told is very popular in the North of England—and some grow upward, budding mainly at the top and forming a single cola—like White Widow or Northern Lights—with smaller buds lower down.

If you want to be an all-year-round grower using natural light then you must commit yourself to using supplemental lighting and to bringing seeds off inside during the winter months. Control the light by using timers to add light volume during the weaker moments of daylight in order to extend the light period to between 16 and 18 hours. No need to use HIDs—simple metal halide or fluorescent lamps from the DIY stores will do. It's just additional light to support growth, so it doesn't have to have intense abilities. Use a natural light program allowing the plant to follow a natural cycle of light. Never allow the lighting to decrease to below 15 hours during the growth period as this could flick your girls into bloom.

If you decide to grow in your window space, greenhouse, or skylight then consideration must be given to photoperiods in a very different way, quite the opposite to supplemental lighting. When you want the plants to go into bloom or bud, then you have to decrease the light using a heavy curtain or the white/black polythene sheeting I have mentioned in earlier chapters. A useful curtain type is that which has the thermal lining. Now you have some minimal control and may shorten the photoperiod at will.

The alternative, if you don't want to pay out anything for the privilege of total control (tight devil) is to simply pick the plant up at a certain time of day and carry it to a darkened room, then bring her out again in the morning—a bit elaborate, but it works. Venetian blinds are a good idea too; they can be manipulated to allow light in and keep peering eyes out. They can also be closed to stop light penetration and used with reflective materials and darkened curtains they can be a great asset to your window garden. If you are going to buy venetian blinds, there are some available on the market that are silver coated, and these are the best to

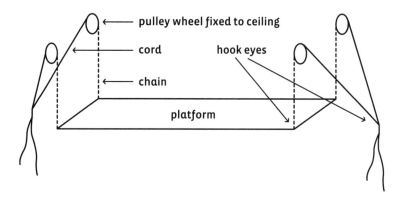

Figure 7.1: Full platform pulley set up for shelf garden.

buy for growing because of their reflective property.

Choosing your window is important! Why? Because the sun changes position in our sky and the available light to your window alters. For that reason, you'll want to choose the window that provides you with the longest period of sunlight. Skylights are constant of course as they're in the top of the house and receive equal light all day, so it may be a great investment to fit a skylight, where neighbors can't peek in and the sunlight can. Your plants can be raised closer to the light or moved away from it by using a table or building block, maybe even a small workbench of some kind; you could even make your own little shelf on chains and a pulley wheel to raise and lower the plants.

Attach 1 ft of chain to the ends of the shelf via bolt hook eyes; screw ones may pull out with the weight of the plants. Fix cord to the chain (alternatively run cord all through), then thread the cord through a pulley wheel fixed to the ceiling. Make sure you screw into the ceiling joist rather than a ceiling board or plaster as there's a lot of weight to support. Run the cord through a centered hook eye screwed to the wall and down to a tie of cleat to secure.

Shelf Gardens

The shelf garden is an excellent choice for anyone who wants a constant supply of weed all year round. As a grower you'll understand by now that you'll need a constant supply of young plants. The easiest way to have this supply is to take clones from your own plants. Develop a room that needs be no bigger than 6' 6" (2 m) square. That is smaller than most box rooms and the size of a small garden shed, so everyone should have a chance here. This type of garden takes advantage of fluorescent lighting or can include some of the mini HID lamps that are now available, offering a simple, cheap and effective way for growing an ongoing crop with a factory-like process. An average height room is around 8' (2.4 m). Fit three shelves, two at 2' (60 cm) wide, to a chosen wall, preferably an outside wall, and one smaller one at the end of the room for your mother plant with a fluorescent lamp fitted over her. Use fluorescent lamps above the top or cloning shelf, and either mini HID lamps or fluorescent lamps for the bottom or flowering shelf; use HID for greater light and more effective cropping. The idea is to use the shelves for different purposes covering the life span of a plant. Shelf 1 at the end of the room will carry your mother plant, which needs very little light but must have an 18–24-hour light period; shelf 2 (the top shelf against the side wall) will carry clones that have first been potted. On the opposite wall place a small greenhouse, available from most DIY superstores these days for around $3.60. You can of course use a propagator instead, although I have found the greenhouse very efficient fitted with 3' (1 m) fluorescent fittings.

To adapt your greenhouse for operation, take out the wire shelf that comes with it and cut a piece of chipboard or similar material to the same size. Fit three fluorescent lamps of a suitable length to the boarding and wire them in together on a loop (that is to say, wired from one to the other to join them) and then to a single 13-amp plug. Take out your tubes while working with the board. Place the board on a flat supported surface, then place the wire shelf provided with the greenhouse on the board in an upside down position.

Place the light fittings on the wire shelf and screw-fix them through the wire into the timber panel; replace the lamps and slide the shelf back into the tiny greenhouse. This will now work as a propagator and bring your clones on to root, ready for the first potting. I say first potting because you may be in a situation where you only have room for a limited amount of flowering plants, so it's easier to pot the clones into small pots for their first shelf life and then replant out into the larger pots to put on your flowering shelves. It is, however, best to plant out rooted clones straight into your chosen size of pot to vegetate. On the other side of the room, you'll have your plants growing in flower. If you're growing with fluorescent tubes, it takes longer but you have a great system here, and once it's up and running you'll have a constant supply of weed for personal use.

Figure 7.2: Healthy clones under fluorescent lighting in nursery area.

The operative idea of this type of garden is to work on constants. You need only keep a few mothers, maybe even just one. You harvest to your needs, unless a plant has got to a stage when harvest is essential to avoid rotting. As you harvest a plant, then place a vegetating plant in the vacant position. This will leave a space on the vegetating shelf, so fill it with a rooted clone. This in turn leaves a space in your propagator, so take another cutting. Simple isn't it? It takes a little time to master the technique and get in tune with your growing needs. Remember, you won't be going for great heights in maturity, this will be a short period of flowering giving you probably one useful cola, although you'll get some smaller ones that will harvest and make up weight of course; they may even provide for the making of hash oil, scuff or space cake (see chapter 16). Place clones and vegetating plants on the top shelves, with flowering and mother plants on the lower shelves since clones benefit more from the heat and humidity found higher in the room and mothers need less heat.

Shelves used for flowering will require a lightproof curtain in front of them to shield them from the light used to bring on other plants in the room, since these plants are on a different light cycle. You can use many ways of doing this. The black/white PVC (plastic sheet material) is a cheap and effective alternative, fixed in place with adhesive-backed Velcro tape or Astrolon or thermal-lined curtains. Remember that when you use a curtain to shield the light, you are trapping in heat, so the use of an extractor is required. A cheap bathroom-type fitting is fine. This is why I recommend an outside wall for your shelving. If you are only growing with fluorescent lamps then you may not have to use a heat exhaust since they give off very little heat.

Vegetative Gardens

These are less popular than all other gardens that are bud productive and are more for the lightweight smoker than the serious grower. With vegetative gardens, plants can be used for several years. Set up your plants in a stable position either in a greenhouse or similar situation using natural light with maybe some supportive light during winter months, since vegetative gardens require at least 16 hours continuous light. Once you have one plant growing, then get a second to run alongside it so that when one is depleted you can benefit from the second and so on, harvesting shoots and leaves when you want to smoke. Since we're not going into bloom there's no real big efforts taken here and no special lighting technique required.

Figure 7.3: Harvested garden of plants stripped of shade leaves.

Harvest Gardens

These are of course the most popular gardens and benefit from varied gardening techniques, using hydroponics, earth or other organic compound. Far the best way to run your garden is by the shelf method or a two-garden technique, with the one garden growing clones and vegetating plants and the other growing bud. The alternative would be to have a small cloning garden, then plant out when rooted into your growing medium. You could bring all your plants into bloom at the same time with a single harvest or create a crop rotations program for a continual fresh supply. Growing mediums and techniques will be covered a little later in the book.

Greenhouses

In this sector we can include outhouses, a lean-to or a sun lounge. There are so many products available to us now other than glass, including plastics and acrylics in opaque, clear or opalescent; flat or corrugated; and even single-, double- or triple-walled sheets when it comes to carbon. If you can't afford any of those alternatives then get some polythene sheeting. Whatever your chosen covering, the techniques are the same, as is the advice on internal preparation.

We still rely on reflective areas when we grow with natural lights and electric lighting. In a greenhouse, the floor may be plain old dirt; if this is the case, then go and buy some white granite chippings or stone. Your local building supplier or garden center will have some, ready bagged. The chippings will reflect light upwards and feed the smaller buds under the plant. Paint any small walled areas with a flat white matte paint. An external quality is recommended for single-skin walls. There are some great little grow tunnels available, similar to those used in commercial horticultural centers but on a smaller scale. These are simple arched frames that join together through the center and at the lower edge and are covered in cheap polythene sheeting. The tunnels come in 6ft sections and can be made as long as your garden by introducing sections as your budget allows.

Figure 7.4: Set-up to grow on clay balls with flood tank.

The main benefit of using polythene tunnels is that you can use opaque poly-thene so that the contents of the tunnel can't be visually identified. If you have an old garden shed that isn't being used, take off the old timber roof and replace it with opaque sheeting made from any of the materials before mentioned. Line the walls with insulating boards; there are several types available on the market including those used for dry lining that have an insulative material fixed to a plaster board. These are quite light to carry and east to work with since they cut with a sharp skill knife; they're also white in color so they don't have to be painted. If you buy the anti-condensation boards used for bathrooms and kitchens, they have a silver lining to them that is a great reflective surface. The only problem with plasterboards is that they don't withstand too much wetting and may break up; however, respect them and they'll last a long time. For instance, never fix them right down to the ground, as they'll act like blotting paper and form a mold growth, then crumble away.

It's also possible to use polystyrene sheeting or rockwool used for attic insu-lation. These are available from major DIY stores or building supply merchants. Cover rockwool insulation with plywood or hardboard sheeting, and paint with a matte white finish. You don't usually need planning permission to erect a green-house but if you add to your existing building with a sun lounge you may attract the attention of your local authority. It may need planning consent depending on construction, so it's worth checking on local planning and building requirements first. Naturally you don't want to get a crop growing and then find that a govern-ment officer turns up following a neighbor's complaint needing to inspect the construction, or worse still with a demolition order.

Whatever structure you use, it's essential to have good ventilation to release heat exhaust. An old drafty shed may be fine, but an enclosed greenhouse or other completely filled-in structure will have lots of heat buildup. Simple cross ventilation may be all that you need, like a small window at each end of the green-house. Lower temperatures reduce the chance of mite infestation or fungal activ-ity. Treat the greenhouse as you would a room indoors regarding heat control.

Growing Outside

If your ground isn't well drained then you have to build yourself a raised area. This can be an elaborate structure created by building brick walls with drainage holes at the bottom, a rockery using random-size rocks and stone, or a simple timber trough; the trough can be bought from most garden centers. A fiberglass fishpond is a great idea too, but you have to make holes in the bottom to allow the water to drain through, and they're often quite expensive. There are cheap ones on the market but they are often a little too flimsy for setting above ground without support. See if you can beg one from a neighbor. Often people throw them away because they're split or they just no longer want them, so try your local refuse dump. If they're split it doesn't matter because you need drainage anyway.

Your garden can be made ornamental and include other types of plants which will hide the fact that you are growing weed. If you plant highly scented plants in with your marijuana, they may mask the smell of your crop as it matures. In a small garden, build your outside plot against a fence or wall so that it shields the plants from the wind, but make sure you choose one which benefits from the longest period of light. There's also the possibility of adding a cover of polythene or Perspex, to use the sun's rays. Soil composition is the same as described for all other uses, the only differential here will be that additional drainage facilities will be installed because the rain will provide more water than is required for your crop and would clog the root system if not drained properly. Again, remember marijuana likes well-draining soil

In deciding how to grow externally we have to look at the plot in a different way than internal techniques in that internally we're able to control every element and so can produce many yields in minimal times; with external gardens you get only one hit, so you'll want to grow them as large as possible before their natural light period takes them into flower or bud. Feed them and care for them with extra-special attention, look at them daily, check for infestation or rot, only plant females or you may end up with your crop going to seed. External growth is cheaper than internal and just as satisfying, but the chances of failure are greater since we're reliant on Mother Nature and must cope with all the crap she throws at us including late frosts, insects, the neighbor's cat peeing on your crop, or a thunderstorm that might flatten it. Given the right care and considerations though, an external garden can give you equal pleasures and concerns, plus you don't get to have the family round for a barbecue because they might spot your plants. (Is that a plus or a minus?)

Guerrilla Cultivating

Initially the term used by growers who took to growing plants outside in remote fields, country lanes and riverbanks, guerrilla cultivating is very popular in most countries because the risk factor of being caught by authorities is low—although the risk of losing your crop to a stranger is high. All the foregoing information on outside cultivation applies to guerrilla growing. All I can add is advice on location, which is just simply based on common sense. Choose the most remote and sunny spot you can find, with access to water being a major plus.

Guerrilla growing has new meaning these days in that many people now rent or lease empty properties and set up a temporary indoor garden growing cannabis until they either feel their safety period is up, which is usually around one year from setting up, or until they are disturbed by police or some other individual. The guerrilla garden is less organized but still as efficient as any professional grow, it's just that it's not put together so neatly and more attention is given to insulation of sound since the properties have usually been empty some time and will have neighbors who are always inquisitive as to what their new neighbors are up to. These gardens are easily and quickly assembled and dismantled to maintain maximum crop supply and often makeshift equipment is used—like a mattress against a wall for insulation, an old dustbin for a water tank, or a cardboard box to house an exhaust fan.

8

Nutrients for Your Garden

When growing marijuana in a complete soil, that is to say a balanced, commercially bagged soil containing phosphorous (P), potassium (K), and nitrogen (N), we're looking for the best balancing available. The marijuana plant is extremely demanding on nutrients; the nutrient taken from the soil by greatest demand is normally nitrogen, so it must be fed back as required. You will need a good EC meter to measure nutrient balance.

There are several proprietary brands of nutrient additives on the market and we will talk about these individually although not exhaustively. These products are made for the job in hand so you don't have to be clever or inventive and create your own secret mixture. Stay away from mixing your own ingredients of manure. These contain bacteria and insect eggs, and promote fungal growth and even root burn in some cases.

Guano

A perfect natural fertilizer is guano, which is particularly rich in phosphorus. Bat droppings or chicken droppings now come bagged in concentrated pellets rather like rabbit pellets or powder for mixing with water to provide a liquid fertilizer better for hydroponic systems. The pellets release nutrients slowly into the soil. Bat guano is collected from the caves in which they live, mainly in Indonesia or Mexico as it forms a deep blanket on the floor. If you find a cave with no droppings but plenty of bats, post a picture of Ozzy Osborne, they'll soon start crapping themselves.

If you're using guano then pellets are easier to use than raw, bagged products; they're more likely to be sterile and contain no disease. Although sea bird guano and chicken guano is available it has been found that bat guano is far the best available.

Guanokalong is product from a company dedicated to providing bat guano. Based in Holland, this company has really done its homework to benefit growers. www.guanokalong.nl

100% natural bat dung is ultra organic, in fact the bats have to look for their own food.

Ripe fruits and healthy insects are all present in the jungle where humans never had any influence. Let the jungle take part of your garden with help of Guanokalong. *This plant fertilizer is excellent to use for growing plants and crops organically.*

How to use Guanokalong-Bat dung

Guanokalong contains a rich and unique combination of macro-, micro-elements and enzymes. The macro-element phosphorus is abundantly present. Guanokalong has a controlled release of minerals and nutrients. In this way roots don't burn. Unique enzymes and a rich presence of calcium/magnesium stimulate micro-life in the soil. In order to fertilize a soil or garden completely, we recommend you to mix additional organic fertilizers:

• Nitrogen (fish = 100% organic, dried cow dung minimum 1 year old),
• Potassium (beet-sugar extract = 100% organic),
• Micro-life (worm castings = 100% organic, or compost as direct plant nutrient),
• Seaweed calcium (100% organic and also rich in magnesium and micro-elements. Calcium regulates the Ph-level in the soil).

Outdoors: We recommend you to fertilize your garden just after the winter season. Be aware that sandy soils wash out quickly. Therefore improve the soil structure by adding worm castings, peats and clay. Pellets release their minerals and nutrients in a very controlled way within a period of one year. Powder releases more quickly, within six months. Mix Guanokalong with the soil before you put in new plants. If the plants are already placed in the soil, then spread the fertilizers and calcium over the soil and rake it carefully. When starting mix 1–1.5 oz. (30–40 g) of Guanokalong with soil in 1.5 gal. (6 L) pots and mix 3.5–9 oz. (100–250 g) with soil for out-door plants. Or take 2.2 lbs. (1 kg) of Guanokalong powder and mix it between 220 lbs. (100 L) (strong) and 550 lbs. (250 L) (medium) of potting soil.

Indoors: Guanokalong can be mixed with all new or used soils. Get started with the best thing available on the market: Guanokalong Potting Soil. The perfect soil has a balanced composition made of different ingredients and guarantees high yields. Used soil can be upgraded with Guanokalong-Soil Upgrademix and worm castings. Always mix and moisten the soil at least one week before planting.

Guanokalong-Extract

This liquid fertilizer contains nutrients that are directly available to the plant. Guanokalong-powder is soaked and pumped around for a period of weeks. Use the extract as a supplement. You can use this once a week by adding it to your feeding water. It adds all natural enzymes and micro elements to your normal fertilizers. There are no additives added like conservatives, hormones, acids and sugars. Vacuum packaging is the solution. This liquid plant fertilizer is excellently used for growing plants and crops organically.

Guanokalong-Potting Soil (Flowering-soil)

This is a heavily fertilized potting soil which is made of 100% natural ingredients. It contains all your plants need for more than 3 months. Just add enough water. This soil has a balanced composition in order to: regulate air and water, release nutrients, adjust ph level and volume perfectly. The composition is made of different black and white peats, timber chops (instead of using perlite), seaweed calcium, clay, lavameal, organic fertilizers including Guanokalong-guano and worm castings. Note, if you feel that this soil is too heavily fertilized for your clones and seedlings, just dig a small hole and fill it with non-fertilized soil.

Advantages for fertile potting soil

1) healthy plants = resistance against illnesses and plagues = great yield,
2) compact growing, exuberant flowering, lots of ripe seeds and tasteful fruits,
3) you need fewer liters of soil per plant for growing long cycles (12 weeks).

Guanokalong-Soil-Upgrademix

It is possible to re-use Guanokalong-Potting Soil and mix up your used soil with the Guanokalong-Soil-Upgrademix, but we recommend you to do this only twice. This package contains a full range of NPK organic fertilizers including Guanokalong and seaweedcalcium. Also mix Guanokalong-worm castings. Re-using your soil on location has more advantages like: no more dragging of bulky kilo's in and out, it's faster and cheaper.

A complete presence of fertilizers: N=2%, P2O5=15%, K2O=2%, S=0.2%, Ca/Mg=15%, mg/kg (milligrams to kilogramme)   Cu =15, Zn=20, Cl=100.

There is also a proven acceleration of root structuring (ideal for cuttings), exuberant topping, and increased resistance of plant against bacteria. It's good for indoor and outdoor use, and it's efficient, practical and odorless.

Use: 2.2 lbs. (1 kg) of Guanokalong is sufficient for 40–50 gal. (150–190 L) of planting soil. Mix guano with soil before planting. Pellets dissolve completely within 10 weeks.

When dissolving in water for faster results, use hot water as guano dissolves quickly in hot water (80° C or 176° F). First mix 2.2 lbs. (1 kg) guano in 1 gal. (4 L) of hot water and then add this to 20 gal. (80 L) of cold water. Use a filter with automated watering to prevent clogging the capillaries. Clean the device with clear water frequently.

Dosage: 11 lbs. (5 kg) Guanokalong is sufficient for 40 gal. (150 L) of potting soil.

Example: For indoor soil (mixing with soil)

Week 1: Mix guano dosage (see above) with used soil or coco and water plants.

Week 1–8: Clean water only.

Example: For indoor soil (dissolving in water)

Week 1: Dissolve 4.5 lbs. (2 kg) guano in 3 gal. (10 L) of hot water, then mix with 53 gal. (200 L) of cold water and pour this substance in soil.

Week 2 and 3: Clean water only.

Week 4 and 5: Dissolve 0.5 kg (1 lb.) guano in 2 gal. (7 L) of hot water, then mix with 40 gal. (150 L) cold water and pour this substance in soil.

Week 6, 7, 8: Water plants.

Example: For indoor soil (mixing with soil and dissolving in water)

Week 1: Mix 8 lbs. (3.5 kg) guano with 264 gal. (1000 L) potting soil. Dissolve 1.1 lbs. (0.5 kg) guano with 0.5 gal. (2 L) of hot water, then mix with 13 gal. (50 L) of cold water and pour substance in soil.

Week 2 and 3: Water plants.

Week 4 and 5: Flowering time! Dissolve 1.1 lbs. (0.5 kg) guano in 0.5 gal. (2 L) of hot water, then mix with 13 gal. (50 L) of cold water and pour substance in soil.

Week 6, 7 & 8: Use water only.

Example: For indoor automated closed water systems

Week 1: Before planting mix 3.5 oz. (100 g) guano per plant with Mapito or Oasis growing medium. Let water run daily for 3 hours in a closed system at daylight.

Week 2–8: Let water run daily for 3 hours in a closed system at daylight.

Example: For outdoor growing

Late spring: Mix approximately 1.8 oz. (50 g) guano per plant in soil.

High season : Dissolve 0.4 oz. (10 g) of guano per plant in water every 2 weeks

To rehabilitate your poor soil with Guanokalong

After harvesting, put 3.5 oz. (100 g) of guano into the soil; this boosts it for getting started on the next crop or season. No need to renew the soil..just give it a boost.

Guanokalong Worm Castings.

These worm castings are especially made for humus (fertilizer use) and not for breeding worms. These worms have digested leaves, different vegetables and aged cow dung. This digested substance contains micro-life and releases nutrients directly to the plants. Guanokalong Worm Castings distinguishes itself from other available products on the market by means of quality, fineness and purity.

Castings have a natural pH level within the range we're looking for (around 6.5). Mix two parts castings to one part guano, then as an additive one part guano/casting mix to two parts soil.

There are so many nutrients to use with your garden. I have chosen those which I consider to be amongst the best and most forgiving. They may not be the best available in the world, but they're the best in my world. The choice is yours and the chances are that you might mess up with your first garden and blame the nutrient (although it'll probably be something completely different), and change your nutrient brand. By the second try you'll probably have the hang of it and get it right being completely sold on the new nutrient, although again, it's probably nothing to do with the nutrient, you have simply got it right now. People usually stick with the first nutrient that works for them, which is quite normal among growers. I stick to Canna because I know what I can get away with and feel comfortable with it, although I have had equally good results with Atami, and even plain old water when I used to grow with compost.

Atami Range of Nutrient and Grow Products

Atami is a research-based organization that observes the growing plant at the cellular level, and studies the stages of growth. They evaluate and compare the various substrates such as soil, Rockwool, Coir (coco) and PU slabs. Atami claim that their primary goal is to increase potential yields for the serious grower by analysis of the growing techniques and by increased knowledge of the plant. The result is a smart range of bio-stimulators and nutrition solutions under the name B'cuzz® Products. Atami strongly believes in the importance of ecological products, that's why all B'cuzz bio-stimulators contain only natural components and are as such harmless to man and plant.

A plant progresses through many stages to develop from a single cell into a plant that eventually creates flowers. In summary: we grow, we prepare to flower and we flower in the final phase. During every stage, the plant has its specific needs. The professional grower has known the changing nutritional needs of the plant for quite some time. There is less awareness of the different needs for bio-stimulators and plant enhancers (e.g., proteins, sugars, enzymes, minerals, amino acids, fatty acids and vitamins). All B'cuzz products have been customized to each other so that their use does not disturb the biological balance. With the B'cuzz product range, the grower can stimulate the plant from seed or cutting to mature plant in such a way that it will lead to a more rapid and efficient fission, coil expansion and cell differentiation (in other words a healthy surplus produce!).

B'Cuzz Bio Defence 1 and 2

Healthy plants will result in healthy produce. Every plant family produces its own defense agents. One of the most important of these defenders are the alkaloids. They are protein connections generated by the plant itself as protection against fungi and insects. B'cuzz Bio Defences 1 and 2 are ecological products that stimulate the production of these alkaloids. This will make life very hard for harmful fungi and insects. The only condition is regular spraying from the start of the cycle with B'cuzz Bio Defence 1 and 2, because to prevent is better than to cure. When spraying, Bio Defence 1 and 2 produce no drops in the process. This will distribute the solution more evenly over the leaves and tops so that it can be absorbed more quickly by the plant. Bio Defences 1 and 2 are spraying agents that need to be used simultaneously.

B'Cuzz Root Stimulator

A good start is crucial for a successful crop. Therefore a fast-growing root system is essential for the grower. Roots are necessary to the plant to provide a continuous supply of water, sugars and mineral nutrients. The larger the root system, the more dynamically the plant can function and grow. B'cuzz Root Stimulator will initiate an explosive root production. The young plant is very vulnerable to disease when it enters the growing cycle. Protection against root diseases such as Pythium and Fusarium is of great importance for the plant's health and growth. B'cuzz Root Stimulator decreases the incidence of substrate pathogens and ensures a healthy, productive root system.

B'Cuzz Nutrition Assortments

This is a bio-mineral plant nutrition range composed of the purest components; it contains elements of "food grade" quality, contains no waste substances, and eliminates the need for washing and draining, which is cost effective. The product is also harmless to the environment, so there's a plus straight off. The nutrient assortments are customized to substrate in such a way that the grower is assured of an optimal surplus product. Atami recognize the need also to stabilize the biological balance in the substrate. Within the products supplied by Atami under their B'cuzz range they have incorporated ideal N, P and K ratios for powerful growth and explosive flowering. The high concentration of active substances makes it highly economical in its light-resistant packaging, which is necessary to avoid light contamination and guarantee quality.

B'Cuzz Hydro Nutrition A and B

B'cuzz Hydro Nutrition is a plant nutrient solution composed on a bio-mineral basis. It's specially developed to enhance growth in hydro substrates such as rockwool and PU slabs. B'cuzz Hydro Nutrition is composed of the purest and most valuable ingredients. It contains no fillers or unnecessary components. Because of this, the serious grower is able to save up to 40% on the cost of the nutrient solution. B'cuzz Hydro Nutrition will stabilize the biological balance in the substrate.

B'Cuzz Coco Nutrition A and B

The substrate coco is conquering the grow market at high speed. Coco fibers contain relatively lots of oxygen and little water. Their pH lies around 5 to 6. Coco substrate responds well to fertilizer substances and is capable of absorbing a great amount of nutrition elements. Tthe latest development in the B'cuzz Nutrition range, B'cuzz Coco Nutrition is a balanced bio-mineral plant nutrition specially developed for growth on coco.

B'Cuzz 1-Component Soil Nutrition

B'cuzz 1-Component Soil Nutrition is extremely suitable for indoor growth, but will also guarantee a successful outdoor growth. This product is very effective for lime-rich soil. B'cuzz. 1-Component Soil Nutrition was awarded the Dutch Hydroponics Award in 2000.

B'Cuzz Booster

The growing and flowering stages of plant growth are quite distinct; the plant produces cells of a different structure for each part of its life. Having examined these phases in a very thorough manner, Atami developed the products to serve the plant's needs through each stage. B'cuzz Booster has been developed specifically to stimulate the growth phase and it's a necessary supplement to normal nutrition. It's a six-in-one growing stimulator, containing micronutrients, aquabacterias, amino acids and proteins. This all-in-one system makes B'cuzz Booster an extremely cost-effective supplement and a must for those gardeners who wish to increase the yield and overall quality of their plants.

B'cuzz Booster is available in six types. Every plant has its own needs and every substrate its own characteristics. The fiber in cocos is totally different from the one in potting compost soil. When a grower ignores facts like these, he will have his end results to show for it. The B'cuzz Boosters are customized to the plant of your choice and the specific substrate in such a way that you can obtain maximum results from both plant and substrate. When using the correct Booster, you will find that the plants show a strong and rapid growth of roots, stems, and leaves. B'cuzz Booster has little or no effect on the EC or pH. In the United States, the B'cuzz Boosters have been granted Best Plant Addition 2000.

Bloom Stimulator

Especially for the plant's blooming phase, Atami has developed the Bloom Stimulator. B'cuzz Bloom Stimulator encourages flower cell production and increases the manufacture and transport of sugar molecules in the flowers. This will lead to big, dense tops and a much better taste. In this way, quantity as well as quality will increase on the final product. Especially for cocoponic cultivation, Atami has developed the Coco Bloom Stimulator. B'cuzz Booster works optimally in combination with B'cuzz Bloom Stimulator. Consult the B'cuzz Bio-Stimulators grow advice for the right dosage in the growing and flowering phases of the plant to obtain bigger tops and more produce.

B'Cuzz Coco Substrate

Atami has developed the B'cuzz Coco Substrate, especially for growth on coco. B'cuzz Coco Substrate is a 100% biological plant substrate that offers many advantages to all those that are professionally engaged in growing plants. The composition of the substrate consists entirely of the purest coconut fiber, which is derived from the processing of coconuts from Sri Lanka. The B'cuzz Coco Substrate is a high-quality product, free of harmful viruses and carefully checked for soil diseases.

The addition of B'cuzz positive microorganisms to the substrate guarantees that soil diseases have absolutely no chance of developing. Because of its smart and well-balanced composition, B'cuzz Coco Substrate can be applied in all growth methods. B'cuzz Coco Substrate has a fine structure and texture because it has been buffered and rinsed so that the plant is enabled to "program" itself to its ideal nutrition conditions right at the very beginning of its cycle. This is a guarantee for an optimal continuation of the growth process. Atami has also developed the B'cuzz Coco Slab. This is pre-packed in convenient-sized slabs to slit open at set intervals and insert a clone.

B'Cuzz Atazyme

This is a high-quality, natural, multi-enzyme preparation that ensures increased nutritional absorption by the plant; root activity is enhanced and therefore also the growth process. Atazyme stimulates activity of microorganisms in the soil, reducing chances of soil diseases and over-fertilization. This product is one of the few that also cleanses dripping and irrigation systems as it works. Atazyme is used as an addition to regular nutrition once a week during maintenance and/or soil rinsing. Suited to soil, hydro and coco.

Use Ratio: 1 of Atazyme to 250 of water using imperial measure of whatever unit is appropriate to your garden (4 ml to 1 L and 40 ml or 38 oz. to 0.3 gal. and 380 oz. to 3 gal.).

B'Cuzz PK 13–14

This is a high-quality phosphor and potassium preparation to help promote a healthy root system and stimulate readiness for flowering to the maximum. It can be directly absorbed into the plant and contains no waste substances. Use PK 13–14 as an addition in the first week of the flowering phase. Wash through with water and enzyme in the final week of the flowering phase. Suited to hydro, soil and coco.

Dosage: Increasing addition through weeks from week one at 1.5 ml per 10 L to 15 ml per 10 L (0.05 oz. per 2.5 gal. to 0.5 oz. per 2.5 gal.) in the final week.

Cultivating with Bio Nova Fertilizers

After having cultivated for 20 years on a professional level Bio Nova started trading in 1993. At the same time a laboratory was equipped for the development of ready-to-use nutrient solutions for amateur as well as for experienced growers. From this long experience a number of products have originated that are of exceptional quality, purity and user-friendliness. Forever working on the development of new products, and the improvement of existing ones, Bio Nova appears to be sharply aware of the worldwide market for new ingredients that could lead to new products. After long testing periods, and only when there is a distinct positive result, these new products are put on the market.

Bio Nova has four main lines in her range of products

Nutri-Nova: A user-friendly mineral A/B fertilizer available on the market, this concentrated fertilizer was developed for systems with artificial substrate such as rockwool slabs, polyurethane slabs, perlite and the like. For some time now Nutri-Nova A/B substrate fertilizer has offered the simplest solution for people who like to grow on an artificial substrate because, among other things, growing and flowering fertilizers have been combined into one product. So you need only two bottles of fertilizer for the complete cycle of growing and flowering. This fertilizer is free of excess salts and contains merely directly digestible minerals. In other words, it's a complete nutrient as easy to use as a chemical A/B with the quality of the best biological fertilizers. The used minerals are all of a "Food Grade" quality and the trace elements are chelated in order to be absorbed in a wider pH range.

The use of this fertilizer is particularly easy and in practice is limited to the simple measuring of the correct amounts of A and B solutions and mixing them, one at a time, in the matching amount of water. If necessary, the pH value of the nutrient solution can be adjusted by using phosphoric acid to a pH of 5.8 (range 5.5–6.3). Nutri-Nova is in my opinion one of the best hydro-fertilizers on the market and its quality surpasses comparable fertilizers

Dosage: 18 oz. per 20 gal. (532 ml per 76 L) of water. The use of PK 13+14 together with Nutri-Nova **isn't advised**.

Coco-Nova, with Nutri-Nova as a basis, specially adapted for cultivating on BN-cocoslabs or those of any other brand. For some time now Coco-Nova A/B coconut substrate fertilizer has offered the simplest solution for people who like to use coconut as a substrate because, as with Nutri-Nova, growing and flowering fertilizers have been combined into one product. So again you need only two bottles of fertilizer for the complete cycle of growing and flowering. The base for Coco-Nova is Nutri-Nova. The minerals used are all of a "Food Grade" quality and the trace elements are chelated in order to be absorbed in a wider pH range. Especially for coconut substrate, various elements have been added to this A/B fertilizer and these elements see to it that the growing and flowering on coconut substrate always take place optimally, certainly when the slabs are reused.

The use of this fertilizer is particularly easy and in practice is limited to the simple measuring of the correct amounts of A and B solutions and mixing them, one at a time, in the matching amount of water. If necessary, the pH value of the nutrient solution can be adjusted by using phosphoric acid to a pH of 5.8 (range 5.5–6.3).

Dosage: 18 fl. oz. per 20 gal. ((532 ml per 76 L)). The use of PK 13+14 together with Coco-Nova **isn't advised**.

For the Nutri- and Coco-Nova products, a simplified fertilization schedule would be as follows:

Fertilizers: Nutri-Nova/Coco-Nova 15–17 oz. (400–500 ml) to 1 L (0.3 gal.) of water (continual).

Plant Feeds: Roots 3.5 oz. (100 ml) to 2.5 gal. (10 L) of water (one off) BN X-cel 3.5 oz. (100 ml) to 26 gal. (100 L) of feed solution (continual) BN-Zym 6.5 oz. (200 ml) to 26 gal. (100 L) of water every 2 weeks.

Hydro-Supermix mineral substrate fertilizer, a one-component fertilizer composed of bio-minerals with added PK 13–14, is also suited for rockwool slabs, polyurethane slabs, perlite, etc. This fertilizer, administered with a drip system, is also used successfully on soil. Growing and flowering components as well as A and B components are combined into one product. This makes growing using **BN Hydro-Supermix** very simple indeed. This fertilizer consists of:

• Macro-elements such as: NO_3, NH_4, NH_2, SO_4, P, K, Ca, Mg, and Si
• Chelated micro-elements such as: Fe, Mn, Zn, B, Cu, and Mo
• Vitalizing plant extracts cell-tissue strengthening bio-extracts.

The elements mentioned above are completely pure and of natural, biological origin, therefore this fertilizer can be absorbed very easily and a low EC will be quite sufficient.

BN Hydro-Supermix causes active soil life, actively stimulates root forming, and supplies the soil with total fertilizing during the growing period as well as the flowering of the plants. During the flowering period we advise you to supply the plant with PK 13+14 as an additional superbloomer.

Dosage: Continuously in the nutrient solution 15–17 oz. (400–500 ml) per 26 gal. (100 L) of water. Though this fertilizer is pH independent because of the applied chelates, it may sometimes be necessary to adjust the pH value (5.5–6.3), preferably by using phosphoric acid. BN Hydro-Supermix is a good combination fertilizer that can also be used for trying out your own ideas and for plants with different feed requirements.

BN Soil-Supermix, a mineral organic fertilizer with Hydro-Supermix as a basis, is the best fertilizer for those who like to use soil for growing. Here too, the combination with BN PK 13–14 is used. The difference with the Hydro-Supermix is the addition of organic ingredients. Because of these organic ingredients, the conservation of a prepared nutrient solution isn't possible! So don't ever prepare more than you need. This fertilizer consists of:

• Macro elements such as NO_3, NH_4, NH_2, SO_4, P, K, Ca, Mg and Si
• Chelated micro-elements such as Fe, Mn, Zn, B, Cu and Mo
• Vitalizing plant extracts

- Cell-tissue strengthening extracts
- Bio-extracts
- Organic components

The elements mentioned are completely pure and of a natural, biological origin. Because of this origin this fertilizer can be absorbed very easily and a low EC will be quite sufficient. At the same time the biological components function as a good buffer. BN Soil-Supermix causes good active soil life, actively stimulates root forming, and supplies the soil with complete fertilizing, during growth as well as flowering of the plants. During the flowering period we advise you to supply the plant with BN PK 13+14 as an additional superbloomer.

Dosage: 2–4 times a week 15–17 oz. (400–500 ml) per 26 gal. (100 L) of water. The number of fertilizing times is variable, depending on the size of the plant, the kind of plant you grow and the climatological circumstances. If you start with well pre-fertilized soil, as a rule you don't need to use a liquid fertilizer for the first three weeks. But if you start up on soil that has been used before, you have to use fertilizers beginning the day of planting, depending on a soil-analysis.

Although because of the utilization of chelates, the working of this fertilizer isn't heavily influenced by the pH of the nutrient solution, it'll sometimes be necessary to adapt the pH of the solution (range 5.5–6.5), preferably using phosphoric acid if you have to lower the pH. As BN Soil-Supermix is partially organic, this fertilizer cannot be used in a dripping system. In the case of such a system the mineral fertilizer, BN Hydro-Supermix has to be used, with the same end result. This fertilizer does not contain the organic ingredients that clog up your drippers. A simplified fertilizing solution using the supermixes soil and hydro are as follows:

Fertilizers: Hydro-Supermix 13.5–17 oz. (400–500 ml) to 26 gal. (100 L) of water (continual); Soil-Supermix 15–17 oz. (400–500 ml) to 26 gal. (100 L) water (2–4 times a week); P-K 13+14 0.8–3.4 oz. (25–100 ml) to 16 gal. (100 L) of nutrient solution (during flowering). Plant Feeds: Roots 100ml to 10 liters of water (one off); BN Excel 3.4 oz. (100 ml) to 26 gal. (100 L) of nutrient solution (continual); BN-Zym 7 oz. (200 ml) to 26 gal. (100 L) water (every 2 weeks).

As an addition to these four main fertilizers I prescribe a threesome of maintenance products that stimulate the roots and the growth of plants and eventually largely increase the produce. At the same time these products cause the plant to be less sensitive to attacks of vermin, fungi, viruses or other pests. For these four methods of cultivating, outlines for fertilizing have been made that give growers something to hold on to as far as usage and dosage go. If all other growing factors are also right, one can expect optimal produce with these fertilizers time and time again!

Bio Nova BN Profi-Mix

For those who like to make their own high-quality soil-mix there is now a low-priced but complete biological mix of fertilizers. It consists of the following ingredients: dry roots, blood meal, feather meal, horn meal, bone meal, hoof meal, chicken manure, cocoa peals, malt germs, AZ bacteria chalk, seaweed, enzymes, amino acids, alfalfa meal, peat humus, iron chelate, iron sulfate, vitamins and glycine. You can see that it's a very complete mix, and in the correct proportions, which is just as important. As a basis one can use potting soil or cocopeat.

A good mixture is: 106 gal. (400 L) of soil/cocopeat + 11 lbs. (5 kg) BN Profi-Mix + 13 gal. (50 L) of perlite + 13 gal. (50 L) of worm castings. Of course all these ingredients should be mixed thoroughly. The definitive EC will be between 1.5 and 2.0. The pH will be about 6.0 and 6.5. (Both of these depend on the potting soil being used.) If necessary the doses of BN Profi-Mix may be adjusted to obtain a correct EC. To raise the pH in case of a soil that is too acid, you must use 7 oz. (200 g) of AZ chalk per 26 gal. (100 L) of soil for an increase in the pH value of 0.5.

BN P-K 13+14 Liquid Phosphorous Pottasium Complex: Phosphorous makes for the development of a healthy, extensive root system and for an exuberant flowering. Potassium prompts the flowering of the plant and the flowering potency.

The combination of these two materials in a mineral shape can indeed be called a superbloomer. In the world of growing this is truly an essential component! In the Bio Nova range of liquid fertilizers, free of excess materials, you have at your disposal a very powerful Phosphor-Potassium combination under the name of BN PK 13+14, which can be directly absorbed by the plants. This fertilizer is used in combination with the Hydro-Supermix or with the Soil-Supermix. The combination of BN PK 13+14 with one of those supermixes gives you a complete fertilizer for either slabs or soil.

Dosage:

1st week of flowering: 1 oz./26 gal. (25 ml/100 L)

2nd week of flowering: 1.5 oz./26 gal. (50 ml/100 L)

3rd week of flowering: 2.5 oz./26 gal. (75 ml/100 L)

4th week of flowering until the last week: 3-4 oz./26 gal. (100-125 ml/100 L)

Roots: The Root and Plant Stimulator

From a great amount of research over an extended period of time on the subject of root strengthening and development done by American universities, it has appeared that in all cases the usage of Roots led to a higher root activity and a resulting higher produce of all treated crops. This stimulator has now been successfully applied for many years already in European horticulture and in the world of growing. Roots can be used on leaves as a foliar spray as well as on the growing medium.

ROOT: consists of, among other things, peathumic (natural chelation) agent for improving the uptake of nitrogen, accelerating root growth and cell forming, and increasing ion transport; 3% kelp for quickly healing wounds, curing chlorosis, and increased chlorophyll and hair root development; 3% Ascorbic acid (vitamin C); 3% Thiamine (vitamin B1); Alpha tocopheral (vitamin E); 5% Myo Inositol (carbohydrate); 1% Glycine (amino acid); and 7% humus acids (enhanced oxygen absorption, faster root cell tissue formation). The dosage for Root is 3.5 oz. (100 ml) to 2.5 gal. (10 L) of water (1:1000); this is enough for 75 plants.

BN Excel Growing and Flowering Stimulant for Crop

BN Excel is a natural growing and flowering stimulant that can be administered to all sorts of plants, which gives you a demonstrable increase in both the quality as well as the quantity of all tested crops. So: more profit of a higher quality. This sophisticated combination of materials gives the biochemical functions a boost on all levels. The ingredients derived from plant extracts advance the processes of the metabolism and especially the photosynthesis, and thus the construction of carbohydrates.

The hormone household of the crop is actively stimulated by the combination of free amino acids. BN Excel contains the following ingredients: various vitamins, natural growing and flowering stimulants, free amino acids, bacteria, trace elements, enzymes, kelp and peat humus acids. From the first day after planting, BN Excel takes an active part in the growing and flowering process. The crops strike root earlier with nearly no loss, a very extensive root system is being formed and at the same time the plant will grow more quickly and vitally. The readiness to flower is stimulated and eventually one can count on a demonstrable surplus yield.

BN Excel is no fertilizer, but it can be combined with all fertilizers that are on the market and it can be utilized in all substrates. Dosage: 0.5 oz. (10 ml) per 26 gal. (100 L) of nutrient solution from the first day to the last week. (During the mixing foaming can arise, but this will disappear as a matter of course.)

BN-Zym Enzymes

BN-Zym is a natural biocatalyst (process quickener), medium composer and improver that is based on several enzymes. Enzymes promote the ability to hold on to water in every medium and to reduce the surface tension, so that the water penetrates quicker and to greater depths. In doing so, BN-Zym supplies the medium with more oxygen. Enzymes are strongly specialized protein molecules and act as catalysts in numerous biochemical processes. Converting sugar into alcohol via the chemical way takes a few weeks or even months. Enzymes manage this in seconds. The functioning of enzymes is always 100% without waste or by-products.

BN-Zym brings about increasing bacterial activity, as a result of which the nutrients and minerals in the substrate are converted in a way that that can be directly taken up by the crop. BN-Zym catalyses the waste products and converts them to once-more usable nutrients. A better balance and less sensitivity for all kinds of diseases are the results. But most of all it will keep the growing medium clean of all kinds of residual salts and ballast materials. This is important during the growing period but is certainly important for soil that is used several times.

Dosage: Medium soil/coco: once every two weeks water with enzymesrinse.

Medium rockwool: once every two weeks with enzymes (1.5 gal. or 5 L per slab). Dosage for all mediums: 6.5 oz. (200ml) per 26 gal. (100 L).

Adjust the pH of the water with added BN-Zym to pH 5.8 using phosphoric acid, or even better, with citric acid.

BN Coco Substrate

After a long period of development, Bio Nova has come up with a superior coco slab that is composed especially for top results. BN Coco is a professionally produced growing medium that complies with the severe R.H.P standards laid at the laps of all European producers. The slab is made up of UV-durable foil filled with finely flaked coco fibers that are pretreated extensively so that the material is without diseases and vermin.

The advantages of using BN Coco instead of rockwool are countless, but the chief obviously is a higher yield. A natural substrate and no longer a waste problem, coconut can be used again as a high quality compost outside. The slabs are ready-made so they can be used directly. Pure material with a very low EC (0.2 ms/s), and an ideal pH value of 5.8, coco has an air proportion of 35%. These slabs can be used again more often.

BN Coco is very simple to use. The BN coco slabs can be simply used in existing substrate systems, as the sizes are the same as those of other slabs: 40" x 6" x 2.5" (100 x 15 x 7 cm). So you see there are many reasons to get going with BN Coco at once.

Bio Nova has developed a special fertilizer for the BN Coco slab, Coco Nova A/B nutrient. This is a two-component growing and flowering nutrient with Nutri Nova as a basis, containing elements for a top produce. Please ask for the particular fertilizing scheme at your specialist shop. If there are any questions about growing on coco slabs please ask your supplier or, alternatively, ask Bio Nova directly.

Canna Products
Specialist Development for the Growing of Cannabis
This brings us neatly to the original cocos product, Canna Coco slabs. This is a product that revolutionized the growing of marijuana, and helped to increase yields with simplicity and cleanliness. If you grow on soil, then you'll love cocos. It lasts forever (almost), and is clean, lightweight, and you don't have to clean out every time you harvest, just take out your old plant root system and mix in your guano or other fertilizer to rejuvenate.

Dutch Hydro Cup Winner 1996
Canna products are specifically designed in Holland for cannabis cultivation on coconut coir, hydroponics, and earth. Canna was recognized as the number-one hydroponic nutrient solution in its class at the Nederwiet Festival, an annual show in Holland for hydroponic and soil growers. They're experts in compound fertilizers for the growing of cannabis in coconut, hydroponic, soil and substrate cultivation processes. Their fertilizer is user-friendly, clean, and simple. Everyone, even inexperienced growers, can achieve excellent results with it! They are well-priced

products that do not harm the environment. Canna is continuously investing in research and development.

Canna has achieved a good reputation among home growers. Canna's special hemp fertilizer is sold to 80% of the Dutch and German grow shops and is also exported to the UK, Austria, Belgium, Norway, Spain, Switzerland and Australia. The ready-to-use fertilizer by Canna is a balanced combination of main and trace elements. Two products for the entire growth cycle have been developed.

Vega

This fertilizer gives the plant all the nutrition it needs during the growing phase. Canna Vega makes healthy, strong plants with healthily growing green shoots. It's also the ideal fertilizer for mother plants that are used for cuttings.

Flores

Canna Flores gives the plant all the nutrition it needs during the blooming phase. Experienced growers love Flores because it stimulates fructification, and ensures unsurpassed THC production and large buds.

Soil: Terra Vega and Terra Flores

All Ruderalis species love nitrogen-rich soil. Terra Vega is rich in directly absorbable nitrogen compounds and high-quality EDDHA-iron chelates. This guarantees maximum absorption from the beginning of the growing process. During the blooming much less nitrogen is necessary. The need for potassium and phosphate, on the other hand, (which are scarcely found in their pure form in nature) is rising. Terra Flores is rich in these compounds in their directly absorbable state and therefore guarantees an excellent bloom. The Vega and Flores containers come with an built-in accurate measuring container in the top. A squeeze of the bottle fills the measuring container, which has its own lid. Take off the lid and pour the content into your water.

Canna Vega and Flores for Hydroponics Culture

Growing in hydroponic cultures, the plant is 100% dependent on the nutritional substances that are contained in the irrigation water. Since mostly tap water is used, Canna products are optimal for this growing process. These products avoid accumulation of salts that are burdensome to the plant and its environment.

Canna Vega and Flores contain everything that the plant needs and thus ensure optimal growth, high potency and a full, round taste.

Canna Coco

This is a ready-to-use fertilizer solution that is made by diluting the A and B concentrates. Again you'll notice the simple measuring device on the bottle that measures 10, 15, 20, and 25 ml (0.25, 0.5, 0.7 and 0.75 oz.). Mix the concentrate with equal amounts of tap water. Fill your feed tank with water and add the Aand B concentrates in the following amounts: 1:250. For an example, take 3.5 oz. (100 ml) of A and 2.5 oz. (100 ml) of B to 6.5 gal. (25 L) of tap water, (20 ml of each to 5 L). Always stir well and let the mixture stand for some hours. Measure the pH level and adjust accordingly to get a reading of between 5.2 and 6.4.

Note: NEVER mix the A and B concentrates together directly as an insoluble combination will occur. As a rule, use 1 gal. of solution per 10 ft^2 (8–15 oz. per plant) or 5 L of solution to every 1 m^2 of garden every day (250–450 ml per plant). The drainage must be minimal when using coco so that 20% of the solution only, leaves the coconut matting. Feeding frequency is 5 times per day, so each feed by any system, whether automatic or by hand will deliver between 1.5 oz. (50 ml) and 2 oz. (90 ml) per cycle.

Canna Coco is an organic product with a homogenous (even) structure free of chemical additives, harmful viruses or soil diseases. In contrast to coconut-fiber, which is also applied in gardening, Canna Coco is free of fiber and comes in the form of fine flakes which are a result of the manufacture of coconut-products in Sri Lanka. Canna Coco has a complex air/water system, which surpasses other substrates. Furthermore it contains a special mold (Trichoderma), which can protect the plant against soil diseases. Canna Coco is developed and created to fulfill all the requirements of cannabis growing. In addition the substrate can be used several times and is environmentally friendly. During the creation of the fertilizer, which Canna has developed especially for this ecological substrate, significant increases in quality and yield were observed. Available in slabs, bags or compressed brick form.

Rhizotonic (RootingHormone)

Canna Rhizotonic is a powerful organic "stress reliever" which stimulates new root development, increases resistance to root-borne diseases such as pythium, and improves the internal and external vigor of the cannabis plant.

Cannazym

This is a high-quality enzyme substance for breaking up the (hemi) cellulose, and stimulation of microorganisms. Cannazym contains more than 12 different enzymes, special vitamins and extracts of desert plants. Cannazym increases the breakup of dead root material, brings more air into the substrate, activates the growth of microorganisms and creates an improved absorption of nutrients, increasing the plant's resistance to disease.

pH Regulators

pH-Growth

pH-GROWTH contains nitric acid and is used to increase the acid content of the nutritional solvent for vegetative plants.

pH- Bloom

pH-Bloom contains phosphoric acid and is used to increase the acid content of the nutritional solvent for vegetative plants. pH+ is a buffer/alkaline combination. pH+ contains potassium bicarbonate and potassium hydroxide and is used to increase the pH in the nutritional solvent.

PK 13–14 Bloom Minerals

Canna PK 13–14 is a dynamic new flowering booster from Holland that will amaze you. PK 13–14 stimulates extreme size, better quality and more numerous blooms with an enhanced sweetness and flavor. The base formulation is an extremely powerful mixture high in phosphorous and potassium. PK 13–14 is totally unique, absolutely safe, easy to use and incredibly effective. Canna PK 13–14 isn't a nutrient; it's a nutrient additive. There are of course several other nutrient manufacturers on the market, like Hesi.

9

Growing From Seed

Following many experiments and studies on structure, anatomy, crossbreeding and chemistry, it was concluded that *Cannabis* is a single true species, Cannabis Sativa. Although many growers may claim that they've discovered several types of cannabis plant, it's declared in a botanical sense that all other plants are simply variants and the result of an unnatural evolution through the transporting to new environments and physical changes brought about by humans experimenting with cross pollination. Over the years many variants have developed with different potency, fragrance, and taste, even different physical attributes, but science says that looks aren't everything and the fact remains that despite all the variants there is only one Cannabis Sativa.

The new age grower of cannabis has at his fingertips the information and ability to develop plants that will suit his or her own tastes, desires and abilities. It's no longer beyond the ability of the common man to develop his own creation. This has been proven more specifically with all the new strains developed in Holland.

Hybrids are available through mail order, or by a visiting a Dutch grow shop or one of the many shops that are springing up in the UK, such as Cannabis Closet grow supplies. It's believed at this time that there have been no prosecutions for the supply, keeping or purchase of seeds. However, if you're buying seeds through the Internet, be aware that this media is used by thieves and con men with a craving to get their hands on your money and they have been known to send out useless hemp seed. You may even have friends who have experienced the Internet fraudsters, and have heard their tales of woe. Learn from their mistakes and only shop at those Internet stores known to be reputable.

Talk to people and ask where they've purchased their seeds. Even advertisements in the many magazines that are available are not necessarily safe; since the publishers cannot possibly know or vet each advertiser, they cannot be held responsible. I have listed a couple of suppliers for you at the end of the book who have always proven to deliver and who have spent many years perfecting their product. Gone are the days of chance. The art of commercial seed manufacture has become sophisticated and you can buy biologically grown strains of seeds and even guarantee females in some cases.

If we accept that Cannabis Sativa is the species botanically recognized then we have to consider three further divisions: Indica, Ruderalis, and Hemp. There are hundreds of variants within these divisions.

Indica plants are short and stocky and rarely reach over 8ft in height. Yielding only small amounts of bud, they have dark green leaves with much broader fingers. Most Indica originate from Central Asia. Flower stigmas go from a pale pink to a deep purple color. Although the harvest appears smaller, the Indica bud is fuller and tighter, giving more weight at harvest.

Sativa can grow up to 22 ft in height and yield around 8–10 pounds of bud (sensimilla). Most tropical plants are known to be Sativa, as are Hemps and can be recognised by their slender, light green leaf blades or fingers, with female stigma being pure white.

Ruderalis are physically similar to Sativa although they're much shorter, rarely reaching over 5ft in height. It can be quite a worry when first growing a Ruderalis, since the leaf system only produces about three sets. The yield at harvest is usually around an ounce or so, and so this is not really a good plant for the commercial grower or the money conscious, although it does mature early so Ruderalis is great for poor-weather countries and it's better to have an early crop with a little bud than a late crop that has died because the plant isn't suited to the climate.

Choosing a Variety to Grow

The most important point to consider when choosing what variety to grow is whether it will suit your intended method of growing. If growing outside, will it mature early and beat the winter deluge of rain and wind? If you're growing inside, then you'll prefer a shorter stocky plant with a high yield; the photoperiod shouldn't worry you since you create that with your electric light system. Important considerations for all growers are those of potency, yield and the period to maturity. Other considerations are those of smell and taste. Maybe you want a cerebral high rather than the debilitating heavy body feeling of apathy. Different marijuana has been described as stupefying and numbing to energizing and uplifting. It has been noted that a plant usually providing a cerebral high at maturity can provide a heavy body feeling if harvests are taken while the stamen are still white.

Your limitation in outdoor growing usually evolves around maturity; yields are a secondary factor. The only limitation inside is space, everything else can be overcome. Many growers prefer Indica to Sativa, the two easily distinguishable by their very different leaves. Indica tend to grow more compactly, with thicker, heavier bud. After some time you may decide to grow several varieties, not just for the choice of taste but because you can! It's exciting to see a plant growing. The cannabis plant gives you a great response and encourages you with its extreme growth rate and durability. How cool will you look when you offer your friends a choice of weed from a small toking box? You can become a connoisseur of weed. The most potent weed used to come from Congolese and Nigerian strains, with as much as 12% THC content. Now, with new understanding and technology, the clever Dutch are finding ways to improve and diversify all of the time, God bless them.

Stay away from Southeast Asian varieties like Thai, as they're renowned for becoming hermaphroditic, although the quality of smoke is high. But what's the good of a great high when you risk losing a crop when the hermaphrodites take over your girls as they grow? Columbian weed is always a good smoke, so you're safe with that one. Indian originating plants are strangely diverse in all respects including physical structure, taste and potency. African strains are usually the most potent and often grow the largest also. It has been known for plants to grow leaves 18" (45 cm) long and plants up to 20' (6 m) tall. The bud however is loose on the plant and therefore does not carry the weight a commercial grower is looking for.

High Quality Seeds (Holland)

Original Haze x Skunk: Of Californian origin, this F1 hybrid has a genetic make-up of 12.5% Indica and 87.5% Sativa. Flowering in 8–12 weeks, it's suited to all growing techniques. A tall plant that gives a bud that has a both sweet and sour taste. Harvesting up to 18 oz. (500 g). This is a high-yielding plant that can give extreme THC content.

South India x Skunk: Of Indian/Californian origin, this stabilized hybrid has a genetic makeup of 12.5% Indica and 87.5% Sativa. Flowering is 9–12 weeks and is suited to all growing techniques. The medium-height, sturdy plant has a sweet smell and taste. Giving up to 18 oz. (500 g).

Swazi x Skunk: Originating in Swaziland/California, this F1 hybrid has a genetic make up of 12.5% Indica and 87.5% Sativa. Flowering is at 9–12 weeks and the plant is suited to all growing techniques. This plant has a small amount of leaf and very tall buds, giving a sweet taste of hash with a good strong high. Plants are usually medium in height, give up to 500 grams of bud, This is a high-quality, high-resin content.

Super Thai x Skunk: Originating from Thailand/California, this F1 hybrid has a 25% Indica content and 75% Sativa. Flowering is 9–12 weeks and it's suited for all growing techniques. The tall slender plant has a surprisingly uplifting high, gives up to 500 grams of bud.

Afghani Hindu Kush: Originating in Afghanistan, this F1 hybrid is genetically 80% Indica and 20% Sativa. Flowering in 8–12 weeks, it's suited to all growing techniques. The plant has a strong bud with lots of resin that smells of sweet hash. This is a short plant, giving up to 18 oz. (500g).

Four Way Special: Originating in Laos, Thailand, California and Holland, this hybrid has genetics of 20% Indica and 80% Sativa. The tall plant flowers in 8–12 weeks with any grow technique. The buds are fragrant and sweet and it harvests up to 21 oz. (600 g).

Original Highway Delight: Originating in California, this hybrid has a gentic makeup of 75% Indica and 25% Sativa. Flowering is enjoyed in 8–12 weeks. Suits all grow techniques. This is a medium height, sturdy plant, which harvests sweet-tasting bud, giving up to 18 oz. (500 g). Northern Lights Skunk cross.

Original California Orange Skunk: Originating in California, this F1 hybrid is 65% Indica and 35% Sativa. Flowering in 8–10 weeks, it's suited to all grow techniques. The strong medium height plant harvests up to 18 oz. (500 g) of sweet bud with lots of THC.

Original Hawaiian Maui Wowie Skunk: Originating in Hawaii, this F1 hybrid is 80% Indica and 20% Sativa. Flowering in 8–10 weeks, it's suited to all grow techniques. This is a beautiful medium height plant with a strong smell, giving lots of resin on leaves and buds. Harvests up to 18 oz. (500 g)

Northern Lights: This is a particular favorite of mine. Originating in California, this hybrid is 90% Indica and 10% Sativa. Flowering in 8–10 weeks, it's suited to all grow techniques. The short, robust plant reaches up to 50" (125 cm) and harvests up to 18 oz. (500 g) of spicy bud in mid-October. This is a very powerful plant. Cost: US $33 (£16) for a pack of 11 seeds.

Durban Poison Amazing Special: This is a South African plant. South Africa has the most different varieties of marijuana. Being a major trade country worldwide, it appears to take on board all comers and the variety of plants reflect the trading scene; its climate lends itself to almost any variety dropped, blown, or planted in its vast lands. A pure Sativa with a flowering time of 8–10 weeks, this plant is suited to outside and inside growing, although it needs height for its tall buds, which are loaded with resin and give off a sweet liquor-like smell. Because of its early flowering it is well suited for outdoor growth and gives between 7 and 18 oz. (200 and 500 g) harvest

South African Durban Poison Skunk: Despite its name, it was developed in California. It's fast growing, has a high potency, flowers early and is an almost perfect stock for any grower. The plant itself can pop up as a small bush about 3.5' (1 m) high or a tree-like 8' (2.4 m). Whichever manifestation it appears in, you'll notice the broad leaf blades or fingers, although the color of stigma varies and doesn't help identify the plant at all.

This plant is an F1 hybrid made up of 87.5% Sativa and 12.5% Indica. It's particulalry suited to indoor growing although it'll grow outdoors and in a greenhouse. Long sticky buds are many on the plant and return 200–500 with a mild taste.

Skunk 3 x A2: Originating in Holland, this homogenous plant flowers in 8–10 weeks and is suited to all grow techniques. Develops to produce a short full plant with a fantastic smell. Harvest up to 18 oz. (500 g).

Purple Tops: Originating in Holland, this Skunk plant is 100% Indica, flowers in 9 weeks, and is suited to all grow techniques. Developing as a big sturdy plant reaching 8' (2.4 m) and giving a harvest of up to 18 oz. (500 g) in September, Purple Tops is very suitable for outdoor use.

Bob Marley's Best: Originating in Holland, this F1 hybrid is 50% Indica and 50% Sativa. Flowering in 8–10 weeks, this plant suits all grow techniques. This is a nice full plant of medium height, with a great smell. Gives up to 21 oz. (600 g) at harvest in early October. Originally created for outdoor cultivation.

Original Big Bud Super Skunk: Originating in Holland, this is a homogenous plant that is mostly Indica. Flowering in 8–10 weeks, this plant is suited to all grow techniques, giving a good flower to leaf ratio and a remarkably sweet, powerful high. This medium-height plant gives up to 35 oz. (1000 g). Best-selling plant well suited for outdoors and a good commercial plant.

Early Girl: Originating in Holland this Skunk plant is 100% Indica, flowers in 7 weeks, and is suited to all grow techniques, but particularly to outdoor growing. The short stocky plant reaches 8' (2.4 m) and has a full potent crop of bud around 14 oz. (400 g).

White Rose: Originating in Holland, this Skunk x White Widow is 90% Indica and 10% Sativa. Flowering in 8 weeks, it's suited to all grow techniques. The bud is sweet with a lot of THC and lots of resin on leaves. Height reaches 8' (2.4 m), harvests up to 500. A plant suited best to outdoor growing.

Ghandi: Originating in Holland, this South Indian x Skunk is 80% Indica and 20% Sativa. Flowering in 9 weeks and suited to all grow techniques, this large, sturdy plant reaches 8' (2.4 m) and gives up to 9 oz. (250 g) of sweet-tasting bud.

Outsider: Originating in Holland, this plant has won the Highlife Cup. It's a Skunk x Durban and 100% Indica. Flowering in 8 weeks, the plant is suited to all grow techniques, but particularly suited to outdoors. This is a sturdy plant reaching 8' (2.4 m) and giving up to 21 oz. (600 g) of very sweet bud . Gives a very large bud and can be harvested early.

White Widow: Originating in Holland, the genetic makeup of this plant is the most fiercely guarded secret in the industry. Flowering is 8–10 weeks inside and 10–14 weeks outside. It's a plant suited to all grow techniques, being very strong and reaching 30" (75 cm) indoors and 6.6' (200 cm) outdoors. Harvest up to 7 oz. (200 g) of great bud. This is a very high-quality plant that must not be given too much nutrition.

High Quality Seeds (Guaranteed Female)

Northern Pride   Originating in California, this pure strain plant is 100% Indica. Flowering at 8 weeks, it's suited to all grow techniques. It's one of the most popular Northern Lights #5 selections; smells and tastes like Northern Lights, of medium height, and gives up to 18 oz. (500 g) of bud. This is an extremely disease-resistant plant.

White Pearl: Originating in Holland, this F1 hybrid is 50% Indica and 50% Sativa, suited to all grow techniques. Flowers in 8 weeks. The buds are white with THC glands even on the large leaves higher up the plant. It gives an excellent high with a mild taste, grows to a medium height and harvests around 14 oz. (400 g).

Serious Seeds (Amsterdam)

White Russian: These seeds produce plants that are fantastic in both appearance and effect. Our most typically Indica strain, White Russian is a stable cross of AK47 and White Widow (a prizewinning Indica clone). Medium height, consistent plants with dense, very resinous flower tops (crystals appear after about 5 weeks of flowering), with 22% THC, likely to be the strongest plant known at present! **Winner of the overall Cannabis Cup in 1996 and Best Bio Grass in 1997.** The plants yield very powerful buds, coated with resin, which give a very strong, long-lasting high, more cerebral than a knockout. This is considered to be a medicinal plant which is mostly Indic. Indoor yield: 12–18 oz. (350–500 g) per 10 ft^2 (square meter).

Khali Mist: The plants' odor is quite strong during both their growth and flowering period.

Arguably the top Sativa strain available today, with 90% Sativa genetic. Kali Mist grows into tall, classically Sativa plants with very few leaves. This strain grows dense clusters of full fluffy buds, producing much higher yields than you would expect. The plant structure and few leaves allow the light to pass all the way to lower branches, allowing bottom buds to develop fully. If planted outside early in the year, this plant can grow very tall. Expect spiralling flowers with high resin content and a delightfully spicy scent. Kali Mist is often the choice of experts for their own stash grows. Also, women in particular seem to like this strain; besides the sheer pleasure of smoking it, we have received several reports that it works great against menstrual cramps. Kali Mist was improved in 2000 to produce bigger yields. In Spain it proved to be very mold resistant, even outside during bad weather. This strain has flavor and a subtle cerebral effect that won it a **Cannabis Cup First Prize** in 1995 (Hydro Cup) and again (with this new and improved version) in 2000, the **Seed Company Sativa Cup!** Without a doubt this is the choice for a connoisseur stash, giving a very strong, clear and energizing high.

Bubble Gum: A plant which is legendary for its sweet smell and euphoric high, Bubble Gum provides a medium height plant, usually not too branchy (sometimes stretchy). And produces compact, crystal-covered buds. Growers in Indiana originally developed Bubble Gum. From there the genetics moved to New England and eventually Holland. It took many generations to finally produce this stable Bubble Gum, with the characteristic, sweet smell (truly resembling a typical bubble gum taste) and euphoric high: the original trademarks of this famous strain. The only inbred strain (no F1 hybrid) in the serious menu. Winner of two awards in the High Times Cannabis Cup of 1994, a 2nd place in 1995 and again a 2nd prize in 1999, giving Bubble Gum a total of four awards from the judges. Type: Sativa/Indica hybrid. Indoor yield: 10–16 oz. (300–450 g) per 10 ft^2 (square meter).

Chronic: Our most commercial variety, this medium height, not too dense plant is the perfect combination of good yield and excellent quality. Smokers who know and grow choose this plant for its combination of appearance and sweet smell. With its Indica background Chronic can produce up to 21 oz. (600 g) per square meter without losing that connoisseur feeling. Chronic grows a single huge central bud, with few side branches. Do not top plants to encourage multiple big buds, as this strain does not respond well. Mild, sweet smell develops while flowering; take care to dry thoroughly after harvest (before packaging) to maintain this subtle fragrance. It took 3rd prize at the High Times Cannabis Cup 1994, improved in 2000. Of the supplier strains, this is the best choice for growers tired of losing quality when increasing yield. Type: Sativa/Indica hybrid. Indoor yield: 12–21 oz. (350–600 g) per 10 ft^2 (square meter).

AK47: This easy-to-grow plant is one of Serious Seeds company's most popular. It's of medium height, produces good yields quite quickly and has an extremely strong odor and smoke. Take extra care for odor control when growing near neighbors. The name was given not out of any idea of violence, but more in association with the "one-hit wonder" that the smoke is. Quality without compromise makes AK47 suitable for commercial grows or home use. These plants have a short flowering period for a Sativa, producing compact, not-too-leafy buds that gleam with a coat of resin crystals. This has won SEVEN prizes in cannabis competitions, including second prize for the Best Sativa in the 1999 High Times Cannabis Cup, proof it's a favorite to smoke as well as to grow. Type: mostly Sativa. indoor flowering time: 53–63 days; indoor yield: 12–18 oz. (350–500 g) per 10 ft^2 (square meter).

Planting Out Your Seeds for Germination

Once you have bought your seeds, you should keep them frozen until you're ready to sow. Most seeds today come packed in airtight containers; if yours are loose, put them in an airtight container prior to putting them in the freezer. Once a seed has been damp it will start to germinate and is no use to you. Seeds will keep for up to three years if they're stored correctly.

If you have bought your seed from one of the reputable traders then you can be almost sure of your quality, however if you have bought them from a lesser-known source then you might want to check them for viability; there's nothing worse than sitting there waiting for seeds to grow and all you get is neckache watching. Check first if they're a decent crop. Fill a cup with tepid water and drop in two teaspoons of bleach. The bleach protects the seed from fungus during the early stages of growth. Take a small piece of toilet paper or other tissue and dip that in the bleached water also, then take a couple of seeds from your batch and lay them on the tissue paper. Fold the tissue over and place it in a dark, warm place, at around 68°F (20°C). Spray the tissue daily to maintain humidity and watch for the seeds to crack. Usually within five days all seeds that are going to grow will have grown. If you have put in five seeds and only two have taken, then this is an idea of what to expect with the rest of your seeds and you'll now know how many to plant out in pots to get at least one per pot that takes.

There are several ways of starting seed germination. One such way is to soak a piece of tissue in the bleach and water solution we just spoke about and leave them to germinate in a warm dark place, then carefully take out the seeds that sprout and replant into your growing media: (CP51–53) earth, cocos or block. This ensures that all the seeds you plant out are fertile and have a kickstart in the pot. Don't let the tiny root get long, plant out as soon as you see the husk crack. If the root is long, then it's too late to plant and the seed will die because it won't be able to get a hold in its growing media when transplanted. Some growers use the soaking method to sow only the seeds that they know will sprout, while others use it to germinate.

Plant out all of your seeds in one go, enough for your whole garden, that way the growth will be uniform and the plant tops level with each other. This avoids the need to place packing under a pot to raise its head for lighting. By doing the initial test of viability you'll know that you have to plant out more than one seed per pot adjusted to the rate of failure in the test. The potency of your seed is hereditary so make sure you have chosen what you like. Don't take a chance on a seed variety you haven't tried or you may get a disappointing smoke after all the loving care you're going to put into the plants' development.

Look at your seeds closely before you buy them unless of course you have bought by mail order in which case choose suppliers carefully. Make sure they're a good color. They should be dark, not light in color, anything from gray to brown. This is one instance where size does matter, fellahs! Make sure the seeds are plump and large; roll them between your fingers and make sure they're solid and not empty. If your seeds are fresh and pass your tests then you should have to plant just one per pot. If they've tested low viability then put up to three in a pot; there's no problem letting them grow together if they all take, all you'll have to do is transplant them once they've become established.

Should you be planting directly into a pot then make sure you keep the surface of the earth moist with a fine spray, using something like an old window cleaner bottle, but make sure it's had the contents emptied and been washed out thoroughly before use. Don't go pouring lots of water in the pot and clogging up the soil, or pushing the seed down so far it can't get out. Moisten the soil by using the spray with warm water; let the water settle in the pot and then press your seed to a depth of around 1/4–1/2" (5–10 mm), no more, cover the seed with fine soil, and put the pot in position. Moisten the top of the earth daily and stretch a piece of clear wrapping like cling film or a sandwich bag over the pot and tape it down; this will act like a greenhouse, keeping humidity high and soil moist without having to wet it daily. As soon as you see the first tiny shoots peeping through the growing medium, take off the covering to avoid the shoot getting too hot and dying. A sensible alternative of course is the propagator with ventilation and inbuilt heat pads. Shoots are very delicate and must have the utmost care. They'll break very easily.

You might choose to grow your seeds in small pots and transplant to larger pots at a later date just so that you can get more pots in a small area to germinate. It's far better though to plant into the pot you want to end up with where possible. The less you move your tiny plant, the more it'll thrive. However, if you have not bought guaranteed females then you still have yet another test to perform, one which I will describe in a while.

Other starter alternatives are peat or fiber pods, although all alternatives are fine and useful space-saving devices. You'll have to take care if you use a tray since the tap root needs room to stretch and search for feed and to take its hold in the medium. If the medium is too shallow then the root will just curl, so use something at least 4" (10 cm) deep (a 2-pt. or 1 L pot). If growing in cubes you must keep an eye on the tap root peeking through the bottom or sides. A strange fact to remember is that restricted growth during early stages will encourage a male plant or hermaphrodite to develop, so if you have been getting all males, this may be the reason.

Testing for Gender

As we have discussed before, cannabis has three possible alternatives in its gender, which dictates its productivity or viability: male, female or hermaphrodite.

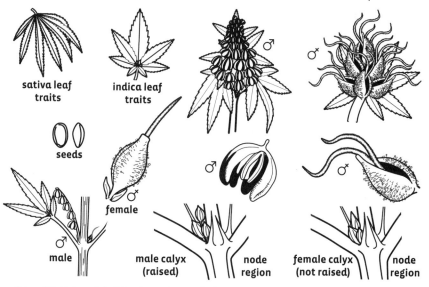

Figure 9.1: Determining gender and type of plants.

Number each pot in order once you have planted out one single plant per pot. Once you have grown your plants to a size where you're able to take clones then do so, taking two or three clones per plant. Select number 1 plant, and take three clones from it, number them 1/1, 1/2 and 1/3. Watch as your number 1 plant grows; if it can't be identified as a positive female then put it into flower, so it'll show its sexing. If it's a male, then throw away all of the young clones relating to that plant (unless you want males of course), and destroy the number 1 plant. If your number 1 plant tests positively female then keep all plants and take further clones for your main crop, leaving your number 1 plant as a mother plant for future crops.

Lighting

It's my advice that lights be left off for a few days until germination takes place. Seeds don't need light to germinate although the shoots need light to grow. Many growers prefer to leave them on immediately. I can see their point in that the earth is kept warm and humidity high, but my view is that unnecessary lighting is just a waste. So I guess by that you can assume that it's not so important, although when you use lights you must keep a closer eye on the soil wetness since the light will dry it out. I usually don't put my lights on until the third or fourth day when the seed is peeking through. Seeds germinate faster with heat so keep the grow area warm or use a heat pad to put the pots on. Good commercial seeds usually show within seven days; generally if they haven't by then they never will.

Peat pellets are a great little starter for your seed whether you intend to use soil or hydroponics. Once the seedling is rooted, simply take the pellet and transplant it to grow. If growing hydroponically you can position a rockwool or expandable pellet into gravel, clay balls or larger grow cube. Plant the seed to a depth of about 1/4" (7 mm) and run your water through as normal. Don't use nutrient at this stage.

There are many items that you can use as a pot: milk cartons, tin cans, paper cups, plastic bags, almost anything—but remember to put a drain hole in the bottom. I can suggest many types of useful receptacles that you will find in the house, although pots are so cheap it isn't worth the worry. I will just say that the plastic bag method is quite good, since you have an instant little incubator or propagator. Pull the top across until germination and then open it up once seeds have germinated. You'll be able to see the root if you use clear bags and when it comes to planting out into a pot, simply take the whole thing, cut up one side with a skill knife and pull the bag away.

Once the seedling stage is past (about two weeks after sprouting), position standard fluorescents about 2" (5 cm) from the plant tops; once they are rooted and ready to start life in their small pot, place your babies under a fluorescent lamp about 4" (20 cm) away for 5–7 days. When you are ready to plant out put them under HPS lamps, position the lamp about 2' (60 cm) from the tops of the plants for 600-watt bulbs and up to 1' (30 cm) if using a 400-watt lamp. Gradually lower the lamp until the plants are getting maximum benefits from the light yet remain in a safe zone. Use fluorescent lamps to start seedlings since standard fluorescents use less electricity and generate less heat. This makes germination cheaper, as well as safer for the seedlings. The fluorescent has a far better light spectrum for seeds and clones to thrive.

When using HID lamps, make sure your light height is adjustable since your plant can grow up to 4" (10 cm) a day in the early stages and in the best conditions up to 6" (15 cm). You can almost watch it move. You will have to watch daily and move accordingly to keep the distance between the tops and the lights safe so as not to burn the top leaves. Keep the plants as close as possible within the safety range to establish a thick healthy growth pattern. A safety rule for light/heat is to place the back of your hand under the light, just above the plants. If after 30 seconds it gets too hot for you then the light is too close. So long as the plants are getting light, that is all that matters during the vegetating period. Refer to chapter 4 on lighting and look at the light area given off by the lamp you're using. Make sure your babies are within that light area (i.e., if using a 1000-watt HPS, within a circle of 2.4 meters or 1 meter if using a 400 HPS).

By this stage you'll be using your timer, which is essential to keep uniformity of the 18-hour photoperiod. As detailed in chapter 4, timers are quite cheap but make sure you use a good quality digital. A timer will cost you around US $12 (£6) for the cheap mechanical version and around US $20 (£10) for the digital version, bought from any good DIY superstore or electrical suppliers—without doubt one of the finer investments to relieve you of some duties. Any timer is suited to fluorescent lighting and you have no need for the relays discussed in HID lighting systems.

Heat

Heat and humidity are essential factors to the success of rooting your seed. There are several aides to assist you in keeping control. The first and to my mind the most important is the propagator. The propagator provides a protected environment for the fragile seed so that humidity, heat, air and light can be controlled. Heat is an important issue since a steady temperature should be maintained. This can be assisted with either a heat mat or a heated propagator. The propagator comes with heating wires set in its floor structure, providing under heat, as does a heat mat. Humidity will be controlled by water in the blocks and its reaction against the heat of the mat or the heat of the propagator.

10

Cloning and Hybridizing

Successful Cloning

The cloning of plants has been practiced for many years and in many forms. Growers of fruit trees have even perfected the grafting of one tree onto another so that one tree bears several types of fruit, although I haven't yet heard any similar stories about marijuana. The options are endless and nature's own resilience, courage and determination to exist will encourage you and help you achieve most things in the world of planting.

One single plant can keep you in clones for many years, with hundreds of clones being taken from it. I have taken as many as 300 clones from one plant 3' (90 cm) high over a week with the plant still maintaining growth and being continually productive. In fact, selling clones can be more profitable than selling bud. An established Durban-Poison-regenerated mother plant is the plant I speak of. This plant has already given two crops and has been regenerated. A regenerated mother isn't as good in quality as a first mother that has been in vegetation for its lifetime, of course. Cloning is a cheap, quick way to get plants. Remember, the clones think they're adult and will perform that way. If you have a year-old plant then all of your clones will believe they're a year old too, and if you want they can be put into bud almost as soon as they've rooted. Clones put into bud at around 4 ins height usually reach a height of 12"–15" (5–6 cm) at maturity if the plant continues to vegetate (albeit far slower) for around three weeks.

Only take clones from your favorite plants. The THC quality will continue throughout all generations of cuttings because each cutting has the same properties as the mother. A cutting can even become a mother plant and have cuttings taken from it and then again and again, with each generation able to be a mother and provide its own clones and go on for more than twenty generations, with the twentieth as good as the first.

It's advisable to use your mother for maybe 12 months of continuous cloning, longer if you only take a few on the odd occasion. When you have finished using a plant as a mother, let her reestablish herself fully and then put her into bud. Each time you take a clone the plant goes into trauma, so take care. If you go on with one plant for too long and take her branches too feverishly then she can go into mutations of many types, including switching some branches to male. Clone only after watering during midday where possible; this seems to work the best, but don't ask me why—it just does. It's one of those things that nature dictates, and it works for me. Of course you'll want to experiment or may find that you aren't available for midday or something stops you. Whatever you try, record your details and see what works best. Depending on which hemisphere you live in you may find also that the moon has a bearing on a clone mortality rate.

It's very easy to take clones and it'll make the planting of seeds much less attractive to the hungry grower. Growing from seed is for the enthusiast or if you particularly want a certain breed that is unavailable to you. Seeding is a slow, expensive, and at this time not very precise process in terms of quality and sexing. Every clone taken from a female will be a female, but with a seed you'll get males, females and hermaphrodites at random.

You will need very little in the way of equipment to take a clone, apart from your mother plant of course and a good sharp knife. Never cut clones with scissors as this will crush the stem and reduce your success rate dramatically. I always recommend using a hormone gel because powders have far less success in marijuana cloning. A rooting tonic such as Rhizotonic gives the plant a vital boost in the watering stage whatever your choice of rooting medium. Rooting medium can be soil, peat pods or rockwool grow blocks. With the rockwool grow block you have the choice of using the clone for all types of gardens, plus roots come through quickly and clearly. The peat blocks are suited better to soil, peat or cocos growing substrate.

Clones develop their roots best under fluorescent light. Fluorescent tubes emit light primarily in the blue spectrum, and using them is less complicated than HID, since fluorescent tubes give off little heat. I usually set the lighting system of three 4-ft. (1.2-m) fluorescent lamps about 4" (10 cm) above the tops of the clones, with a lighting regime of 18 or 24 hours per day. If the clones are not in a heated area, like a bedroom or heated garden shed/greenhouse, then leave the lights on 24 hours a day or they'll shock from the evening chill and die, especially during the winter months. I keep 60 plants in 2-pt. (1-L) pots under this amount of lighting and use a ploythene sheet to drop in front of the shelf to keep out the chill.

The planning of clone crops can be decided exactly, since your experience with the first clone crop is applicable to the second and all future crops. With some experience you can maintain a growth regime suitable for your needs. For instance, if your clones usually take ten days to root, and then seven days to establish themselves in the pots, you can plan your garden's vegetative stages. Decide how long you want to vegetate, allow six to eight weeks for flowering and you have set your cycle. The vegetative stage is very much a choice here since, as we have already seen, clones are adult plants and can be put into flower immediately. I put mine in flower as soon as they've established root in the growing medium and are around 6" (15 cm) high.

Clones form roots best at a temperature of 77–78°F (25–26°C), and a relative air humidity of 70–75%. Check temperature and humidity constantly in all growing stages by using a combined humidistat/temperature gauge. Temperatures and humidity remain constant throughout the plant's life until the flowering stage, when humidity should be decreased to avoid rot in your growing area. Molds, pests and insects must never get a chance. If the climatic conditions are kept at optimal conditions, then mold spores won't cause you problems. Clones from the marijuana plant could take up to a month to become established although seven to ten days is the average.

The best points from which to take a clone depend on your plans for the plant and your garden. You could take clones from a smaller plant just before you put it into bud—you don't always have to have a full-grown mother. If you do clone from a constant mother then take your cuts from the extreme end of any branch, next to a shoot so that the shoot you leave on the plant then grows to become your next clone CP65 and so the circle will continue for as long as you wish. If you are taking clones from a plant that you intend to put into bud, then take them from the small branches at the bottom of a donor plant; usually these branches won't give you any crop worth having so you're not wasting them. Maybe you have a garden of 25 plants in a vegetative state: simply take a cutting from each plant, just before you change your lighting to put them into flower. That way you'll have 25 clones to put into vegetation while your older plants bloom. Keep repeating the process for as long as you need. If you take 25% extra cuttings, that allows for a failure ratio; if they all survive you can either give the extras to a friend or just choose the strongest and throw away the rest. If it's legal in your country then sell them.

The length of a cutting isn't a huge issue; sometimes a small cutting can grow to be the most fruitful plant at the end of the growth period. Cuttings taken from lower, slightly green shoots root the fastest. If you plan on taking cuttings, refrain from adding any nitrogen fertilizer for one or two weeks prior to taking cuttings since they'll root more readily.

Many growers cut the branch underwater so that no air bubbles will form in the stem of the new cutting. If air enters the stem it'll prevent the stem from carrying water and the cutting will die. Dipping the cut end of the stem immediately into a rooting gel also solves the air bubble problem. If you are using a powder the cuttings must be wet so that the powder will adhere.

Should you decide that you just want to take as many cuttings as possible from a plant and then discard it to grow another, then cut away the small branches from the main stem. You can of course take lots of clones leaving just a few tiny branches at the bottom of the plant, then let the mother grow again before going back for more although this could take several weeks and you may just as well grow a new mother rather than try to get your old one going again.

When cutting a clone, make one clean sharp angular cut at the base of the stem, leaving two pairs of true leaves on the clone if possible. An angular cut leaves a larger area of stem surface, which must be kept moist. Once cut, the cutting can be dropped into a glass of water to keep it moist or dipped into a rooting gel (Clonex or similar). Place immediately into your chosen rooting medium, then moisten (don't soak) with clean water. Whichever method you choose to take a clone, do it in as sterile a condition as possible. Once the clone has been taken, strip the lower leaves, leaving two full sets on the clone, this way your little lady doesn't have to feed too many shoots or leaves and it keeps her from the damp medium so that no rot sets in. Cut back larger fan leaves with scissors so they don't shade other clones from the light.

When you're using rockwool cubes, although they come ready holed, it may be necessary to use a toothpick, nail or other suitable item to make the hole larger and break the skin formed inside to make it easier to push in the cut stem. It's important not to crush or bend the tender stem in any way. Remember these few pointers. Try and make the hole about the same size as the stem to be inserted, make the hole a little larger just for the first 1/2" (10 mm) so that the gel isn't wiped off as you push the cutting in and Rockwool can be difficult to pierce; if it's too hard then the stem of the clone will bend and the cutting is no use. If you break the rockwool skin in the way before described, then it goes in easy. When using rockwool, cut the stem into a point then dip it in the Clonex and push into the block. Once all of your clones have been taken and watered, then place them into the propagator under your fluorescent lighting system and leave them for two to three days. Keep a check on the dampness of the rockwool; don't let them dry out too much but don't overwet them as the stem will rot. When the block requires water just dip it into a solution a little way so that the tiny roots go searching for nutrition.

During their rooting stage, if any leaves dry or begin to die, pinch them off and increase the humidity by adding a little water and heat. The use of a heat pad or heated propagator is recommended for the first three days, but you'll have to keep a closer eye on the water in the block when using heat as it does dry out quickly. If leaves yellow or any mold appears, decrease humidity (open the small slides on your propagator). As long as there's a living top shoot, the clone has a good chance of eventually rooting.

It's so exciting when you see those little white shoots peeking at you. Once the root is showing through then the clone is ready for planting. The more times a plant is repotted, the greater the trauma it experiences. If you have the space, then plant straight into the final pot you intend to use for growing. If you're plant-ing into rockwool for hydroponic growth then do that now also. Take care not to damage the small hairy roots. When ready, simply drop it into a 3" or 4" (75 mm or 100 mm) rockwool block and place under lights for rooting through. If you are using HPS then lift the lights as high as possible at this stage. The receiving block is presoaked in Rhizotonic or similar product to encourage rooting.

Water used for feeding your clones must be correct to get optimal growth. The pH value must be 5.8–6.0 and the EC value 0.8 to 1.0. Always clean your scissors, knife and growing trays with a disinfectant after you've used them. Once the two- or three-day waiting period is past you have to check the clones daily for possible rotting. Rotting leaves or stems must always be removed, so that molds won't take hold. Never oversoak your clones. Overwatering will not encourage rooting, a stem will develop what appears to be a bulb rather than send out roots. Too much watering can also causes pythium, a fungus on the roots.

After a couple of weeks, healthy cuttings will have enough roots to be transplanted. In principal, approximately 80% of the cuttings will root. Allow the cuttings that have no roots after two weeks one more week. These cuttings can produce a plant of less quality. If no roots have grown after three weeks, throw them away. The root systems of the young plants are very tender, and can easily be damaged. The extremely small root hairs are very important for a healthy plant. Rough transplanting has ruined lots of cuttings. The roots of plants don't like light. They grow in the dark but can dry out quickly.

Growing from clones means that you'll harvest more bud sooner. Many people who start a garden these days know someone who will give them a few clones for the simple pleasure of sharing a good thing. Some people sell clones, often growing an exclusively vegetative garden without ever flowering. These growers keep a variety of select mothers from high-quality strains, and grow them on a continuous 24-hour light cycle. They can make a great income selling trays of rooted cuttings. If you don't have fluorescent lights then you can place your rooting clones in a bright space or within the periphery of your vegetating grow room. DON'T put them in a flowering room because the lighting regime is too short.

Creating a Hybrid

Breeding your own stock is the ultimate desire of the seasoned grower. Once you have experienced the growing, cloning, seeding and experimenting with many varieties, the final achievement is to create your very own hybrid. The best smoke, the biggest bud, the bushiest plant—whatever you think is important is what you'll want to achieve.

It has been said that the ultimate smoke has been made with White Widow, probably the closest guarded secret of content ever known in the world of weed. Then someone got really inventive and crossed White Widow with Northern Lights, my own personal favorites. This crossing created the K2 plant for which I thank you, O Mysterious One, and will remain forever grateful. Now I have my two favorite plants, giving a good yield, on a strong Indica frame. The K2 is a stocky plant that matures quicker than most. THIS plant is worth growing, the design of a great inventor. Now you'll understand what drives growers to want to develop a hybrid of their very own. This is a way to become almost immortal. Another consideration for those wanting to grow outside is that of creating a hardy plant that matures early.

Of course you'll need stock to start with, and to have something in mind for your creation. You can't just go in bashing away and cross-pollinating to hit pot luck. You must have a plan and develop the new plant by monitoring, tasting and developing, sometimes for several years before you get exactly what you want. During the search for your ultimate dream smoke there will be disappointment, with disease and defects. It's far easier to cross-pollinate than you could imagine simply by using saved male pollen to fertilize a female and leaving nature to do all the work.

Begin your creation by finding the qualities you want from two or more plants. The easiest way is to take clones of the sexes you require and of a proven quality plant. If you can't get the clones you require then you must go through the laborious process of growing from seed. I imagine creating something like Kali Mist and AK47 as a hybrid; giving the yield quantity of Big Bud would be quite something. That's a hybrid to die for, although for now I will be happy with K2 because I just don't have the patience or the time for the work that goes into creating such a masterpiece. To create a hybrid worth its salt will take several generations before the plants give up a true quality seed.

There are several elements to overcome and decide about when hybridizing. I would stay away from the notorious Asian varieties they can give you the unwanted hermaphrodite and so any plant created from these will carry the same undesirable effects. A second and very important element is to actually find a source of female pollen that suits your needs. You must find a variety of plant that has the genetics of a female, even those that may give off the odd male flower. Once you have done this, then collect the pollen and fertilize an exclusively female plant.

The male flower can be induced to form on a female plant in several ways, one of which is to apply gibberellic acid to the shoots of the female plant by foliar spray. Use approximately 0.5 mg (0.008 gr.) per plant for two weeks. The formula to use is a solution of gibberellic acid in distilled water with added sodium hydroxide—the mix isn't precise but don't make it too strong. You will notice elongated shoots and mixed flowering within a few weeks.

By growing all of your stock indoors you can create all the seasons, day and night, and so find the perfect grower, even for outside growth, by using lighting techniques and creating effective day/night periods. Cut the photoperiod to an low; the first to flower will be the one you're looking for to get an early outdoor harvest.

Male plants die after promoting their pollen so you have to get the timing right or learn how to store for that maximum period of potency as pollen loses potency with time. Since all plants have varying maturing times, the pollination process is a precise art and although the actual pollination isn't hard, getting potent pollen from all your plants that are ready at the same time is very frustrating. To hold your male plant back from pollinating too soon, tell it to think of its mother, works for me (just kidding). Simply cut it back when the flowering shoots first appear. The male will produce new growth and therefore produce fresh pollen for when it's needed.

The male plant, like mother plants, does not need an awful lot of light and before the flower opens move them to another room. They don't even have to have HID lighting. Once male flowers have opened and provided you with pollen, they can be cut from the plant and stored in water. Make sure you keep the male and female plants separated. Keep the water fresh and the capillary open to keep a fresh and continuing supply of pollen. You may have noticed with flowers bought for mother, wife or girlfriend that the flower continues to mature and open even when cut. This is so with the marijuana flower; hang it upside down with its head in a paper or polythene bag—if you use polythene make sure you pierce the top side of the bag so as to allow air in. The pollen will fall into the bottom of the bag. If it isn't falling fast enough, just give the branch a little shake. Pollen can be stored for about four weeks before it loses potency, so keep it in a container; something like a plastic sandwich container would be ideal. Most importantly, keep it dry and cool. Don't put on the airtight lid, just cover it loosely and let the air circulate to avoid mold growth.

If you have to through circumstance, freeze your pollen; it could last as long as 12 weeks and still be potent. Do it properly and take care of it and it could store for a year or two. Once you have your dry pollen, place it in sealable air-lock bags—the ziplock type that's used to sell weed in small quantities—then freeze immediately. To use, let it thaw at room temperature just the way you would anything else. Using a microwave doesn't save time and you don't want to contaminate or aggravate your stock of pollen; only use one if it's really necessary.

To pollinate you need to take your female to the male, away from any other females that you're growing for weed. Put your chosen females near the male plants and give the male a shake or two to get the pollen to go airborne and fertilize the female. You can even pick up the male and hold him above the female, then give it a shake. Once you have pollinated, the female can be taken back to the garden with the others unless you have the luxury of a neutral space. If you're taking them back to the garden then it would be a good precaution to secure the pollen on the females by a light misting of water so that the pollen bonds to the chosen female and no pollen shakes loose on the other plants.

Pollinate lower branches rather than top buds if you're pollinating your female with more than one variety of male plant. If you do the top buds, there is the chance that pollen will fall on lower branches. A female plant can be pollinated with four, five or even six varieties if you wish and each bud will give you up to 100 seeds to plant on. Each branch must be labelled though, so that you'll know what seed crosses you're taking when the time comes. If you want to pollinate with various varieties then use a small brush to distribute the pollen exactly where you want it. Wash the brush and your hands thoroughly before going on to the next variety, or better still use a new brush for each application since they're very cheap anyway. Always make sure that you do this job in a breeze/wind free area.

Seeds should form within a period of two to five weeks. Once seeds start to split the casing of the pods (or bracts), then harvest. Take the darkest seeds only; the lighter ones are still immature. If your plants are outside make sure you harvest before the ripe seeds get damp as they may start to germinate on the plant, and these won't be any good to store. A good recording system of the seed and its history is essential to maintain a high-quality and controlled development program. Try all your newly-grown plants once harvested and start the process again if you haven't got it right first time, which I doubt you're doing except for sheer luck. Go first for potency; this has to be your first deciding factor since it's no good growing a weak plant. Your second deciding factor is to grow a hardy plant that resists diseases. Since you're going to be playing with genetics, you'll need a hardy plant to play with. Consider consistent production of these factors and finally, the harvest time and quantity.

11

Hydroponics and Soil Cultivation

Now that you know the technical stuff, let's get into the practical options of growing.

Soil versus Hydroponics

Soil Hydroponics

In soil, bacteria has to break down the dirt into the basic elements of nitrogen, phosphorus and potassium as well as trace elements. Balanced plant food (the nutrient solution) is dissolved directly into water so the plant may receive perfect nutrition at all times.

Soil isn't able to produce as much nurient per area as the root system is able to take up. Hydroponics takes the desired amount of food directly to the root rather than making plants' roots look for it.

Soil loses its nutritional value and is difficult to measure in terms of pH and fertility. The pH and nutritional value of the water are easily measured and maintained, so plants always have enough to eat.

Only when you water your soil plants, the basic elements can dissolve into the water. In a hydroponic system, moisture is present for extended periods of time or for all the time.

Soil plays host to many nastly little creatures. Hydroponic growing mediums are inert and sterile making a very hygenic environment for the plant and owner. Soil requires a lot more watering, has a higher occurrence of pests; plants grow slower, need more space and constant maintenance. Hydroponics increase plant growth and yield per area; decrease pests and diseases and the need to water plants.

Hydroponics covers a varied range of growing techniques and is a means of growing with water but without soil. This can be done in a crude DIY manner with bits of guttering, a water tank and a fish tank pump or you can go whole hog with pumps, filters, trays and elaborate drainage.

Hydroponics:

From the Greek for "water working" (hydro = water and ponic = working)

Hydroponics goes way back in history to the Hanging Gardens of Babylon and the floating gardens of Mexico. The mass technique is still applied today in countries like China, where they have tiered gardens of rice fields. All you smokers out there who think that it has been invented for marijuana gardens, think again. In the summer season probably 60% of the vegetables you eat are grown by hydroponics and certainly commercial flowers are grown this way on an even higher percentage level.

Today this technology is widely used to grow lush, healthy indoor plants and premium-grade vegetables, fruits and herbs. The physiological requirements of plants can be met without the use of soil or natural sunlight. Plants are rooted in an inert medium and nutrition is provided by water and soluble mineral elements. Through years of research determining which elements and their combinations affect plant growth, scientists discovered the first hydroponic formulas. This allowed for greater control over plant nutrition and therefore increased production. With the use of proper nutrients and the right artificial light source, today's indoor gardener can achieve amazing results. The plants can have an ideal environment since the gardener determines everything that is normally up to Mother Nature. Hydroponics may also be called "controlled environmental agriculture." In a complete controlled environmental agriculture system you control light, temperature, water, CO_2, oxygen, pH and nutrients.

Organic?

Many growers (like me) prefer the taste of soil-grown plants because they're grown organically. Now I will argue against myself in saying that with today's available commercially prepared nutrients, better plants can be grown "organically" in hydro systems than in soil.

An atom of nitrogen is an atom of nitrogen, whether it comes from a pile of compost or a sack of chemical fertilizer. There is no nutritional difference between a marijuana plant raised organically and one grown chemically. Minerals that a plant requires for growth are absorbed by its root system after they've been broken down into their elements and dissolved by the water. In soil, this breakdown process includes weathering, animal waste, leaching, bacterial decay, and dead plant material. By the time the plant ingests these mineral elements, they're no different from prepared chemical elements.

Many organic gardeners are put off hydroponics because of the use of chemical, nonorganic nutrients. The widespread and negative overuse of chemical fertilizers for soil agriculture has destroyed essential bacteria and other organisms in the soil, as well as having contributed to excessive runoff and the pollution of rivers. Too many nitrates can destroy the bacterial balance in soil and prevent it from being able to continue its normal regenerative process of creating minerals. It becomes *dead* soil, and will only support decent plant growth if further huge doses of fertilizers are added.

Hydroponics may still include pot culture but with the use of inert materials such as clay balls, gravel, vermiculite and even rubber. There are so many materials now available on the market and even more are being invented by growers using materials freely available to them. Growing in today's market is made easy for you. Nutrients are supplied in a specially developed formula for the system, inert slabs are prepared and complete home systems have been developed; you hardly have to use your imagination.

For one of the most superior modes of hydroponic growth, plastic trays are laid out side by side on a slightly tilted surface; not too tilted or all of the nutrient will drain out too quickly rather than soak the slabs. Each tray has two drainage pipes at the lower front end that will take excess nutrient away, sometimes back to the storage tank which I personally believe to be bad practice and a false economy since any deficiency will be recycled. It's far better to dispose of waste or excess feed. Nutrient solution is fed to the plants via a main feed pipe and pumped from the tank and distributed from that pipe via feeders which may have one, two or four outlets, into a smaller diameter pipe and then to the capillary that directly feeds the plant. In each tray a slab of rockwool or rubber is laid; it can also be filled with loose material, but the slabs are made for the job. There are rubber conglomerate slabs that can be used time and again for several harvests. They're more expensive initially but save you money in the long term. The reusable slabs should be cleaned of the main rooting when they've been used and the next growth will use the enzymes trapped within the slab to encourage new growth, although bear in mind that they can also harbor disease. Once you have grown your plant initially

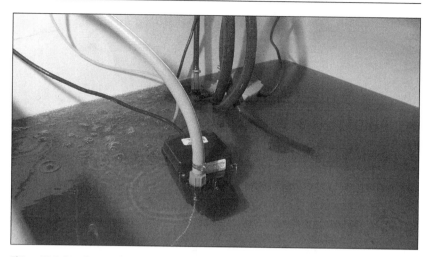

Figure 11.1: Nutrient tank with pump, attached feed tube and capillary.

in a 1' (25 mm) or 2' (50 mm) rockwool cube, this is of course transferred into the 3' (75 mm) or 4' (100 mm) rockwool block. When roots have been encouraged to pierce the cube it will be put on to your grow slab in the tray. Take a capillary feed and push it into the grow block, piercing it to the slab underneath. The capillary is then attached to the tiny feed tube, and this will carry nutrient from the main feed pipe that comes from the tank via a suitable pump lying in your nutrient tank. This is a fully automated scheme, providing good results.

The benefits of growing in hydroponics are that there's little chance of deficiencies or toxicity, since the nutrient balances of commercial supplies are perfected for your use. Providing you follow the guidelines and don't get tempted to "add a little bit more for a treat," then all will go fine. Yield is usually far greater than that of soil-grown plants and water usage is about 10% of that used for irrigations. There are no diseases or bacteria contamination that can exist in soil, it's environmentally compatible, safe, cleaner, more convenient, more sanitary and transplanting offers the minimum of problems. Finally, if there does appear to be a problem with nutrition, just empty the tank and refill: problem solved. The downside for me is that the taste does suffer slightly. I think organic, soil-grown weed gives a better high and a better taste, but then I am just an old traditionalist I guess. The other downside is the initial cost of an elaborate system.

Apart from the slab method, other popular inert, sterile, modern alternatives used as growing mediums are clay pebbles or perlite, although plain and simple nutrient-enhanced flowing water is used in many cases. Remember growing the daffodil or hyacinth bulb in a jar of water at school? What would your teacher say now if she knew you were turning that innocent, child-taught process into a dope growing operation?

The principle of hydroponics is quite basic: where soil-grown plants have to develop a root system and search for their feed, developing and stretching constantly, hydroponics put more of the plants' energy in growing the upper branches rather than the root system as the feed is just there, no searching required. Plants are maintained with free-flowing nutrient, air and water giving enhanced rates of development.

Plants grown hydroponically are given precise amounts of each nutrient required for specific development of vegetation and flower, and they'll use all that nutrient; any extra would burn the foliage. Because they don't need huge pots to reach greater size, plants can be grown closer together and so many more can be grown in a smaller area, providing you don't mind losing side shoots and lower growth where many small buds develop. Just go for the big cola. Poor support is a problem with hydro growth, especially where only water is used and a broad-holed net must be stretched over the plant tops so that they can grow through and use it for support.

Hydroponic systems can be divided into two distinct types: passive or active

Figure 11.2: Clay ball beds hold moisture but must be cleaned.

systems. An active hydroponic setup is one that uses a pump system to supply the nutrient on a regular basis. In terms of management this system of recirculating the nutrient solution is the finest and most-used. We'll look first at active systems.

Nutrient Film Technique (NFT)

The purest form of highly developed hydroponic grow system is the Nutrient Film Technique (NFT). The nutrient is fed into tubes, tanks or tunnels in shallow amounts, from which the roots draw it up. The excess drains by gravity back to the reservoir. A thin film of nutrient allows the roots to have constant contact with the nutrient and the air layer above at the same time. This system can be created simply with plastic guttering, provided you cover the guttering to shield solution from light contamination, and let your plants grow through the covering by making holes the size of the grow block you use.

You can also use electrical contractor's industrial trunking from a contract supplier. The 6' (150 mm) UPVC section available has cap ends, angles and connectors. Put the parts together and run feed pipes through the end, leaving one end open to drain off. Take your grow block and mark around it with a pencil or fiber tip pen to give you a size to cut out. Drill a quarter-inch hole in the corner of your template and insert a jigsaw or pad saw, then cut out the square to give you the effect of the tray. The channel should be raised at the end so as to encourage the solution to flow back to the tank. Your tank needs to be as large as possible to act as a buffer against a blocked return. If the flow rates don't meet each other's need then you'll get problems. You don't want to empty out a tank as it pumps through. More importantly, a larger tank provides a buffer for the changes in pH conductivity. The buffer is a way of expressing excess solution with the correct pH balance so that small changes go unnoticed. The solution should be supplied at 2– pt. (1–2 L) per minute and allow 8.5 pt. (4 L) per plant in the nutrient tank.

Drip or Micro-Irrigation

Today's greenhouse irrigation systems employ, to an ever-increasing extent, the concept of drip or micro-irrigation. It entails a principle of minimized water consumption with maximized plant benefit. There are literally hundreds of emitting, dripping, trickling, spraying, and micro devices on the market today for the commercial or hobbyist grower to choose from. A submersed pump feeds nutrient solution through header tubes to secondary feed lines connected to drip emitters at the plant stem. A controlled amount of solution is continuously drip-fed over the medium and root system. Another tube is connected to the lower part of the garden system to recover the solution.

Aeroponic

An aeroponic system works by misting the roots in a chamber. A pump pushes the water/nutrient solution through revolving mist sprayers, wetting the roots and providing a maximum amount of oxygen. This is a first-class technique for propagating cuttings.

Deep-Water Culture

Deep Water Culture is another form of aeroponics. The root system of a plant grown in deep-water culture is immersed in nutrient solution with a bubbling aerator within the tank keeping the roots oxygenated, which is crucial to healthy plant growth. Root inspection and pruning is easy. This technique is very good to use with plants that are heavy feeders. The simplicity and affordability of these very active systems make them popular with home hobbyists and commercial growers alike. They're easily made with available products from your local DIY store or can be purchased from a grow shop.

Flood and Drain (Ebb and Flow) System

Flood and drain systems are similar to NFT systems. This is ideal for multiple plants growing where an individual plant inspection is difficult. A plastic tray BW38 is flooded periodically by a pumped water supply connected to a digital timer. Medium and root system are soaked then drained (by gravity) at specific intervals. Various mediums can be used; rockwool is the most popular with this system. The tray has a capacity for a predetermined amount of solution that is pumped up from below, flooding the roots and pushing out stale oxygen. As the solution drains off then oxygenated air is drawn in from the top. Flood and drain systems are effective because of the dramatic changes and interaction of the moisture and air in the root. Your tray must be set level and well supported in the center. The weakest point is that the tray must have equal amounts of solution and any defect in level will take feed away from higher areas.

Setting up plumbing is simple, the main consideration being that you must be sure that the pump you buy allows the solution to flow back through it, as some

Figure 11.3: Bud-intensive professional grow room. Plants are leaf stripped, grown in clay ball beds, set in rockwool and watered by ebb and flow system.

pumps have a non-return valve. If you're using a pump you already have or have been given, then make yourself a small bypass system so that the solution runs through a pipe directly into the tank and not back to the pump. Make sure also that you have an overflow pipe; this avoids flooding in your growing area and allows you to be careless in timer setting: so long as the timer comes on four times a day, it doesn't matter if it runs slightly longer than the recommended time indicated on your ebb and flow package. I would say that the best medium for the ebb and flow system is the clay ball: they're clean to use, easy to store and efficiently cleaned. A general rule when using pumped systems is to cover the solution well and avoid light contamination. The black/white plastic that we discussed earlier for reflective values would be great as your plants will then benefit by the undersides of its branches receiving reflected light. The sheet protects the water from algae growth and extraction of required elements. Water stored in tanks must be kept covered, aerated and in all cases kept at 79°F (26°C). If you use rockwool or similar solution-retentive mediums, set your pump to come on at shorter periods; clay balls drain down quickly but some materials like rockwool or sponge hold the water longer.

Passive Planters

This is probably the most commonly known form of hydroponics. These systems don't require a water or air pump and are therefore called passive systems. Passive planters have been used in office buildings and restaurants for many years. *Hydroculture* planters utilize a clean, porous growing medium to support plant roots. A nutrient reservoir in the base of the growing container allows the plants to take as much or as little water as they require. Water level indicators show exactly when and how much to water. Clean, odorless and nonallergenic, hydroculture or passive planters are ideal for every environment. A passive system has the nutrient supplied periodically, allowed to sit in a reservoir and be drawn by capillary action via the plant whenever it's required. As a commercial option the passive system is a nonstarter. The pot culture that I mentioned much earlier is a passive system and is a cheap alternative in the field of hydro growing.

Soak your transfer rockwool block in a solution of rooting enhancer (like Rhizotonic) before you transfer your rooted clone. Fill a bucket, sink or bath to take your solution, drop in the transfer blocks with the holes in them to soak, then take them out and drain them of the mass of fluid. When they're drained and feel quite light put your small plants gently into the block taking care not to damage the roots. Place all of your plants under a fluorescent or use a single HID about 1 meter from the plant top until the roots show through the larger block. Once the roots show through, put your blocks out to grow and gradually lower the lights. Use aeration blocks and an air pump in your tank to oxygenate to your feed solution. This advice may sound familiar because it has been used before in another growing situation. I am covering it again since you may have skipped that method to find one you prefer.

. In any system of growing, it's advisable to use an oscillating fan, and not just for cooling. It's also useful for blowing air through the developing buds to stop any mold forming and especially advisable in a hydroponics system as the humidity gets higher. A fan has additional benefits: if you use it during vegetation the plants get blown gently, which tears at the fiber stem making it stronger as it heals itself. The plastic louver grill turns, directing the airflow multi-directionally. There are three speeds and the oscillator system can be switched off. Another alternative would be a fan on a large stand, but these do take up a lot of floor space.

The most important elements to consider in hydroponics are the simple ones,

Figure 11.4: Fanned cooling system stimulates plant strength.

chief of these being pH and conductivity; a good understanding of their effects is important. These elements will determine which nutrients will be absorbed and how the plant absorbs them. Keep pH values at around 6.0 to 6.8 using the plus and minus products we discussed in chapter 7. Rockwool cultivation can be a little lower at 5.8; a safe practice in all cases would be 6.0. If you're using a recycling system to grow your plants then it's essential that a pH meter is used regularly. If

Figure 11.5: Adjusting the pH of your water using plus or minus additive.

you're growing in passive hydroponics and use perlite or rockwool with a hand-fed system, make up large amounts of nutrient solution at a time, say 53 gal. (200 L). Once you have the correct strength (conductivity), the pH can be checked and adjusted accordingly. Record the amount of pH added to find your best quality and use the same formula to make your next batch. A store of nutrient solution will not change its pH value unless something is added to it or it's used in recycling drained solution. Just as a note, remember the acid/alkalinity in water differs from county to county or town to town so if you move, start your records again. If you're advising a friend who lives quite a way from you, your applications may not apply to his water.

Hard water has high levels of bicarbonates and it makes itself known by depositing lime scale in kettles, so have a look in your kettle for a clue on the quality of your water, and remember if it leaves deposits in your water, and it goes unadjusted in your storage tank, it'll leave a deposit in your capillaries, blocking the feed getting to your plants. A pH plus will be needed to neutralize the bicarbonates. Amounts of pH should be applied in small quantities, as its effects are dramatic. If you decide to use phosphoric acid to neutralize then you'll create another problem in that there will be a buildup of phosphate in the nutrient tank, and this will inhibit any uptake of salts like zinc and cause a nutrient imbalance. Stick to proprietary pH+ and pH- products such as those provided by Bio Nova and Canna.

Controlling pH and Conductivity

pH Down A concentration of 81% orth-ophosphoric acid (HPO) is the content of pH Down, which is very strong, so handle with care. Some products on the market are considerably weaker so check the concentration before you buy. This is a very dense liquid and should feel much heavier than water.

pH Up Potassium hydroxide (KOH) is the content of pH up. This is a very caustic liquid and should be handled with extreme care. Always check the label before you buy for best value. An obvious solution is to change the nutrient regularly. This reduces the chance of phosphate accumulation and keeps a good nutrient profile. Frequency of changes will depend on tank size and number of plants. In very hard water areas, you'll need huge amounts of phosphoric acid to correct pH when nutrient is first made up. It's possible to use nitric acid to control pH; that will solve the problem of phosphate accumulation. Nitric acid is a very unpleasant and dangerous liquid, and it should never be handled by anyone who is not experienced. Nitric acid will

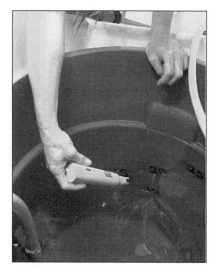

Figure 11.7: Using a pH tester on your water supply is highly recommended.

solve only the phosphate problem; it won't make the slightest difference to high levels of calcium or other minerals that accumulate.

The best solution is to use a specific formulation, usually based on more acidic components. Hard water nutrients were formulated in response to demand from growers. Various residential areas have very hard water. Another solution would be a reverse osmosis filter (RO unit), which will remove the mineral ions by passing water through a very fine membrane. The water produced can be very pure and will allow normal nutrients to be used with complete confidence.

pH and Conductivity in Rockwool Systems Readings in the tank rarely reflect the value in the slab. Squeezing slabs out regularly and testing the retained solution can test measurement of nutrient within the slabs adequately. In a well-maintained system there won't be too much variation between tank readings and those obtained from slabs. If conductivity rises in the slab it's an indication that irrigation is either too infrequent or too short. Nutrient needs to trickle into slabs for just enough time to achieve 10–15% run drainage. The timer should be adjusted to provide this amount of nutrient at least four times during the photoperiod.

Frequent irrigation may benefit the growth program. As plants grow they'll take up more solution and the cycle of watering will need to be lengthened to suit. The regular check of nutrient from the slab itself is the most important routine for the rockwool grower. If conductivity begins to rise then the grower will increase irrigation to ensure runoff at each watering cycle. If conductivity remains high then it's a simple matter to flush the slabs.

Conductivity The conductivity of a solution is the capacity of the solution to conduct an electric current. Distilled or deionized water conducts virtually no electricity and has a conductivity reading of zero. The conductivity of the solution increases as salts are dissolved in the water. The conductivity of a nutrient solution is a measurement of its strength indicated by the actual amount of salts dissolved, and is usually expressed in terms of CF (CF standing for Conductivity Factor). Units of measurement are usually millisiemens, microsiemens or siemens. The difference between these is purely in the placing of the decimal point. There are a thousand microsiemens in a millisiemen.

A CF unit is equal to a hundred microsiemens so there are 10 CF units to a millisiemen. CF meters usually read in millisiemens or CF units but for the grower it's a matter of getting the decimal point in the right place. As a rule of thumb, it can be said that a good conductivity level for most purposes would be 2.0 millisiemens (expressed as 2.0 mS/0.4 sq. in. or 2.0mS/cm^2). This is a standard working solution. Therefore: standard working solution = 2.0mS = 2,000jLiS = 20 CF units EC. Conductivity is sometimes expressed as EC (Electrical Conductivity). Units of EC are now identical to CF; however, as most nutrient solutions have approximately the same ratio of constituent salts we can make an approximate conversion: lmS = lOCF units 5-640 ppm. Standard working solution = 20 mS = 20 CF-1280 ppm meters for pH and conductivity. If all that is beyond understanding or just too boring then get yourself one of the many types of meters available on the market. The most popular has been the Truncheon over past years but the market is now flooded with alternatives. Meters are calibrated by using pH buffers and CF standards. These are liquids with a known pH, usually 7, which can easily be used to check and correct the accuracy of your pH meter. CF Standards are solutions of a known conductivity, which are used to calibrate your conductivity meter.

Aeration

Aeration is extremely important and your second main consideration. Stagnating water is ruinous. Solutions must keep moving and be aerated by a pump. Roots can actually drown through lack of oxygen. **Salt** builds up unless you use an inert medium, and even these should be flooded occasionally to flush through. **Nitrogen and potassium** ratios are your final thought. Your balanced nutrients supplied by any commercial supplier can be affected by light—its duration and intensity. If you're growing in a greenhouse, during the summer you'll need about double the nitrogen to potassium and in the winter you'll require equal amounts. Fortunately you're able to buy these elements individually and can adjust the needs. This information is really for those of you who want to get deep into the growth needs. Most of you won't need to mess around with this problem. It's just nice to know as extra information for a later date. Most of the larger suppliers now have buffers in their products to allow for these deficiencies and in any case indoor growers have the edge, since it's always summer in their gardens and the hydro products are formulated to give the best performance in those conditions.

Substrata
Soils and Cocos

Marijuana grows an extensive root system, so by prohibiting its network of rooting by growing in small pots or failing to water correctly, you may produce stunted or deformed plants. However the pot is not such a restrictive factor if you're using the right amount of nutrient and water. You could in fact grow the same size plant in a 1-liter pot as in a 20-liter pot, but the restrictions are too great and not practical. It's far better to use the biggest pot practicable for your grow room. Transplanting from smaller plots slows down growth for a period of about one week.

Unless you intend taking this all very seriously and want to create your own strains or get your own seeds, then never keep male plants; they're just too much trouble. Seedlings and clones will take up very little space, so if you have the facility to grow them to a respectable height prior to transferring them to another area for the maturing process then you're fortunate.

The size of pot you require depends on how you decide to grow. Either use the Sea of Green method, where as many plants as possible are fitted into your grow space to maximize turnover; or grow just a few plants in a cupboard for your own use. If you use the Sea of Green method, a 1 gal. plastic pot is enough; that will give you about 25 pots within a 1 sq. yd. and yield around 0.35 oz (10 g) per plant on a short bloom period, giving you around 10 oz. (300 g) of bud on a 7–8 week cycle, providing you're using clones. On the other hand you could get 4 good-sized plants in the same area and have around 1.5 oz. (40 g) off each plant, giving you around 10 oz. (300 g) in a 12–14-week period. The difference here, apart from the fact that Sea of Green will harvest a greater annual yield, is that if you get a visit from the authorities, you may get a fine or community service for four plants but if you have 25 you could get a custodial sentence, as it could be considered that you're growing with intent to supply either socially or otherwise. Even though harvest is around the same it's the number of plants that is often taken into consideration.

If you insist on growing illegally the chances are that you may get caught. If this unfortunate event should happen, make sure all of your plants are bagged and kept. This will have bearing on any prosecution and defence. A good drug agency or defence lawyer will assess how much yield the plants would likely have given. Rather than the prosecution trying to impress the court with their assessment that your 25 plants would have returned a kilo of weed, a drug agency will consider the size and variety of plants and assess quite accurately what a true yield would have been. In many cases the true yield could have been as little as 200 grams. This could make a lot of difference when it comes to assessing personal or social supply against being a full-blown supplier and subsequently affect whether you get a custodial sentence or a walk.

Rather than planting out in pots you may decide to plant in a trough or tray with spacing of 1" (2.5 cm) between your plants. This is an equally good method although it's restrictive in some ways, more specifically with harvesting, watering and having plants at different stages of growth. The tray or trough method can be good in other ways though, since you can seed the tray, thin out as the plants develop and then grow to full maturity without ever removing the plant or restricting its growth. A taproot can be 4" (10 cm) long within days of the seed germinating and will sink to around 1" (2.5 cm) during maturity so a shallow pot does restrict early development. It benefits you and the plant to get it right the first time, although the seedling does recover once transplanted.

If growing from seed it's better to use a rockwool block or peat pod rather than the fiber pots that are available since the seedling may not be able to penetrate the fiber. This will benefit you with space since the fiber and peat pods come in small trays and are ready for you to drop into your growing medium as soon as the roots peek through.

Most recommendations are that the ideal size of pot should be at least 1' (30 cm) across the top and a minimum of 4" (10 cm) in depth. Now you could rush out and buy yourself expensive clay pots, but it's recommended that you use a cheap plastic pot since you may be moving the plant around and at the very least will transport it through the house to harvest, and a clay pot could be easily broken. Plastic pots are cheapest and are flexible for squeezing into places or for repotting. It's also possible to find alternatives for free, such as old plastic pots of emulsion or paint, plastic buckets or even a polythene bag. If you use any plastic container don't forget it has to have drain holes in it; drill these out because if you try to make the holes with a nail or other sharp instrument the plastic will just split and the container will be no good to you. If you're using an old metal paint can however, a 4" (10 cm) nail and a hammer will do the trick. I have also used things like the plastic tray designed for bread delivery and storage containers from a removal company. In fact anything that is about 1" (2.5 cm) deep, comes for nothing and doesn't break is fine.

Another great invention of course is the Gro-bag, which lends itself nicely to the marijuana plant, requires no feeding, needs just a little water, stands easily in a corner, comes in several sizes and can even lie on a balcony with its readymade cut-out holes to get the spacing of plants right. If you live in a flat and have a small balcony, growing dope is easy and relatively safe. Fill in the front of your balcony by forming a timber frame and cover it with polythene or plastic sheets from the DIY store, put in your grow bags and grow away. The police will be hard put to detect you.

Your harvest will be your creation and the fruits will reflect the care and consideration and patience you bestow upon it. Give it love and you'll get a great harvest, ignore it and you'll get little or nothing. You're the provider here and must ensure that water, nutrients, light and heat are given in the right proportions. Too much nutrient is in many cases worse than too little; it can effectively poison your plant. I have found that there is no perfect, across-the-board condition for the marijuana plant; each variety has its own peculiarities and its own preferences. What I am trying to do in this book is to give you a rule to grow by that will suit all plants, yet may not be perfect for any particular plant. This perfection comes with experimenting and there are many contributing factors within your own living area.

Soil must be well drained, have a balance of nutrients and a near neutral pH of around 6.8. PH is controlled by external means and measures so that your own water condition will be treated by a pH+ or a pH- solution; this is the acidity (sour/bitter) element of the soil. Most commercially produced, bagged soil comes with all its trace elements. Watch out for some cheaper organic soils, as they may contain something that you don't want in your pots, especially those formed from mushroom compost. Go for something like Levington's, or some other known brand. Look for the pH and the listed trace elements, although not many list them on the bag; that's why I stick to the larger brands and pay a little extra.

If you grow outside or inside, make sure the soil texture is right. I have said several times throughout the book that the soil required for marijuana must be free draining. A lack of oxygen to the roots cannot be compensated for and will ruin your plant by drowning. The roots must be free to seek the soil for nutrient and oxygen. A waterlogged soil leaves no room for that activity. The use of additives with premixed soils is essential; something like perlite or vermiculite is perfect since perlite holds water and feeds the soil. Sand, lava rock, pea gravel or the small grit that is used for ponds and fish tanks are fine; crushed cockleshells are great too and can be bought very cheaply. Make sure everything you use is washed thoroughly or comes sterile. To determine the suitability of a soil, dampen it and squeeze it in the hand gently. If it clogs together in a solid lump then it requires an additive; if it loosens when you let your grip go, or with a gentle prod, then it's fine and suitable for your purpose. The use of perlite serves two purposes: it breaks up the soil allowing aeration, and it retains moisture.

Unless the soil in your area is exceptional I wouldn't even think of using it, bagged compost is so cheap (as little as US $8 per 15 gal. or £4 per 4 L, it's just not worth skimping; plus you may be getting diseased soil, contaminated soil and several types of weed in there that will all take away the nutrient your plant needs.

Pearlite is very cheap, at around US $18 (£9) per 20 gal. (26 L) bag depending on your supplier (I have paid as little a US $12 or £6). Silvapearl is just one of the many providers of perlite and the promise appearing on their bag is that it's inorganic, inert and sterile; it doesn't decompose; lasts for years; is almost neutral pH; is free from disease, weeds and insects; is nontoxic and not a fire hazard. They also say that it stimulates root initiation and vigorous growth, holds moisture but does not become soggy, prevents compaction, improves aeration and drainage, insulates and minimizes temperature fluctuations and can be sterilized by steam, flame or chemicals. A huge claim, but I have yet to fault it.

When raising seed, use a standard-grade perlite for marijuana, it'll encourage quicker germination and improved seedling growth with less check when you're pricking out to pot on. Sow on a well-watered mixture of equal parts of perlite and sphagnum moss peat (50/50) or add one part perlite to two parts of a ready-mixed potting compost. Perlite may, of course, be used 100% provided it's kept wet at all times by capillary irrigation or inter-mittent mist. Sprinkle fine peat all over the seeds, and cover with glass or plastic to retain moisture until seeds have germinated, and then feed.

If you're growing from a blocking situation, use superfine grade perlite with a fine peat, also use it for sprin-kling on the surface of the seeded blocks as a light reflective dressing. Mix approximately 15% by volume into blocking compost for improved texture and blocking performance. Aeration is also improved and sogginess prevent-ed, giving stronger seedling root sys-tems. Should the blocks become too dry perlite aids rewetting. Cover seed

Figure 11.9: Fox Farm Ocean Forest potting soil is a blend of fish, crab meal, shrimp meal and earth-worm castings.

blocks with a 1/8' (2–4 mm) layer of perlite superfine using a simple curtain feed hopper attached to the blocking machine. The benefits of perlite as a block dress-ing are that it insulates the seed from extreme variations in air temperature and excessive sunlight, improving germination; it discourages insects, birds and rodents from attacking the seeds and seedlings; and it holds moisture and pre-vents drying out of the seed and the surface of the block—plus it reflects light to the underside of the growing seedling promoting quicker sturdier growth, partic-ularly when natural light is poor.

Perlite speeds up rooting and reduces the risk of damping off, providing an optimum balance of air and water. This makes waterlogging almost impossible, and minimizes damage to roots and check to growth during transplanting. For soft stem cuttings use a mixture of equal parts perlite and sphagnum moss peat. For harder cuttings, and for fragile plants, increase the proportion of perlite up to four parts perlite to one part peat (80/20). Under mist irrigation perlite may be used 100% where sterility is essential. Keep well-watered but ensure drainage. Plants should be fed as soon as roots develop.

Because of its sterility and unique rooting properties, it's ideal for the critical stage of establishing plantlets raised by micropropogation techniques such as

Maristem or Tissue Culture and Twin Scaling of bulbs. Silverpearl mixed with Agar Gel or used 100% with nutrient solution is an excellent rooting medium for plantlets. Silvapearl special seed or standard grade mixed 50/50 with sphagnum moss peat and nutrients is the ideal compost for growing on as it encourages root development and facilitates transplanting. Special seed grade is an inert growing medium for demonstrating the effects of the nutrient and of toxic chemicals.

Perlite standard grade can be used wholly or partly in place of sand or grit in potting compost where it improves aeration, drainage and insulation, and it also facilitates rewetting. Perlite can be used to open up ready-mixed loam or peat-based composts. For soilless composts mix 3 or 4 parts of sphagnum moss peat with 1 part of Silvapearl (75/25 or 80/20) plus limestone and nutrients. For loam-based composts mix equal parts of sterilized loam, peat and perlite (1:1:1) plus limestone and nutrients. Alternatively, a 1:2:1 mix may be used. Mix thoroughly then water well after planting, and feed as appropriate.

For NFT and hydroponics, use a super-coarse grade for maximum drainage and aeration; being an inert, sterile and neutral lightweight aggregate, the high air- and water-holding capacity of perlite is perfect, and it can be sterilized for reuse by steaming, using a flame gun or by treating with steam and chemical sterilizer. For capillary watering, use at least a 1' (25 mm) depth of Silvapearl standard or special seed grades in place of sand or gravel in suitable trays lines with plastic sheet material. When using perlite with underground heated cables then mix with 50/50 sand to prevent overheating.

To mix perlite, use in a 50/50 combination with peat. Pour your peat onto the floor and then tip the perlite on top, and spread both evenly. Soak perlite with 20 liters of water, using the whole 100-liter bag, then leave for about an hour to soak; then mix thoroughly the same way you would mix cement.

Vermiculite

This is another suitable product to mix with your soil; although it does contribute some nutrient, the pH is near neutral. Vermiculite will hold three times its own weight in moisture and provides a good buffer against pH deficiencies. Where there is an extreme pH situation the vermiculite can reduce the problem by holding nutrients and releasing them into the soil as needed. The expected properties of vermiculite are potassium and magnesium irons. If the water in your area is alkaline (hard), sphagnum or peat moss will work better for your soil than vermiculite. If your water is soft (acidic), then avoid sphagnum and peat moss, and use vermiculite or perlite to condition your soil.

Rockwool

Recognized as an insulation material, this branded product made of a mixture of rock, limestone, and coke looks like fiberglass insulation but has not yet had the fiberglass added and is therefore less irritating to the skin—however precautions are still to be taken. Rockwool is produced as granulate in bags, and as various-sized planting blocks or slabs. Always wet rockwool when using it, so that its fibers will be less airborne. During handling of a dry product you could inhale fibers, which may cause an allergic reaction. Blocks or slabs of rockwool for hydroponic gardens are quite good, although I prefer the conglomerate sponge slabs personally.

Use 1' (25 mm) rockwool blocks for rooting clones, or seed planting, then transplant to 3' (75 mm) blocks using the soaking methods before described, and later place them on either rockwool slabs or conglomerate sponge slabs; these are slabs of sponge made up of pieces of scrap and shredded sponge, easily recognized by their variant color. The advantage of rockwool blocks is that the roots become visible very quickly through the sides or bottom of the block so that you can identify at the earliest time when they're ready for planting out. The blocks are then placed into a larger block that has first been soaked as before described. The roots then grow out of the larger block and into the sponge or fiber slabs. There is no transplanting and no interruption of growth. Water and nutrients are fed through the block and drained into the slab; the roots then feed from the slab giving the plant stability and good growing conditions. There are many kinds of substrate. All have their benefits yet all have a similar purpose: they are the anchors for your plants, supporting the root and main stem, and they are home to the growing elements, air and nutrients.

If you're looking for the perfect soil for marijuana as a plant, don't bother because it doesn't exist. Each variety has differing needs. As a general rule of thumb, look for good fertility medium that's well-aerated and as near neutral in pH as possible. This can all be created artificially and to near perfection without too much trouble with today's commercial products. Buy your bags of soil from a garden center or similar place; if the label doesn't tell you what's in the bagged product then look for one that does or ask an attendant. If you still don't know then you can run a few tests but most products today list the nutrients as a complete nutrient mix and the information on pH should be available. Don't be afraid to ask—the average gardener or hobbyist

Figure 11.10: Grodan Rockwool blocks come in varying sizes to support clones and full plants.

would ask the same question, so they won't instantly suspect that you're growing cannabis. Once you know what's in the bag, you know how to prepare the product for your best needs. If the soil texture is too tight or becomes too compact, it'll suffocate the roots and inhibit their development. Every effort you make after the damage has been done will not get you back where you started.

Dry soils like coco should not crack or form a crust; they should feel spongy or lightweight and have a fibrous texture that will hold a lot of water when wetted. This is where coco is perfect. Soils that compact must be mixed with any of the following products: perlite, sand, lava rock, or other aggregate. Your main concern is that the soil retains some water, and drains excess water. If wet soil is too dense, compact, or sticky, the roots will not be able to penetrate and will not access oxygen, and plants will grow very poorly or worse still die.

If you want to dig and manufacture your own soil then look for the best naturally fertilized soil available, like that in ditches, along fences or hedges, or in areas where leaves and plant debris tend to collect and degrade to form a rich natural humus. Screen the soil and take out any nondecayed matter and stones. Sterilize the soil by putting it in a pressure cooker at 15 lbs. (7 kg) pressure for 15 minutes, or by baking soil in an oven at 200°F (430°C) for 30 to 40 minutes.

Adjusting the pH of Soil

Take a mixture of soil wetted with distilled water because distilled water will not adversely affect the reading and influence the true pH value; wait an hour and then test with a pH soil meter. If the pH is lower than the ideal range then add fine dolomite lime and retest. If it's still low then keep adding the dolomite until it's at 6.3. Dolomite lime acts very slowly. If you want faster results then use hydrated lime in small amounts. Approximately 1 pt. (500 ml) of hydrated lime will raise the pH of a 20 gal. (75 L) bag of soil by 1 full point (from 6 to 7). Try adapting the

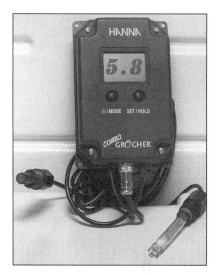

Figure 11.11: An electric in line pH meter hangs in water and hangs nearby.

equation to a smaller amount, say 1.3 gal. (5 L), and test that quantity rather than mixing a full bag. Once you have the ratios right then it'll be simple to do the same mix next time as commercial mixes remain constant. If you change your brand of soil then start your tests again. Always record your findings for later reference.

If you wish to lower the pH then use either gypsum or iron sulphate in the same quantities and test by the same method. Always use a pH meter; there is no other accurate means of measurement. Any soil that tests above 7.25 should not be used as the amount of added elements required to get to an acceptable level will cause chemical reaction and adversely affect your plant growth. To adjust your pH during the vegetating period, you'll have to rely on a water solution, as obviously you can't take out your soil. Add a teaspoon of hydrated lime to 1.3 gal. (5 L) of water, water an area and retest.

Cocos

Those of you who don't already grow in cocos, **GO AND GET SOME!** You will love this stuff; its texture is perfect for growing marijuana, it comes with a neutral pH and it has no nutrient in it whatsoever so you start with a clean slate and create your own growing environment.

Cocos slabs are convenient-sized, polythene-encased, cocos compound—rather like grow bags. Printed on the slab covering are small markings for you to cut and slip in your plant. The slabs can be watered by hand or have a pumped supply using the capillary feed system. There are of course several types of capillary drip feed that will suit your needs. Lay your coco slabs out on a tray or covered shelf, plant out your growing plant, attach the water droplets and water in well, allowing the excess solution to drain off. It's very important that you water plants in whatever substrate you use, the water in the rockwool cube or peat pod will be sucked out by the substrate.

Cocos bricks have to be soaked in a bucket of lukewarm water; they immediately start to expand to several times their compressed size. Cocos can also be bought in a convenient bagged, loose form ready to use straight away to fill your pots, and ideal if you're going for a filled tray method of growing. You have to feed cocos because it's inert. (This was described in chapter 7.) A tray or pot method of growing can be used with cocos and work very successfully. Cocos is reusable after harvest as it only contains what you put into it, so the nutrient and pH are perfectly balanced if you do it right, and it drains down easily. There is no root clogging with cocos because its structure creates aeration.

12

Flowers and Flowering

We have already determined that there are four divisions of the cannabis plant and that we are really only interested in two, Sativa and Indica, which by now you'll know by their easily recognizable and distinctly different leaves.

Having found out how to identify the diversity, it would then be quite nice if we could identify strains, which in many cases is quite difficult until they flower, although there are a few varieties that are identifiable from their leaves. Plants grow in a distinctive pattern; some grow as a huge bush, some treelike and some of imperfect design.

You will notice, looking at a Sativa plant, that the branches grow in a perfect pattern. They grow in alternate pairs at 90°angles from each other. Reminding ourselves that the marijuana plant is normally dioecious, that is, it bears either male or female flowers, it's pretty much assured that there will be a single determined sex in most cases. If you have grown from seed then you'll probably get around a 50% split in sexes, although there is the distinct possibility you'll have a plant that is a hermaphrodite. Recognizing the flowers of these plants is essential to the well-being and balance of your garden. You as a smoker are looking for the female plant, as this is the only flower that turns into the bud you want. You can smoke a male bud, but these are not so good and very low in THC. The only value a male has as far as I am concerned is for breeding (which most girlfriends or wives will probably confirm). The hormone that induces marijuana to flower (phytochrome) is locally produced by each part of the plant and does not travel around the plant. To induce your plant into bud, reduce the light period to 12 hours. If you find on the first harvest that the plants take some time to begin flowering, then next time give them a 24-hour dark period on their first day, then lighting of 11 hours for the first week and 12 hours a day thereafter.

Male and female plants change growth patterns just before flowering. The tops of the male plants elongate about a week before the first pods appear. By elongating and ultimately growing taller than the female, males ensure that when they release their pollen, it falls upon the female. Male top shoots are thin and sparse, unlike the female tops, which thicken and branch to provide you with a good show of bud.

Male flowers are small pods as shown in the earlier pictures, and about 0.3" (8 mm) long before they open. As they develop they become clustered (cymes) mostly at the top of the plant and on the ends of branches. Pollen develops within the anthers or sacs, and resin glands form along the sides of the anther slit, which drops the pollen. It's said that the resin on the resin glands dissuades insects and microbes from attacking the reproductive area of the plant.

Females begin to flower eight to ten days after shortening the photoperiod. They are small and insignificant at first but, continually forming for six to ten weeks, develop into tightly packed clusters (racemes), the bit we've been waiting for, the buds or colas, sometimes referred to as YeeeeeeHaaaaahh! A single female flower consists of two small (0.3"–0.5" or 8–12 mm) fuzzy white stigmas raised in a V sign and growing out of an ovule enclosed in a tiny green bract (pod).

Figure 12.1: Frame and ties supporting heavily budded plants.

Figure 12.2: Adult plants in the early stages of bud production.

Pollen that lands on a stigma grows a germinating tube down to fertilize the ovule. Most of the resin glands, which contain the active ingredient THC, develop on the bracts, which cover the ovule. The resin glands on the bracts are visible with good eyes a few weeks after the flower appears. Sometimes because of an abnormal environment, the plants respond by producing male flowers on a female plant, or female flowers on what should be a male plant. Often the cause of this defect is an erratic photoperiod. These are hermaphrodites.

If you are growing just a few plants, a week before you put your plant into bud, just nip out the top shoot. There is still a three-week growth period after the plant goes into flower and by nipping out your top shoot you'll develop four or more shoots that will form the top of the plant. This will maximize on yield if you have only a few plants and are stuck for space. Pull off all the weak lower branches. They won't return much bud; maybe you can make clones from them; if you don't have the space for them all then give them to a friend or if it's legal sell them. That way the four or five top shoots get all the energy from the nutrient pumped into them. As branches grow, and buds appear, gently bend the branches over and fix them in position. There are several ways of doing this. You can push wire into the earth and tie the branches to the wire with ordinary ties from a garden center, or the little twists from sandwich bags; you can use string tied from the garden floor to the ceiling and fix your branches at random to that, or use the retracting clips that have been devised to support the tops of the plants. Plants will be encouraged to bush if you cut off several sections during the vegetation state, leaving at least five sets of branches. This will provide you with a short wide plant rather than a sprawling great thing that becomes undernourished or unmanageable. Don't be fooled by the thought that you have to have a tree growing for a good harvest. You are far better off to go for a smaller plant giving good bud, and grow more often rather than labor forever waiting for a smoke. In the long run the smaller quicker harvests will return the highest yield.

Once the first signs of budding appear, start to feed your little lady with a bloom nutrient (see chapter 8). The EC can be increased and feed time also. It's a good idea, if you are using slabs, to flush the slabs through with clean water every two weeks; also check your pH and EC levels at regular periods to ensure a balance is being maintained; your drainage water will be a good indication of what's going on in the root system. In the last week of the budding or flowering period only feed your plant with clean water. This will make the plant use up the last of the nutrient in the system and provide you with a smoother sweeter smoke, since your bud is made up of a high percentage of fluid. You won't want it filled with nutrient, will you? So no more nutrients use, and no more pH adjustment. **Keep it clean.** The budding cycle is very rapid in development and extremely interesting. Even after many years of growing I find it exciting trying to anticipate how much yield I am going to get from each plant.

13

General Care

Air Control

You can do a lot of things to improve the air conditions in your grow room or cupboard. Just because you can't see the air doesn't mean it doesn't matter; it'll make a noticeable difference to your harvest and growth rate if you get it right. Obviously if you are growing outside this section won't interest you since you can't do a thing about the world's climate. If you grow in a greenhouse or garden shed you should still read on because you are, for the purpose of air values, concerned—although simply opening a few windows may be all you'll have to do, but read on and choose what you can benefit from.

Cupboard growers must invest in a small mechanical vent, similar to a bathroom vent. They are very cheap and will give your plants enough air changes to increase the oxygenation and growth rate. Drill a couple of holes in the bottom of the door, either five at about 1" (25 mm) wide or a letterbox cut with a chrome or plastic meshed vent over it—these are sold by your local DIY store. The mechanical or bathroom vent is put either in the ceiling, if there is a roof void above, or if your grow room is downstairs, put the vent in the wall or the door. **SECURITY ALERT** *(1) Don't put it in an outside wall unless you use a filter. Remember the air you blow out will smell of marijuana. (2) If you put in a vent, seal the vent against light.*

Never close off your plants and let air stagnate. It won't kill them, but your crop and growth will suffer, plus lack of airflow will encourage fungal rotting, especially when your buds are forming tighter groups, and encourage the dreaded *spider mite*. (Oooooooooooooohh yes, you haven't read about those yet, have you? The spider mites will ravage your whole crop if you aren't careful; they are the locusts of the marijuana grower.) Even a small, cheap fan will make a difference. You have to imagine how hot it's getting in the room with the lights going, creating humidity with solution interaction. Mechanical vents and exhaust fans really are the best way to control the air quality of your room or cupboard and should be considered a real investment. In fact everything you spend on your plants is an investment since it'll come back to you in cash or product one way or another.

Temperature

Temperature control should be no problem. Marijuana grows well at room temperatures of 70°–84°F (20°–28°C) with 82°F (26°C) being the optimum during light hours and around 66°F (18°C) during darkness. Again, your plants won't die if the temperature is even at the most extreme from these points, from 30°F–230°F (0–100°C), but the plant yield will suffer and what we are trying to achieve is the perfect growing environment. I can always tell when the plants aren't happy, because I am not happy. Quite simply, if it's too hot or too cold for you and you are feeling uncomfortable then so are your plants. The best way to keep temperatures balanced is to suck warmed air from the home into the garden and blow heat exhaust into the attic space or outside. If the room runs too hot then open a small window to let cooler air flow through the fans.

An important item in all this is the minimum/maximum thermometer. This will record the temperatures at their extremes so that you'll know what has been happening at the coldest part of night or during the hottest time of day. Place your thermometer among your plants for a true, effective reading. Once your room is set up you can easily control the temperature. If the heat is too high, then adjust the control on your extractor and if it's getting too low then adjust the thermostat on your heater. To operate the minimum/maximum thermometer, simply press either button to get a reading on the screen of your highs and lows for the past period. If a thermostatic controlled unit is fitted, then management is even simpler. If you use an electronic heating device then link it up with a room stat. It's very important that there be no huge differences in the day and night temperatures. Although there will be some drop as in a natural environment, a huge deficiency will cause weak and poorly formed plants. In the colder parts of the year there will be a huge deficit to worry about and the introduction of heat will be required. The best form of heat would of course be a propane catalytic heater, as this provides carbon dioxide to feed the plants' needs, and this is a safe and clean method.

Propane is the most beneficial heat source since it gives off the grow gas CO_2. Ordinary gas, central heating, or electrical heat is OK too, but keep a close eye on humidity because of the dry heat they produce. Never use paraffin-type heaters, as the fumes they produce are harmful to the plant and to you when you are in the room. An oscillating fan can direct the heat from the plants.

If you are finding it difficult to maintain low temperatures during the summer

Figure 13.1: Min/max thermometers show the highest and lowest temperature of the day.

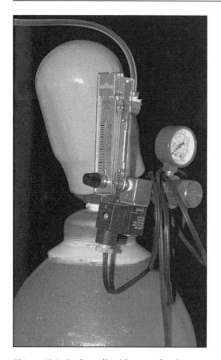

days, then swap your grow period. Just because it is daytime outside the garden, it doesn't mean it has to be daytime inside. Switch your lights on at night when the external temperatures are low and off in the daytime when the outside temperature is higher. The air sucked into your grow room during the day should be house temperature and good for the plants. Remember you have the fullest control; if it's still too hot, get an air-conditioning unit.

Figure 13.2: Carbon dioxide auto feed to maximize air quality and bud development.

Carbon Dioxide (CO_2)

CO_2 is an inert gas essential to plant growth produced by both plant and man during their natural processes of "breathing," and an essential element of photosynthesis. Photosynthesis (**photo** = light and **synthesis** = produce) is the means by which plants create energy (Don't you wish you listened in school biology now?) taking water through the root and carbon dioxide from the air. The process takes place within the chloroplasts (green pigment). Green plants are the only plants capable of producing their own sugar. Greenhouse growers or those with farms or small gardens that draw their air from outside will have ample CO_2 available to them, and so have saved a fortune already. All gardens must be ventilated where possible. CO_2 only affects growth rate; your potency however will not suffer. If a plant is a good smoke then it'll stay a good smoke, you'll just have less of it.

CO_2 enrichment to your garden will increase productivity and maximize your yield. Supplementing CO_2 will make your plants produce more dense buds, and can reduce the growing period significantly. There's no point in introducing CO_2 to your garden unless all other factors are correct, especially heat, since this affects the values of CO_2 as an addition that aids biochemical acceleration. If you are growing indoors then you must have at least 30% extra HID lighting and prepare for an increased use of nutrient solution of about 50%.

Measuring CO_2 levels has been made a lot easier these days since the huge global interest in hobby growers. A billion-dollar industry now thrives around marijuana. There are available on the markets small CO_2 tester kits that only laboratories had use of at one time; now there is no reason why you should rely on guesswork. Today's grower treats CO_2 as one of the most important elements of the grow room, using a quick measuring procedure with a pump analyzer, syringe and the analyzer tubes measuring in 300–5000 ppm. The higher the content of CO_2 in a plant, the less heat affects the plant growth. A test reading of .3% or 300 parts per million is a normal reading to be expected, but increasing the ppm to .15% stimulates growth dramatically, especially in an inert substrate like rockwool or cocos.

CO_2 can be introduced quite simply through the use of bottled gas. There are two ways to do this. The cheapest way is to buy a pressure regulator that can be adjusted after ventilation to release the right amounts of CO_2 inside. You will have to calculate the right balance of CO_2 introduction yourself by the following calculation procedure:

Length x Width x Height of the room = cubic volume.

Multiply the volume of the grow room by the volume of CO_2 required. For instance, a 10' x 10' x 8' grow room has a volume of 800 cu. ft. 800 x .0012 = 0.96. It will take 0.96 cu. ft. of CO_2 to raise levels to optimum in a garden this size.

For those of you who work in metric measurement, here is the formula to calculate how much CO_2 you'll need to add to your grow room: One cubic meter is equal to one cubic liter, so if you want to increase carbon dioxide concentration from .3% to .15% you need to add .12% carbon dioxide. If your grow area is 2 m x 2 m x 3 m, then the total cubic area equals 12 m^3. If 1 m^3 is 1,000 L then 12 is 12,000 cu. L. Now I have to take out a calculator for the next bit. To increase 12,000 L by 12% I will have to introduce 14.4 L. If you aren't sure how to work this out, take your calculator, put in the cubic liter volume, which in our case was 12,000, and then press the times button and punch in .12; now press the divide button and punch in 100; that gives you the liters required:

12000 x .12 = 1440 ÷ 100 = 14.40

Introduction of gas needs to be done after every exhaust period and only during the "daylight" hours since plants only use carbon dioxide during the photoperiod. You might want to plug your CO_2 system into your lighting timer. A 2 lb. (1 kg) bottle of carbon dioxide is approximately 132 gal. (500 L), so a room of the size we discussed here requires two 22 lb. (10 kg) bottles for its growing period.

Oxygen (O) is produced by photosynthesis, during which plants produce more oxygen than they use in respiration. In fact, the oxygen in the earth's atmosphere is produced by plants. That's why there's such a fuss made about tree planting and felling, and the abuse of the rain forests. Sitting with your plants increases CO_2, since you are producing it as you breath—but don't rush out and fill your grow room with six of your friends just to get the CO_2 flowing through.

Some home gardeners have invented many ways of injecting CO_2 to their gardens—by using fermentation, or sublimation of dry ice, or the burning of a paraffin (kerosene) heater or a small gas-filled camping light. All of these options do however present problems for the user and the plant since fumes can be very dangerous. These methods can work in the small garden, although by the time you take out your labor time and materials, long-term costs are greater than getting yourself kitted out with the real thing. The most practical method of adding CO_2 to your room is through compressed gas and is relatively inexpensive.

Use either a generator or an injected CO_2 system. With any good system, it's easy to control the amount of gas released into the garden. The compressed gas units that are sold should come with a regulator, a solenoid valve, a flow meter, and a programmable timer. They may include tubing, but if not, that is cheaply obtained at your local store.

Clear and simple instructions for calculating the flow rate will be included in your kit. Your gas bottle will have to be rented from a gas supply company, but look in your phone book for suppliers and check their prices as they do vary. Always make sure the room is enclosed and ventilation fans are off when introducing gas, otherwise your CO_2 will vanish out into the open air. The best way to run the system is to disperse of CO_2 a few seconds before your lights come on, then switch off wait a while for the CO_2 to be used up, and then switch on the ventilation system. Repeat the process through the photoperiod. This will require programmable timers. If you don't use the alternating process you'll run the risk of rot or insect infestation.

CO₂ Generators

The Growth Gas Generator® is a dedicated carbon dioxide production unit designed specifically for the small growing area. Controlled by an electric solenoid, it burns propane gas to produce carbon dioxide. The grower can set his generator to provide CO_2 during the hours of brightest "sunlight," when plants get the benefit. Generators can be used with a CO_2 sensor to maintain precise levels in the hi-tech growing environment. The Growth Gas Generator® is provided with suggested

Figure 13.3: Gas generator enables smaller growers to generate their own CO_2.

timer settings to provide the best CO_2 levels in area up to about 43 square meters. This product is designed for gas production rather than heat, and heat production is kept to a minimum.

Don't mistake the generator for a heater, and don't rely on a gas heater alone to provide your CO_2 needs; the latter are designed purely for heat, carbon dioxide is just a by-product. Most gas heaters in a grow room will be thermostatically controlled, so they will produce more gas as the temperature drops. Unfortunately, this means that most of the CO_2 is produced at night when plants can't use it. Gas generators are designed to produce CO_2 and can be set to produce it during the daylight hours. It's possible to provide CO_2 at high levels. Modern research has shown that levels up to 1500 ppm can be maintained in a grow room.

Negative-Ion Generators

These are quite inexpensive units that hang unobtrusively in your garden, freshening and revitalizing the air at a very low running cost. They also remove dust, cigarette smoke, pollen and bacteria. A complete overhaul of the air is carried out, cleaning out polluting particles by creating billions of negative ions. (We have discussed this product in the security section as it also rids the grow room of smells.)

Some expensive ion generators include a collector that pollutants settle on, and some generators automatically alternate between emitting negative ions and collecting pollutants; many have reusable filters. One factor you must be aware of

Figure 13.4: Professional dehumidifier. Humidity levels are important for the growth of happy, healthy plants.

with ionizers is that they may activate a fluorescent lamp if they are too close, just enough for it to glow or flash. If this happens, then your plants will either not go into bloom when the time comes or they'll go very slowly. Go into your room during the "night" period and check. If you find a problem, first try moving the ion generator away from the lamp or turn it off at night.

Humidity

I personally don't see this as a huge factor with marijuana unless it's far too high, as marijuana seems to grow almost standing on its head, but if the room is suffering from a very dry atmosphere through the heat system you have provided then the addition of humidity may improve your greenery a little. If humidity is too low, increase by using a humidifier. Marijuana likes humidity between 40° and 80°, 40° for flowering and 80° for vegetation. If you use a humidifier, you'll find growth more luxuriant in appearance, leaf blades larger and broader, and plants a little taller. In a dry atmosphere, development is more compact overall, and the leaves are smaller and thinner. I take humidity more seriously when I am germinating or cloning, but since I do this in a propagator or mister, it is very easily controlled. In terms of humidity as a problem, during the later stages of flowering when buds are tightly packed and subject to rot, if the humidity is too high then rot sets in quite quickly; use a fan to get it down. With high humidity, there is also a danger of fungal growth. Use a dehumidifier in short spurts, since you don't want all the moisture to be taken from the room.

Water

Eighty percent of a plant's weight is made up of water, that's why you'll see so much shrinkage when you hang your buds to dry. Water is a fundamental component that fuels the growth of all green plants through photosynthesis, keeping them erect. Water is the means by which nutrients are carried. Your watering program very much dictates the success of your garden. Too much water suffocates the plants' roots and they can develop rot, fungus, or nutrient problems. Too little water and the root system may never develop fully; even with a good root system, consistent underwatering slows growth and maturation of the plant.

The rapid growth of a marijuana plant needs a continuing and ample supply of water, and since the space around the plant is limited by the pot's size, you'll need to water regularly, keeping the substrate moist. Rainwater contains carbonic acid and is perfect for growing plants, removing salts and alkaloids from the soil. It also contains a natural growth nutrient of dissolved nitrogen, being near neutral pH, but consider your storage or collection methods to maintain that level. Water high in sodium requires one teaspoon of gypsum to five liters of water to level it off. Sodium may eventually poison the plants. Counteract any acidity by mixing about one teaspoon of hydrated lime per five liters of water. Check the pH of your water regularly and add only enough lime to bring the pH into the acceptable range. Never use water that's been processed through a water-softening device

Chlorinated water should have no adverse consequences, but if this is of concern to you, simply solve by displacing the soil's oxygen by over watering. Plants

Figure 13.5: Surface leaf watering or pest control should never be performed while the lights are on as this can burn the plants.

may give symptoms resembling nutrient deficiency these symptoms being the yellow, gray, or copper/brown areas on dying leaves. The worried grower will try to battle the phantom deficiency by adding more fertilizer, which of course comes with more water and so a vicious circle begins. The first test when you see these symptoms is an easy one: test the wetness of your soil with the cheap tester described earlier in the book. Transplanting is your only course. If you have trouble with discolored leaves or signs of nutrient deficiencies on very young plants, try starting them again, using purified or distilled water.

The plant's watering needs naturally increase with growth, and once the plant has reached middle growth, water to saturation, then allow the top 2" (50 mm) to dry before you water again. The best way to test is to water one pot a bit at a time, then just when the water begins to run from the bottom, you'll have a measure of the capacity required to water that plant.

Too much water causes plant cells to become too rigid because of the water pressure within them, if the soil dries out completely, the cells lose water pressure and their rigidity. First the bottom leaves droop, and the condition works upward until the top of the plant flops over. Water immediately, you'll see your plant spring to life almost instantly. Marijuana is a hardy plant and will last through most droughts, dropping a few leaves on the way.

14

Harvesting Your Plants

Now the Good Part...

You've loved them, cared for them, suffered anxiety attacks when they wilted and gone through stages of paranoia every time a helicopter went over or there was a knock on the door; now it's time to benefit. This is the best bit of the whole process. I love growing the plant. It has become a great hobby, almost a way of life really, and when you start to grow you'll understand what I mean. It seems I am always in with the plants, I even talk to them. The rapid changes and speed of growth of the marijuana plant fascinate me throughout the process and I am in awe of the plant—but harvesting is still the best bit for me. Harvesting is such a buzz, although there was a little disappointment when my first ever crop dried out, as it seemed to shrivel to nothing when the moisture was drained and what was once 2 lbs. (1 kg) suddenly resembled 1 oz. (28 g) but hey, who cares? It's mine: I planted it, I grew it, I picked it and now I am going to smoke it.

The first question is "When do I know the plant is ready to harvest?" EASY ONE! When the stamen turn to orange/brown over 80% of the bud and the bracts (buds) are swollen with a few new white flowers at the top, you can harvest. You will feel the cola hard and heavy to the touch.

You can of course be selective and just take off the ready buds and leave the rest to mature, but I usually wait until the whole plant is ready. About a week before she is ready to give up her fruits, the small white stamen on the bud begin to turn orange. This is a time when you might want to strip out a few of those fan leaves that have been shading the lower buds. Many growers strip out all of the stemmed leaves from their plants during the flowering period. I think this stripping of your plant is a bad practice; if you are going to strip them at all then keep them on until the buds are maturing and then only take off the leaves that are shading a bud. Stripping some leaves may maximize maturing buds, allowing the light to get through. Buds that have not matured will give you a different smoke so another consideration would be your preference in smoking too; try an early bud and compare it to your mature bud. I have found with the varieties that I have grown that white stamen buds will give you what I call a "body smoke," a sensation all over as the effects spread. The mature bud will give you a more cerebral smoke, the reason being that THC is degrading to other chemicals such as CBD. It is suggested that the THC gives you the high and CBD gives you the heavy, lethargic feeling, although there is a school of belief that says CBD actually gives nothing.

Don't be tempted to harvest too early: stamen start to turn orange and your mouth starts to water, but let common sense prevail. Let the weight of your yield rule your brain and not the desire for an early sample. Since most of the weight of your bud piles on in the last week or so, an early harvest will be stealing from yourself. You'll want to flush out all of the nutrients by feeding plain old water so you get a sweeter, cleaner smoke, and additionally, if you prefer the mature full richness of a bud that is ready to burst with THC, then WAIT. Watch your plant closely in the last few weeks: if you have fallen buds or the plant turns to darker brown quickly, then harvest immediately.

How It's Done

What will you need for your stripping process? A good, sharp pair of **scissors** is essential. If you have a number of plants, then make sure you get comfortable scissors with soft handles like the pair in the picture. You'll also need **Baby Oil** (don't get excited it's for your hands). Rub your hands with baby oil and the resin from the leaves and buds won't stick to your fingers. Resin on your fingers makes it difficult to work for the first 40 or 50 plants although it does coat over and goes powdery after a while. It's best not to have any of the resin in your skin, *SECURITY ALERT* especially if you want to go out and buy a Big Mac or some KFC while you are working. You will probably get the munchies since the resin will penetrate your skin while you are working and give you a high. When you harvest, make sure you have food and drink around you and if you have to go out during harvest change all your clothes, because even if you can't smell the resin on you, others will. Lastly, make sure you have some **white spirit** to clean your scissors with when you have

Figure 14.1: Drying a harvest should never been done in the grow room. Do not rush the drying period.

finished or even during harvest as they get coated with the heavy resin.

Once your plant is ready for you to harvest, don't chop her from her water supply until you're ready to clip. If you have grown on larger rockwool blocks, cut the root under the block, keep the block moist and your plant will remain workable for longer. As soon as you cut off the water supply she will start to wilt and be harder to clip. If you have grown in pots, then only cut the stem when you are ready to sit and work; don't be tempted to cut and set aside for later. Handle your buds as little as possible as the heavy touch of the hand will fracture the tri-chomes that hold the beads of resin, and will degrade the THC at an earlier rate. If you have a garden that requires you to transport your plants to a suitable place to clip, then bag them in garbage bags having first given the leaves a mist spray.

Before you chop your main stem, strip the plant of ALL stemmed leaves, that is to say all the leaves except the ones tightly peeking out from between the bud; we

Figure 14.2: Example of a bud ready for harvest. Squeeze gently to feel the plumpness. Mmmm.

Figure 14.3: Full plants hanging to dry. The plant on the left has not been properly stripped of leaves.

will clip those, unless you are growing large amounts for supplying of course, in which case most of the shoot leaves can be stripped by hand and then trimmed after. For those of you growing in pots, strip your main leaves while the plant is still in the soil, then cut her for clipping. If you are a commercial grower, you'll have copious amounts of clippings; save these to make scuff or oil. If you are just growing for yourself, keep the clippings to dry out later and either use them in place of tobacco or smoke them on their own, they are infused with resin and will make a satisfying toke for all but the heavy smoker. ***SECURITY ALERT*** Put all of your leaves in a garbage bag or a small plastic bag if there aren't that many, but make sure it's not see-through. DON'T put your leaves in your garbage can! Remember the nosy garbage collector? He could inform the police, or his friends. Take your leaves to an apartment block where they have communal garbage, burn them in the garden or take them into the country and spread them somewhere different each time, they'll break down and compost the soil, so you aren't littering.

Once you have taken your harvest, leave the buds on the stem for drying out. Hang them individually (as shown on page 199) in a cool, dry area. A humidity of around 40–50% is fine with a room temperature of approximately 66°F (18°C). It's possible to have a quick sample of your bud by force drying on a radiator, in the boiler cupboard (airing cupboard) or the microwave, but the smoke will be a little harsh and shouldn't be taken as the true value of your harvest. Wait for a natural drying process before you evaluate. To dry in the microwave, use a 650-watt unit on medium heat for 15 seconds; take the bud out, feel it for dryness and put it back for a few seconds if it isn't quite ready.

If your bud is dried with the heat too high or the humidity too low then it may go crispy on the outside. If this happens, put them in a bag for a couple of days to make them sweat up, opening the bag a couple of times a day to stop them from fermenting. Hanging your plants is easy: set yourself up a small string or thin wire line out of the way somewhere, hang your plants and wait. Five days is the average drying period, depending on the room temperature and the size of bud, sometimes it can take as long as 10 days. A good rule is to wait until the main center stem can be snapped clean. If you have to wait for some time keep checking for mold; this can creep up on you if you don't check. Once the mold sets in you'll lose your bud and if you try to sneak it into a bag of bud to sell then it will infect the whole bag—"one rotten bud spoils the bag." You won't get away with it because the bad bud will give itself away by its odor.

Another way to dry your bud if space is limited for hanging and you only have access to say a cupboard-sized area, is to buy yourself one of the drying trays available, which is great because they dry evenly and no part of the bud is closed off from the natural air-drying process. Spread your buds evenly over the netted tray and wait.

Storing your bud requires an airtight container; exposure to the air will deteriorate your bud. Zippy bags or an airtight jar are ideal. If you want to keep the bud in the fridge then make sure you have waited for the right period of time for it to dry. If you freeze a bud that still has moisture in it, you'll lose your bud because when you thaw it, it will become moist again. It's possible to save a harvest for years if it is kept airtight and the buds do not contain more than 5% moisture. Light and temperature diminish THC factors so make sure the airtight container is kept

Figure 14.4: Dried bud stored in small containers ready for freezing.

cool and dark; a coat of black paint over the outside of the jar will be worth considering if you want to store it in a cupboard that is prone to light. If you freeze-store, make sure that there are no small holes in the snap-fastening bag and that as much air as possible has been removed from the bag prior to sealing. You can suck the air out with a straw and seal the already snapped bag with tape so it does-n't open by accident or rough handling. If you store underground for security reasons then make sure the hole you dig is waterproofed and the container is damp proof. A good storage tank is a plastic cooler available from most major stores. Wrap it in a garbage bag before burying. Don't bury it too deep or you'll knock yourself out digging it up again. If you store in the fridge or freezer, remember the smell can still escape and visitors will detect it in the house. You will get used to it but a visitor will notice in a second.

After the drying process you may be a little upset because the full, rich, huge buds that you hung to dry are now a shriveled semblance of their former selves, since they have now lost 80% of their weight and close to 40% of their volume from moisture loss. Be prepared for this factor and you won't be quite so disappointed. A good test to see if the bud is ready for smoking is to take a sample from the center of a cola. A properly dried bud should allow a cool even burn without the need to relight.

THC in marijuana is THC acid (THC-COOH); this is not psychoactive, but when it is burned, it decarboxylates inactive THC-acid into an active form of THC. That's why all recipes containing marijuana involve a process of heating the bud before it's used in the recipe processing. If you make your spliff too fat then some of the bud doesn't burn evenly and your THC is lost. A "percy" (personal) spliff is the better option, smaller and slimmer; you lose the sociability of passing around but you get a better smoke and you won't catch herpes.

The last word goes to Kermit—no, he isn't still chasing Miss Piggy, he's resurrected in the form of a clipping machine (named after the loveable green character) that is worth its weight in gold if you've got a number of plants to clip. It's simple to use and bags all of your clippings ready for scuffing or drying out, no mess, quick and clean on your fingers. Cost is approximately US $350 (£170) but it's worth it if you have more than 100 plants to clip. These machines are available to rent also.

Regeneration

So, you've had your fun growing, you've had your bud, and maybe you don't have another plant to carry on. Well, don't fear for your future, you can rejuvenate the plant you have been nurturing for months.

Look at your plant before you harvest, decide what amount you can take without completely dismembering it, then cut all the way down toward the lower branches, leaving your chosen few branches on the plant with a couple of scraggy buds clinging to them—this amount must be left on the plant to rejuvenate her.

Once you have had your harvest, put the plant back into an 18–24-hour light regime for around 6 weeks and you'll notice the plant begin to regrow its leaves and branches, finally to be reborn into its former self, at which time you can put her back into bud. This process can be done several times, although quality and potency of bud diminishes each time, it would be a good idea to take clones on the second growth period if you forgot the first time, or just didn't have the courage to make the first cut.

15

Troubleshooting for Growers

There are several things to watch out for when growing marijuana. You'll have heard horror stories of all kinds from friends, but you needn't worry if you work cleanly and heed the words of this book you should have trouble-free harvests. Although there are chemicals you can use to kill off insect infestation, I prefer nature's way with a suitable predator.

Insect Infestation

Spider Mite

The most damaging problem that nature can throw at you is the two-spotted mite or spider mite *(tetranycbidae)*. These are almost invisible to the naked eye and undoubtedly the greatest nuisance that you'll ever come up against in your growing experience. Their numbers grow at an alarming rate, and they are often unsuspected until they swarm on your crop and devastate it.

There are two varieties, the common spider mite and the fruit spider mite; the difference is not visible unless observed through a microscope or magnifying glass. A fully-grown female only reaches the size of a grain of sand but can lay close to 100 eggs. Spider mites live and lay their eggs under the leaves of your plants, so keep vigilant. Small white spots on your leaves are the first visible sign that these unwanted visitors exist; this is where they have sucked the fluids out of the plant. If humidity is too low in your garden, the mites will begin to spin webs and eventually cocoon the whole bud if you aren't on top of the situation. It's possible to smoke the pests out with a fogger that you can buy or rent from any good grow shop, or you can spray with an insecticide, although neither of these methods are 100% successful since the mite develops an immunity. The best and most natural way is to introduce a natural predator like the *Phytoseiulus Persimilis*, another mite that lives entirely on two-spotted mites. This predator will multiply to suit his feed availability so if there are a lot of spider mites then the predator will multiply to eat them and once the food source diminishes then so will the predator, creating a healthy balance in your garden. If the pest situation begins to exceed the predator, adjust humidity and temperature to suit the predator. You can buy the predator from your grow shop—ask for SPIDEX.

Other insects that may infest gardens are pretty standard, and you probably have heard someone in the family complain of them in their garden:

• thrips (Thripidae)
• plant lice or aphids (Aodidina)
• moss flies (Sciara and Lycoria)
• whitefly (Aleurodina or Trialeurodes vaporarium)

Thrips at full size are about the same as the head of a pin, with two pairs of wings. They are hardly noticeable but can fly so well they can cover the whole of your garden in seconds. They live, like the spider mite, under your leaves. The natural enemies of the thrip are predatory mite, lacewing flies, spiders and ladybugs.

Aphids have several hundred varieties, and multiply as quickly as the spider mite. The distinction between the spider mite and the aphid is that the latter do not lay eggs. Rather, they produce one tiny baby each day of their lives by virgin birth. They usually live on the stem of the plant but may be found on the leaf also. Aphids make themselves visible as they group together with their young. The natural enemies of the aphid are ladybugs and their larvae, the larvae of the ichneumon fly or parasite wasp, lace wing flies and their larvae, glow bugs, predatory bugs, and earwigs.

Moss flies grow to around the size of a head of a pin. They are a small mosquito that lays hundreds of eggs in moist soil. The larvae then eat away at the small roots of your plant in the early stages and can kill the younger plants. They are easy to control and get rid of: buy a "yellow strip." The natural enemies of this mosquito are little eels and spiders.

Whitefly is almost as big a pain as the spider mite but still not unbeatable. It grows to the size of a grain of rice and has two sets of wings. The female lays two or three eggs a day on the lower side of your leaf. The larvae will feed on the juice of the leaf. The natural enemies of the whitefly are ichneumon flies or *Encarsia Formosa* and spiders. The tiny wasp known as the ichneumon fly is available to purchase as the product En-Strip. They will go on to lay their own eggs and control the whitefly population themselves.

Never introduce biological warfare to your garden as a means of prevention; wait till there is an attack. The predators you introduce will go for survival rather than extinction and will never rid your garden completely of the pest you wish to fight. They will maintain a steady food supply.

Poor Management and Deficiencies

Most of the problems you'll find in a garden will occur due to poor management or lack of knowledge, so take care. Don't pet your animals before you walk into your garden. Don't bring in nonsterile earth or sand from outside (this may carry bacteria). Don't walk through bushes or plants before you go into your garden (you may pick up some of the pests we have talked about and introduce them to their new restaurant). Any other problems that you might have could be caused by over-neutralizing, under-watering or burning; you can never under-fertilize, the plant will grow quite happily on water—so putting too little nutrient won't cause a serious problem.

The most common problem is over-neutralizing the solutions. You might think a little extra will give you a better crop but it doesn't. The formula you have bought for your plants has been designed for marijuana and the recommendations on those containers are precise, given a few variants regarding the plant, environment and water. Nutrient companies spend millions of dollars on getting it right and if they say solution is best mixed at 200–1 then that's what it is. If you want to change their recommendations then go for less rather than more. Another common problem is under watering during the flowering period. Turn your back for one day and that will be the day your pump packs up. Visit your plants daily and check that everything is OK; check the electrical connections, make sure the pump is pumping and there is water in the nutrient tank, see that capillaries are in place and not blocked with salts. Give them constant care. Never leave your garden for more than a day.

Bud Rot

Bud rot is a fungal growth know as Botrytis (gray mold). If this problem should arise, cut off the affected buds beyond the visible mold, decrease humidity, increase ventilation and if necessary spray with a safe fungicide. Make sure the garden is kept clean, picking up and disposing of all dead and dying leaves as they drop. Botrytis attacks yellow leaf more quickly than a green leaf. If you see a yellow leaf growing from a bud then give it a sharp downward tug to pull it off and inspect the inside of the bud area; if it is soft and spongy then you know you have some form of rot. Remove any affected cola from your plant immediately and take them from the room. If you stop feeding your plants nitrogen they'll start to yellow. Some growers prefer a less green bud, and although this gives you the coloring you want, it does leave you open to fungal attack.

Excess Nitrogen/Over-Fertilizing

Excess nutrients can burn your little ladies. Too much nitrogen (N) causes many problems. Too much nitrogen will change the osmosis properties of a plant so much that it reverses, drawing water out instead of taking it in. Even though your soil is wet, the leaves will droop, turn brown and die.

A major change in your plant will be chlorosis, which is a lack of chlorophyll (the green in your plant). Plants suffering from chlorosis can be saved. The symptom is the leaf will go through all shades of light green to white. Treat chlorosis by providing a sufficient replacement of any diminishing nutrient, (providing you can identify what it is). The best treatment is to leach the plant if you are growing in soil— that is, thoroughly wash it through with clean water, no nutrient at all. If you are using a nutrient tank then empty it and reassess the qualities of your water. If your plants are suffering from necrosis, the tissue is dead and there is no chance of breathing life back into it. To identify the deficiency in your plant can be difficult, but I do have some guidelines to offer. Identification of a problem begins with locating the starting point, either the top or the bottom of the plant: this is our first clue. Primary and secondary symptoms of a deficiency start at the bottom of a plant and micronutrient deficiencies start at the top. If the problem is at the bottom, the fan leaves are the first to show signs. If the problem is at the top, then it affects the topmost shoots first and then travels to all other shoots rapidly moving downward.

Nitrogen Deficiency (N):

This begins with the gradual yellowing of the lower stem leaves, where brown tips start to form (necrosis). In smaller plants the whole thing may go a lime-green color with red stems, lower yellow leaves dying and dropping, slow growth and smaller leaves. Add nitrogen to your feed and watch for improvements to older leaves. See your garden center for their nitrogen injection products which may be based on a fish emulsion. Too much nitrogen will delay growth, so get the balance right, and stop feeding once your plant has recovered—but keep an eye open for recurrence, if it has happened once it may happen again.

Phosphorus Deficiency (P):

This is very uncommon but none the less possible. The plants may look healthy but will have a dull, dark blue/green color with the undersides of the plant purple. Before you diagnose this as your problem, make sure that it isn't just a trait of the variety you are growing. Check lower leaves for blotchy areas before they turn yellow and drop off; the plant may suffer growth problems; blade tips will curl and edges become brown. It could also be that the water or soil is acidic, so be sure to check the pH.

Potassium (K):

Symptoms start at the bottom of the plant, and again you see the yellowing of the leaf. Blotches appear in spots or mottled areas. Stems may go red or purple. There will also be a possible burning of the leaf edge. The problem is most likely in low-light gardens, rather than those using HID. A good tip for this problem is the addition of a wetting agent like a detergent to the water, just a few drops in five liters of water will do.

Calcium (Ca):

This deficiency manifests itself as a dark green, slow-growing plant. Symptoms are crinkled leaves, curling at edges and gnarled. The leaves and shoots usually die before they grow properly. Dissolve one teaspoon of dolomite lime in five liters of water.

A good example of this disorder would be leaves beginning to curl; necrosis setting in, and the plant being eaten by grubs.

Magnesium (Mg):

This starts at the bottom of the plant and will progress to the growing shoots. Chlorosis develops between the veins of the leaf, sending them white to yellow in color. The veins remain green. Leaf tips curl and die with dying tissue between the veins apparent. The remedy is to add a teaspoon of Epsom salts to five liters of water. Use a foliar spray to the underside of leaf also for a quick improvement.

Micronutrient Deficiencies (Fe, Mn,Zn,B,Cu,Mo)

The most commonly found deficiencies are from Fe, Mn, and Zn, (iron, manganese and zinc), most commonly in areas with alkaline (hard) water. Adjust the pH. On the other hand a plant too high with micronutrients will suffer from root injury, stunted growth and necrotic leaf tissue. They are the vitamins of the plant world, the minerals that promote health and vigor.

An iron deficiency is recognized by the yellowing of the leaf and the existence of the green vein; chlorosis starts at the base of the leaf and spreads. Iron deficiency only affects the growing shoot, where manganese affects leaf and shoot. Manganese deficiency appears at the top of the plant, and in all newly growing shoots, older leaves are rarely affected. In a manganese-deficient plant the leaves remain green at the outer edges, yellowing in the center and green-veined. If zinc is your failing element then chlorosis starts between the veins of top shoots at the bottom of the leaf. A zinc deficiency has an unmistakable characteristic in that the leaf curls horizontally in a twisting mode. Upward growth could cease completely and a sort of knotted top appears to develop on the plant. A good general fertilizer for all the above is Miracle-Gro or other brand of tomato fertilizer solution. In all cases check the pH.

Some General Advice

Check the Water Crusty taps and shower heads mean your water is "hard," usually due to too many minerals. Tap water with a TDS (total dissolved solids) level of more than around 200ppm (parts per million) is "hard" and should be looked into, especially if your plants have a chronic problem. Ask your water company for an analysis listing, which will usually list the pH, TDS, and mineral levels (as well as the pollutants and carcinogens) for the tap water in your area. This is a common request, especially in this day and age, so it shouldn't raise an eyebrow. Regular water filters will not reduce a high TDS level, but the costlier reverse-osmosis units, distillers, and deionizers will. A digital TDS meter (or EC = electrical conductivity meter) is an incredibly useful tool for monitoring the nutrient levels of nutrient solution, and will pay for itself before you know it. They cost about $5 and up.

General Feeding Tips Pot plants are very adaptable, but a general rule of thumb is to use more nitrogen and less phosphorous during the vegetative period, and the exact opposite during the flowering period. For the vegetative period, try an N:P:K ratio of about 10:7:8 of and for flowering plants, 4:8:8. Check the pH after adding nutrients. If you use a reservoir, keep it circulating and change it every two weeks. A general guideline for TDS levels is as follows:

Seedlings = 50–150 ppm; unrooted clones = 100–350 ppm; small plants = 400–800 ppm; large plants = 900–1800 ppm; last week of flowering = taper off to plain water. These numbers are just a guideline, and many factors can change the actual level the plants will need. Certain nutrients are "invisible" to TDS meters, especially organics, so use TDS level only as an estimate of actual nutrient levels. When in doubt about a new fertilizer, follow the fertilizer's directions for feeding tomatoes. Grow a few tomato or radish plants nearby for comparison.

pH The pH of water after adding any nutrients should be around 5.9–6.5 (in rockwool, 5.5–6.1). Generally speaking, the micronutrients (Fe, Zn, Mn, Cu) get locked out at a high pH (alkaline) above 7.0, while the major nutrients (N, P, K, Mg) can be less available in acidic soil or water (below 5.0). Tap water is often too alkaline. Soils with lots of peat or other organic matter in them tend to get too acidic, which some dolomite lime will help fix. Soil test kits vary in accuracy, and generally the more you pay the better the accuracy. For the water, color-based pH test kits from aquarium stores are inexpensive, but inaccurate. Invest in a digital pH meter, preferably a waterproof one. You won't regret it.

Cold Cold weather (below 50°F or 10°C) can lock up phosphorous. Some varieties, like equatorial Sativas, don't take well to cold weather. If you can keep the roots warmer, the plant will be able to take cooler temps than it otherwise could.

Heat If the lights are too close to the plant, the tops may be curled, dry, and look burnt, mimicking a nutrient problem. Your hand should not feel hot after a minute when you hold it at the top of the plants. Raise the lights and/or aim a fan at the hot zone. Room temps should be kept under 85°F (29°C)—or 90°F (30°C) if you add additional CO_2.

Humidity Thin, shrivelled leaves can be due to low humidity; 40–80% is usually fine.

Figure 15.1: Shriveled leaves often indicates poor humidity or calcium deficiency.

Figure 15.2: Check around the base of plants for mold or shrinkage. Keep water feeders clear.

Mold and Fungus Dark patchy areas on leaves and buds can be mold. Lower the humidity and increase the ventilation if mold is a problem. Remove any dead leaves, wherever they are. Keep your garden clean.

Sprays Foliar sprays can have a "magnifying glass" effect under bright lights, causing small white, yellow or burnt spots that can be confused with a nutrient problem. Some sprays can also cause chemical reactions.

Insufficient light Tall, stretching plants are usually caused by growers using the wrong kind of light. Don't use regular incandescent bulbs ("grow bulbs") or halogens to grow cannabis. Invest in good fluorescent lighting or HID lighting because they supply the high-intensity light cannabis needs for good growth and tight buds. Even better, grow in sunlight.

Figure 15.3: Foliar spray. Never use under light.

Clones Yellowing leaves on unrooted clones can be from too much light, or the stem may not be firmly touching the rooting medium. Turn off any CO_2 until they root. Too much fertilizer can shrivel or wilt clones—plain tap water is fine.

Quick View Guide to Problems

To use the guide simply start at 1. When you think you've found the problem, check the nutrients information in chapter 8 to learn more about it. Diagnose carefully before making major changes.

1. If the problem affects only the bottom or middle of the plant go to 2. If it affects only the top of the plant or the growing tips, skip to 10. If the problem seems to affect the entire plant equally, skip to 6.

2. Leaves are a uniform yellow or light green; leaves die and drop; growth is slow. Leaf margins are not curled up noticeably. Nitrogen(N) deficiency. If not, go to 3.

3. Margins of the leaves are turned up, and the tips may be twisted. Leaves are yellowing (and may turn brown), but the veins remain somewhat green. Magnesium (Mg) deficiency. If not, go to 4.

4. Leaves are browning or yellowing, with yellow, brown, or necrotic (dead) patches, especially around the edges, which may be curled. Plant may be too tall.

Potassium (K) deficiency. If not, keep reading.

5. Leaves are dark green or red/purple. Stems and petioles may have purple and red on them. Leaves may turn yellow or curl under. Leaves may drop easily. Growth may be slow and leaves may be small. Phosphorus(P) deficiency. If not, go to 6.

6. Tips of leaves are yellow, brown, or dead. Plant otherwise looks healthy and green. Stems may be soft. Over-fertilization (especially N), overwatering, damaged roots, or insufficient soil aeration. Use more sand or perlite. Occasionally due to not enough N, P, or K. If not, go to 7.

7. Leaves are curled under like a ram's horn, and are dark green, gray, brown, or gold. Over-fertilization (too much N). If not, go to 8.

8. The plant is wilted, even though the soil is moist. Over-fertilization, soggy soil, damaged roots, disease; copper deficiency (very unlikely). If not, go to 9.

9. Plants won't flower, even though they get 12 hours of darkness for over 2 weeks. The night period is not completely dark. Too much nitrogen. Too much pruning or cloning. If not, go to 10.

10. Leaves are yellow or white, but the veins are mostly green. Iron (Fe) deficiency. If not, go to 11.

11. Leaves are light green or yellow beginning at the base, while the leaf margins remain green. Necrotic spots may be between veins. Leaves are not twisted. Manganese (Mn) deficiency. If not, go to 12.

12. Leaves are twisted. Otherwise, pretty much like 11. Zinc (Zn) deficiency. If not, see 13.

13. Leaves twist, then turn brown or die. The lights are too close to the plant. Rarely, a Calcium (Ca) or Boron (B) deficiency. If not...you may just have a weak plant.

(Information supplied by Overgrow for distribution)

16

Waste
to Taste

After you harvest, you're stuck with a huge amount of waste. Throw away your root, stalk and fan (shade) leaves. Keep the smaller leaves and your clippings. We have uses for these and it depends how much you have as to what we can do with them. Keep them fresh by putting them in an airtight bags. Put the clippings in the bag, hold the top corners and spin the bag round in your fingers to make the top tight and trapping in some air, tie a knot in the top of the bag to hold the air in or use the wire ties that come in the sandwich bag box. Now put the leaves in your fridge; don't freeze them. Each day, give your bag a little shake to let air around the leaves; maybe you can put a lettuce leaf in there to keep it fresh but make sure there is no mold on the lettuce, it'll rot your leaves. You won't be able to leave it too long, this is just to give you some breathing space between harvesting and having some more fun so you can maximize on your harvest. At 16.1 you'll see just what you're wasting when you throw away your clippings.

The amount of waste you have will depend of course on what plants you are growing, how big you grow them and how many you grow. Let's say you grow something like White Widow, a non-bushy plant that grows small and harvests well with mostly top bud. The height at harvest will be around 18" (45 cm) and yield around 15 oz. (45 g) of good bud. You will find that you'll also have about 1 oz. (28 g) of usable clippings. This is your bonus and it's wasted by most people. I am going to tell you how to use those leaves to their maximum potential, which will give you more to smoke, alternative types of smoke and even something to munch. This is great news for the non-tobacco smoker.

Dried Clippings

When you were growing and prior to harvest you saw how much resin (snow) had formed on your leaves around the bud. That doesn't go away; its still there and can give you a great smoke, more mild than the bud but good enough for most people to enjoy a daytime joint while buzzing around the house or shopping.

NEVER **smoke or use cannabis when you drive or have responsible activities to perform, like looking after the children,** directing the traffic in Times square, being the judge in a murder case or if you were the Queen of England when knighting one of your subjects at the palace. As a non-tobacco-using lover of the herb, I use my clippings to roll instead of tobacco and add bud as normal. Lay the clippings out, spreading thinly on a sheet of newspaper and let them dry. When they are crisp, take them between the palms of your hands and rub until they powder and flake. Bag in a lock-seal polythene bag and keep in the fridge.

Hot Buttered Bhang

"In a saucepan, melt about 3.5 oz. (100 g) of butter. Crumble a good handful of marijuana tops or leaves, about 1 oz. (25 g). Stir the grass into the molten butter. Continue stirring over medium heat for one minute. While it is hot or sizzling, add 8 oz. (237 ml) of vodka. Be cautious that the hot butter does not make the mixture spatter. It is best to pour in the vodka swiftly. Continue to boil for 30 seconds or more, stirring all the while. A pinch or two of powdered cardamom seed may be added during the boiling...

After boiling as much as desired, strain the liquids. Press the mash in a strainer with the back of a spoon to remove all the juices. Discard mash or boil it again in fresh vodka to salvage more materials. Sweeten to taste with honey. Pour the liquid into wine glasses when cooled. This mix provides two servings. This is one of the most swiftly absorbed cannabis concoctions. The effects of the grass may be felt in less than 15 minutes.

Hash Oil

This is better than any import of course because it is fresh and pure. Oil burns slower than weed and at a lower temperature. It can be made of pure bud if you are not a grower with access to clippings; it's stronger (I believe) in many cases and makes a bit of bud go further—almost three times as for in ready made joint terms—and the smoke is quite different, very trippy. There are several methods of making oil. I personally favor the following because the mix ferments and takes in as much resin as possible.

Figure 16.1: 'Snow' on the trim leaves.

You will require several items of kitchen equipment: a heavy bowl suitable for the oven, something in the Pyrex® range maybe; a large frying pan or pot that is bigger than the Pyrex® dish; muslin if you can get it, an old pair of tights or a coffee pot filter will do equally as well; and some Isopropyl alcohol or denatured alcohol that is 99% pure from the chemist (Isopropyl is also called rubbing alcohol).

WARNING ! *ALCOHOL IS HIGHLY FLAMMABLE SO DO THIS OUTSIDE IF POSSIBLE. TAKE ALL PRECAUTIONS TO AVOID COMBUSTION*

Take your filter (or tights) and place the fresh clippings in it. It's wise to use two or three filters inside each other as the alcohol and the squeezing weakens them and they may split. Put the filter over one of the filter bowls and pour alcohol over the weed. Let it drain at its own speed. When it stops dripping, give it a little squeeze to encourage the last drop.

Now take a fresh filter and place it over another bowl, transfer the weed from the first filter to the second and pour your once-used alcohol from the first bowl over the weed again, letting it drip through into the second bowl.

Do this over and over until all the alcohol turns green. Then you are ready for the second stage of the operation. By now your mouth will be watering and your smoker's palate twitching.

Put a small amount of water in to a metal frying pan or large saucepan and place a Pyrex (or similar) bowl in the water; this protects you a little from putting the pure alcohol over direct heat, which could cause ignition. The way I have described allows the alcohol to warm through the water, but don't let the water run dry at any stage.

DO NOT USE AN OPEN FLAME (so quite obviousl use an electric stove)! Always make sure you have good ventilation as the fumes from the alcohol could ignite. Do not smoke or light a naked flame while you are working with or in the same room as this operation. This means your friends also.

Put the alcohol slowly into the Pyrex dish and allow it to simmer gently on a low setting, keep an eye on the water. Top it up as you need to with boiling water from a kettle. As the alcohol simmers, it'll evaporate into the air and leave behind your hash resin. Ensure that evaporation is slow by keeping the heat low, and be patient.

Once all of the alcohol has evaporated, you'll be left with liquid gold, pure hash oil from the resin in your leaves. Take a razor blade or something sharp that will not damage the dish and scrape the oil from the bottom and sides, and place it in a glass or plastic container that may be sealed airtight for storage—a small plastic tablet box for instance with an airtight lid. If you are using plastic or glass, make sure the oil is cooled before storing.

Figure 16.2: Resin taken from the shakings of trim leaves. Press to make Scuff.

Scuff

This is the best smoke you can have if you like a heavy buzz. It's mild on the throat for the non-tobacco smoker. If you buy this in any of the coffee shops you'll pay around twice the cost of any other weed. Scuff is made from waste trim leaves, tumbled slowly to release the resin. There are several small personal machines made available these days although a large machine for large amounts of waste would cost around US $700 (£350). An approximate for the amount of scuff you'll achieve from an average yield is about 1.5 oz. (35 g) if you do one 5-hour tumble. If you want to break it down then you may get 0.25 oz. (7 g) on the first shake, 0.5 oz. (14 g) on the second and 0.5 oz. (14 g) on the third, maybe higher if you are grow-ing resinous Indica strains, which give a dark sticky scuff.

The store-bought machines are of a very simple, almost primitive design, con-sisting of a geared-down electric motor, a cylindrical frame stretched with a fine mesh and a small tray underneath. The drum is driven by a small plastic ferrule attached to the motor. Place your trim leaves and any pieces of bud that aren't worth smoking or selling in the drum via a small door in one end. (Make sure your leaves aren't too dry; if they start to crumble, place them with a handful of fresh leaves in a plastic bag to rehydrate, just for a couple of hours.) Place the drum back into the box and switch on low for about an hour. If you're a more discerning smoker and want to break down the tumbles into stages, make a first tumble of 15 minutes; this is said to give you the very best tumble with prime resin collection. I would find it hard to tell the difference between an hour tumble and a 15-minute one.

The results of the first tumble will resemble a very light brown sugar and can be used immediately in any way you wish, as can any tumble. The ideal room temperature in which to tumble is around 65°F (18°C). Ensure there are no pieces of leaf in your scuff. Pour a small amount of freshly extracted scuff into your hand and rub it lightly until it begins to form together. Sativa is less oily than Indica. Keep rubbing and putting in more scuff as it comes together, constantly rubbing; if you don't rub long enough then it'll become too crumbly and you should only be able to crumble under heat application. Don't be shy about working the piece. It will get smaller as you continue and some people may think that they are getting less, but in fact you are getting a better product that will be very potent.

For tumble two, continue to tumble for four hours, then take the scuff from the drum mesh with a plastic spatula, add it to that in the collecting tray and bring it together. Wrap it in cling wrap and heat it in the microwave for a few seconds only. Take it from the microwave while it is still warm, lay it on a table or worktop surface and take a heavy chopping board and press it by applying all of your weight. You will then have a block of hash fit for a king.

I have to say that I usually do just one tumble for four to five hours and call it a day, but you can get a third quality tumble from the leftover. It comes out a little leafy, but it'll hold together and is still a better smoke than any soap bar or commercial Lebanese. It's worked and prepared in exactly the same way except that it needs a little more heat in the microwave and a bit more pressure to press.

Holland has done it again! An Amsterdam manufacturer, The Pollinator Company, is marketing an improvement in resin-collecting devices, called the X-TRACTOR®. Traditionally resin was collected by drying high-quality cannabis, sifting it through progressively finer screens until the powdery residue was left, and then heating and compressing it into blocks of hash. In more recent times machines like the one pictured were developed to do a more efficient job in less time.

The X-TRACTOR® maintains the basic principles of those methods that have gone before, but instead of tumbling cannabis through air to dislodge the resin glands from the plant matter, it agitates it in a cold-water bath to achieve the same results. Resin is heavier than water and also insoluble. This makes it possible to use the liquid as a medium for removal. To use the X-TRACTOR® , fill it with ice water and leaf clippings or bud, agitate it, and the water gets cloudy as resin breaks away; it then falls through the water, where it is funnelled into a glass bottle after settling through screens that filter and separate it from any tiny bits of plant matter that may drift downwards. The result is a bottle of water clouded with pure resin, which can then be separated and dried, using a coffee filter. The dried resin is then ready for processing. What makes this system unique is that by using water as the medium of extraction, it can process either dried or fresh plant matter—making it much more efficient since, if fresh cannabis is used, much less resin is lost during drying, when many glands would be knocked off due in handling. Also, because THC resin is oil, it gets less viscous as the temperature falls. Using cold water hardens the glands and softens the plant matter, making their separation easier, meaning more resin can be collected from the same amount of fresh or dried cannabis than if done the old way.

The X-TRACTOR® can be used to extract essential oils and fragrant resins from other plant species for use in aromatherapy, medicine, cosmetics and foodstuffs. The device comes in several sizes, for the personal connoisseur or the high-volume commercial producer.

NEVER FREEZE SCUFF...no matter what your friends say.

Space Cake

Now a dope book wouldn't be a dope book unless it included a recipe for Space Cake, and here it is.

If you like it trippy, this is right up your street, and it's made from all the crap you usually throw away so you don't lose anything. I usually make myself individual cakes and take half a cake at a time; I really can't handle any more. It's not a treat you want to be on your own with; take a small cake and have half each with a friend, sit back and wait for an hour or so and you'll have four to five hours of nutty tripping of the best kind. If it all gets too much then take something sweet to eat, maybe sugar in a cup of hot water, and the feeling goes away. Eat your cake on an empty stomach.

Take 3.5 oz. (100 g) of waste leaves, tops or clippings (avoid fan leaves); put 1 lb. (400 g) of butter/margarine in a pan with a little water, apply heat until the butter/margarine has melted, then add clippings and simmer for 45 minutes, stirring occasionally. When finished, strain the liquid through a fine mesh to separate the weed from the liquid; there must be no visible leaf at all. Put the melted mixture in the fridge until it hardens. When it's hard, pour off the water, which leaves you with a butter/margarine mix ready for cooking. You can either buy a cake mix or be really adventurous and mix your own. The cake mix isn't the important thing, the preparation of your butter/margarine is.

Sponge Cake
Ingredients
- 4 oz. (115 g) of self-rising flour
- 1 teaspoon of baking powder
- 4 oz. (115 g) soft butter/margarine (Our Mix)
- 4 oz. (115 g) granulated white sugar (castered cooking sugar)
- 2 large eggs

Making the mix
1. Preheat the oven to 325°F (160°C)
2. Sift the flour and baking powder into a bowl. Add the butter/margarine, sugar and eggs.
3. Stir briskly with a wooden spoon for two to three minutes. The mixture should be pale in color and slightly glossy.
4. Spoon the mixture into paper cake trays bought from your store. (Alternatively this mixture will make a large cake of 8" (20 cm) round; before pouring in the mix lightly grease pan with ordinary butter/margarine. Baking time is the same.)
5. Bake in the center of the oven for 20–30 minutes.

To test if the cake is cooked, press lightly in the center. If firm the cake is done, if soft cook for a little longer, keep checking. Alternatively, insert a skewer into the center of the cake. If it comes out clean then it's done. Take from oven and leave to cool on side. Don't put them in the fridge to cool. If you don't think you are cut out for the mixing procedures, just buy a standard cake mix from your store and add the special butter/margarine you have made.

Flavorings
Chocolate: Add 1 tablespoon of cocoa powder mixed with 1 tablespoon of boiling water into the cake mix.

Lemon: Stir 2 teaspoons of grated lemon rind into the cake mixture.

You can add iced topping or chocolate topping, cherries, currants or nuts to your own taste. In fact once you have the formula right, you can use your imagination to create all sorts of flavors and tasty additions.

Remember my advice: this is real trippy and if I were you I would only risk taking half of a small cake until you master the feeling; the affect is far stronger than a spliff and I ain't no lightweight. Since I am a non-tobacco smoker myself, I have a special interest in this method of absorbing cannabis and can see the need for tasty morsels that will create a stress-free me! These can be yogurts, desserts, cakes and cookies. Mmmm, I'm hungry already.

Save your lungs and eat yourself into a *BUZZ!*

17

Cannabis in Commerce

Drug Testing

Drug and alcohol abuse costs American employers billions of dollars in decreased productivity, increased liability insurance and higher workers' compensation insurance premiums. Employers may be liable for the negligence of an employee under the influence of drugs or alcohol and they may also be liable for negligently hiring an employee with a history of abusing drugs or alcohol. Furthermore, drug and alcohol abuse is also blamed for high employee absentee rates. All of these factors give employers an incentive to test their job applicants and current employees for illegal drugs or alcohol. The more these tests are required, the more we will become accustomed to them. It follows that as we become accustomed to drug testing, then those tests will become even more pervasive. Today, individuals subject to drug testing include government employees, military personnel, those involved in the transportation industry, athletes, and countless other employees who consent to drug testing as a condition of employment and continued employment. Drug tests are almost routinely required as a condition of probation, or parole.

A private employer may require an employee to submit to a drug test (without suspicion) as a requirement of continued employment. Depending upon the facts of how and why such a test is conducted, an individual who believes his or her employer has conducted an unreasonable drug or alcohol test could possibly sue the private employer for an invasion of the employee's right to privacy. An employer may be found civilly liable for such an intrusion if a judge or jury decided that the required drug or alcohol test pried upon the private affairs of the employee in an objectionable manner. For example, an employer who directly observes an employee providing a urine sample might be liable for an invasion of the employee's privacy. Asking an employee to submit a urine sample as a condition of continued employment would be unbelievable and most certainly it would be considered an invasion of the employee's privacy even as little as ten years ago. Today, such testing is becoming so commonplace that it generates almost no opposition. *The Wall Street Journal* reported that about 90% of Fortune 200 companies have drug-testing programs. Society now readily tolerates what would have been considered an invasion of privacy. The remarkable aspect about employment drug and alcohol testing is how acceptable it has become in such a short period of time.

High Times magazine advertizes such products as the *Whizzinator,* a device used to fool authorities when giving a urine sample. The Whizzinator comes as a prosthesis for both men and women. It comes in a range of colors in shades of white to black and is complete with a warming device for the self-mix synthetic and pure urine. The head of the company who sells the Whizzinator called me with a great story about its origin that I have to share with you.

Having been locked up in a Federal Penitentiary, the proprietor of the Whizzinator company sat worrying during the later years of his long sentence as to what he would do for a living when he left prison. All he knew was bank robbery and obviously he wasn't too good at that because he got caught. His cellmate was an Englishman who had been locked away for his part in drug smuggling, and they became great friends until it was time for the drug smuggler to go home. As a parting gift the Englishman gave his prison friend the idea of the Whizzinator, but there was one hitch: the penis had to be shaped the same as the Englishman's. They spent the last few hours together in prison sketching his member. All of you who purchase a Whizzinator will be pleased to know that you have an exact replica of Howard Marks's penis in your hands (depending on color of course). Yes! Howard Marks, our own Mr. Nice, was the originator of the idea.

A similar, less elaborate or convincing alternative is the *Urinator.*

Most drug testing is broken down into two categories, urine testing or urinalysis, and hair testing. The labs are not looking for drugs in urine samples; they are looking for drug metabolites. Once the body takes in a substance, the end product looks much different, once it passes through. Alcohol goes in as beer, gets oxidized by the liver, and comes out as water. Drugs go in the body in the psychedelic form and come out as a metabolite. The psychoactive ingredient in marijuana is tetrahydrocanibinol (THC). This is oxidized by the body and comes out as 31 different metabolites. The most prevalent form is 11-nor-D-9-tetrahyrocanibinolic acid (THCA)

Marijuana is passed from the lungs to the bloodstream, and while the drug is freely floating in the body in sufficient quantity, a high is felt. Marijuana is *liposoluble*, meaning it absorbs into fat cells. The drug is stored in the fat cells indefinitely until the body burns the fat cells for energy. When the cell is burned, the drug is metabolized and released back into the bloodstream. This is why marijuana can be detected for 30 days after a substantial usage.

The following information has been provided by Spectrum Laboratories®, who manufacture and sell products to help you pass any drug test with a 200% money back guarantee. Spectrum is to be found at www.urineluck.com, and their products can also be purchased from our own Website at www.cannabis-closet.com. Apart from marijuana testing, Spectum® also provides a test kit that covers THC, cocaine, opiates, amphetamines and barbiturates, called the Five Panel Kit®.

The five panel kit that tests for all of the drugs mentioned before costs around $40 and is probably the most comprehensive around. There are of course many products on the market but those from Spectrum are recommended by me personally. **Quick Fix®** is a synthetic urine mix that you heat and pour into a transfer bag for a prosthesis such as the Whizzinator.

Absolute Detox®, is a drink that flushes the system. It requires one hour to take effect. Spectrum® also makes **Get Clean®** shampoo for hair testing, **Quick Fizz®** one-hour detox tablets, and a home-test kit. Employers or institutions, in an attempt to cut costs, will only use drug screens occasionally. The screen is always performed first and is usually Urinalysis

Urinalysis is typically separated into two separate sections: the drug screen and the drug test or confirmation. There is a huge difference between a drug screen (EMIT) and a drug test. Most drug testing procedures utilize a drug screen and test (GC/MS). However, some are followed by a test or confirmation. Drug testing is broken down in the following percentages:

Hair Testing—5%

Screen with GC/MS—80%

Screen Only—5% FPIA (Screen)

GC/MS = Gas Chromatography/Mass Spectrometry—5%

FPIA = Florescence Polarization Immunoassay—Abbott Labs version of a screen—5%

Blood Test

Often people will be given a blood test and a urinalysis. These are for two totally different types of tests being performed. Blood is normally drawn for detection of diseases such as AIDS. Drug toxins can only be detected for 48 hours in the blood after consumption. For this reason the urine is tested for toxins instead of the blood.

Hair Tests

Toxins are circulated throughout the body via the bloodstream. The blood feeds the hair while it is in the growth stage at the scalp. As the hair is formed the toxins are trapped inside the hair follicle. The toxins then grow away from the scalp as time passes. If the use of toxins is stopped, the hair by the scalp is clean, but the middle of the hair or ends of hair will retain the toxins until cut off. The level of toxins is greatest near the scalp. Sunlight and chemicals added to the hair in dyes or shampoos will oxidize the drug metabolites over years, and can reduce the level of metabolites by 75%.

For this reason, the hair sample is clipped from the back of the neck (nape), near the scalp, by the examiner. Once sent to a laboratory the hair is dissolved with organic solvents. Once in a liquid solution, the toxins are freed from within the hair follicle. Extraction is performed on the liquid and drug toxins are removed. Once the drug metabolites are isolated a GC/MS is performed with urinalysis testing and a quantitative level is provided.

The most common type of drug screen on the market today, manufactured by Dade Behring, is called the EMIT (Enzyme Multiple Immunoassay Test). A typical screen will be referred to as SAP 5-50 NIT. This means substance abuse panel, 5 panels (drugs), 50ng/ml cutoff, and with nitrite check. This type of test is a competitive binding assay, which utilizes enzymes for the conversion of NAD+ to NADH. The conversion process is measured on a spectrometer to give semi-quantitative measurement of a specific drug metabolite.

Competitive binding assays utilize two types of drug metabolites competing for one antibody. The two possible sources of drug metabolites are from the donor and the lab. The reaction is very complex and difficult to comprehend. Three reagents are added to the urine sample to complete the test. Reagent 1 contains IGG anti-sheep antibody which is specific for the drug metabolite being analyzed. Reagent 2 contains the enzyme G6PD (Glucose-6-phosphate dehydrogenase) attached to the drug metabolite being analyzed and NAD+ (Nicotinamide Dinucleotide). Finally, the substrate G6P (Glucose-6-phosphate) is also added, which is just an intermediate compound that is neither produced nor consumed, but required for the reaction to proceed.

The reaction proceeds under two mechanisms dependent on the sample being positive or negative. The key result is whether the antibody reacts with the drug metabolite from the donor or the drug metabolite added by the laboratory. If the antibody reacts with the donor's metabolite, the sample is positive. If the antibody reacts with the lab's metabolite, the sample is negative. The lab's metabolite is attached to the G6PD, so when the antibody attaches to this metabolite, it blocks the active site on G6PD. When the activation site is blocked on the G6PD, it cannot attach to the NAD+, which is required for the production of NADH and thus a positive result.

Positive

Reagent 1 is added to the urine sample, which contains the antibody that binds to the donor's drug metabolite. Reagent 2 is then added which contains the G6PD attached to the lab's metabolite. The antibody has been consumed by the donor's metabolite in the sample and cannot react with the lab's metabolite on the G6PD. The G6PD's active site is free allowing NAD+ to bind and subsequently be reduced to NADH. The NADH gives off a distinctive color, which is absorbed by light at the 340nm wavelength. The spectrometer measures the change in absorbance per minute and determines whether the sample is positive based on a previous baseline of the urine being analyzed.

Negative

Reagent 1 is added to the urine sample, which contains the antibody. The antibody does not bind with anything because the sample is clean. Reagent 2, which contains the G6PD attached to the lab's metabolite, is then added. The antibody reacts with the lab's metabolite. The antibody attaches to the metabolite, which is attached to G6PD. The antibody binds to the active site of G6PD. Because the site is blocked, the NAD+ cannot bind and be converted to NADH. With no NADH present, the spectrometer reads a nominal absorbance change, and the sample is negative.

The test is usually performed on a Hitachi 740 spectrometer at 340nm wavelength of light. A spectrometer is a piece of scientific equipment that shines a beam of light through the urine sample. The amount of light that passes through the sample is termed "transmittance," i.e., transmitted through the sample. The light that does not pass through the sample is termed "absorbance," i.e., absorbed by the sample. The change in absorbance per minute is the parameter measured to determine if a sample is positive or negative. A baseline is run on each sample to determine the absorbance, because each urine sample is unique and different. Therefore, every sample has a different starting and ending point of the absorbance per minute to determine if a sample is positive or negative.

Confirmation with GC/MS

The GC/MS (gas chromatography/mass spectrometer) is actually two pieces of equipment used in conjunction. The pair of equipment is very complex and very costly. For this reason, they are usually found only at universities and hospitals.

The GC performs the separation and the MS allows the chemical identification. The GC separates the drug metabolites from the thousands of compounds found in the urine. Every compound has a specific molecular weight and charge, which allows for each compound to be separated and identified, based on these criteria.

To begin, an organic solution is added to the urine sample, and it then attaches to the drug metabolites. This process is called derivatization. The derivatization process changes the drug metabolite to a form that will react with GC. The sample is then heated to change it from a liquid to a gas. The gas then flows through a hollow tube on the GC referred to as a column. The GCs have columns specifically suited to isolate drug metabolites found in urine. Each distinct chemical of the urine comes off the column at a known interval of time and is collected. Once the drug metabolites are collected, the sample is moved onto the MS.

The MS (mass spectrometer) determines compound identification by molecular weight and charge. The sample is first ionized to a cation (positive charged particle) by bombarding the sample with electrons. The sample is accelerated with an electric field and passed through a slit, which allows only certain particles to pass through. The sample then passes through a magnetic field with a known strength. The sample and the magnetic field have opposite charges, which causes a repulsion or deflection of the sample. The sample is then passed through another slit and into a collector. Because the strength of the electric field and magnetic field are controlled and known by the operator, the mass of the cation can be determined with great accuracy

Some companies will give an individual a day's notice of a pending drug test. This is usually a sign that the donor will be providing a sample off-site. The collection site and laboratory where the urinalysis is performed are usually two different places. Less than 5% of all samples have a drug test with a GC/MS performed in the same facility where the sample is collected.

When the donor arrives at the collection site, a nurse or lab technician will ask for photo ID for proof of verification. The technician will then transfer the donor's information on the laboratory paperwork and give the donor the sample cup. The donor is usually asked to empty his or her pockets and leave all personal items in the lobby area. The donor is then escorted to the restroom. The technician will make a quick check of the restroom and might inspect the donor's fingernails or ask the donor to wash his hands before voiding (urinating). This is to ensure that the donor does not have salt or other additives under his fingernails. The water in the restroom sink is turned off and the toilet water is dyed blue.

The donor is given instructions on how many samples to provide and told not to flush the toilet after voiding. Each lab is different on the sample size. Most labs require a minimum of 1.5 oz. (45 ml) of urine. The accepted sample size can vary from 1–5 oz. (30–150 ml). Usually the donor is left alone to provide the sample. The technician will wait outside the stall or in the hallway while the donor is urinating. Rarely does the technician view the genitals while the sample is being delivered, except for the military and a few cases of criminal probation. The donor is then instructed to wash his hands and proceed to the final paperwork. The urine sample is never supposed to leave the technicians sight in this stage of the test until the final paperwork is completed.

The technician will get the sample from the donor and do a quick integrity check. This consists of temperature and maybe a test strip, to check pH, creatinine, and nitrite. The sample must be in the 90–100°F (30–35°C) range, with a pH in the 4.0–9.0 range and creatinine > 20mg/dl, and nitrite < 500ng/dl. The sample is then split in two; if there is a dispute on the first set of results, the second sample can be sent in for a second analysis.

The donor must sign his or her name or initials several times in a chain of custody. The chain of custody proves the sample was not tampered with after the donor left, or that samples weren't mixed up in shipping. The samples are sealed

This stunning specimen basks in the warm rays of the afternoon sun.

The lower branches of these plants have been trimmed to concentrate light, and therefore growth, to the main top buds.

A high calyx-to-leaf ratio means this plant will have very little to trim.

Clones given little vegetative growth before flowering take up minimal lateral space.

These buds were manicured fresh and now hang on strings to dry.

Healthy plants are less susceptible to pests and diseases, particularly mold.

Without its supports this plant would have toppled from the extreme bud weight.

Individual drippers are placed directly into the Rockwool cubes. Keep an eye open for clogged drippers.

Bud matter left on the plant to dry turns brown due to a significant breakdown of chlorophyll.

This brown furry looking spot is a sign of the onset of botrytis.

Watch those colas closely. Larger, dense buds are the most susceptible to molds.

These distorted and twisted leaves are a tell-tale sign of trouble on the horizon.

These plants, still in the vegetative stage, are enjoying their environment.

The collection of gland heads for hash makes for a great finale.

Buds are placed in paper bags for the final few days of drying to even out moisture levels.

Fresh weed weighs a lot. Don't forget to support it adequately.

Beware of high humidity levels (65%+) while drying.

A cool, dark area with a good amount of airflow is optimal for drying.

Getting the perfect balance of nutrients, environmental factors and growing method can be challenging but look at the rewards.

Just enough space has been left to manoeuvre between tables and reach the plants.

The flowering room is being used to dry the harvest utilizing the carbon filter for odor concerns.

Particularly during the final weeks of flowering the buds should be inspected regularly.

Proper storage of the stash will maintain potency as well as taste and smell.

A vacuum sealer is an excellent way to store cannabis and contain the odor for extended periods of time.

A smooth, non-porous should be used to collect the gland heads from the dry sieve screen.

After the dry sieve process a thick layer of gland heads is easily scraped into a pile with a card.

This mound of powder (often referred to as kief at this stage) is ready to be pressed into a piece of hash.

Hung buds usually take about 7-8 days to fully dry.

They're ready when the stem in the middle of the bud makes a snap sound when bent.

Pointing a large fan directly on the buds may dry them too quickly but airflow is important.

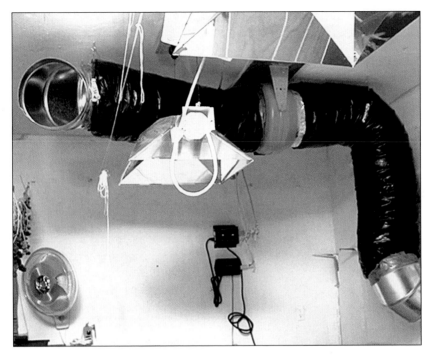

Each bend in the line lowers a fan's output so keep the ducting as straight as possible.

A quality reflector increases the amount of lumens traveling from the bulb to the plants below.

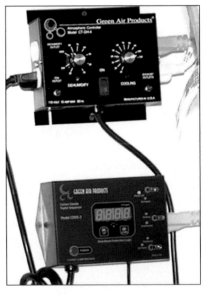

Control units for ventilation and CO2 systems are popular because quality air is as important as lighting and vastly impacts the environmental conditions.

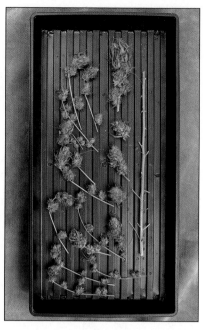

A dried plant about to be manicured.

Side branches are cut from the main stem to make handling them easier while trimming.

Manicuring is being done over a screen to collect the falling gland heads for hash.

An organized trimming area makes the job far more enjoyable.

These will be bag-ready in a few quick snips.

A bountiful harvest of finely manicured buds and a bowl of quality shake to be processed into hash.

A potent Cannabis plant has some of the most tantalizing flowers you'll ever see!

with special tape. The donor signs his initials to the tape confirming the identity of the urine and indicating he has witnessed the sample splitting. The urine is then placed in a special transportation bag that the donor also initials. After a final signature on the chain of custody form, the donor is finished. The entire process usually takes less than 15 minutes.

Probation Drug Testing

A probation test is a little different than most types of drug tests. During probation an individual forfeits certain inalienable rights, such as the right to vote, bear arms, normal search and seizure, purchase alcohol, and a fair drug test. For this reason, there really are no rules or regulations for drug testing individuals on probation.

Most probation tests are screens or FPIA screens. This means no GC/MS will be performed as a confirmation to a positive screening result. The individual on probation will fail the screen if taking high levels of ibuprofen or certain over-the-counter sinus medication. With no GC/MS to back up the screen, the individual goes back to jail for simply taking too much of or the wrong medications.

If taking a probation test the best choice is abstinence. If the individual chooses not to follow this path, the two best choices of products are Quick Fix synthetic urine or the Absolute Detox Drink.

Inconclusive Lab Reports

There are several types of results on a drug test other than pass or fail. Two of these are *sample too dilute,* or *unable to obtain valid results.* These two results sound similar but are very different from the laboratory's viewpoint.

Sample Too Dilute

This simply means too much water or liquid was consumed before the test. The creatinine and/or specific gravity were too low because the sample was too diluted. This can happen for lots of reasons, like drinking coffee, exercising in the morning or intentionally diluting the sample to pass a drug test. When this happens, the labs ask the individual to return and provide another sample. By law, an individual cannot be fired for continually providing samples that are too dilute. For a preemployment drug screen, most employers will give a candidate only two chances to provide an adequate sample.

Unable to Obtain Valid Results

These results are from a smoker who fit in one or more of the following categories:

1. Tester is a heavy smoker (daily).

2. The tester took the test in the morning.

3. The tester skipped breakfast.

4. The tester is more than 20 pounds overweight.

5. Tester used Urine LuckTM additive.

6. The lab was unable to find an adulterant.

The tester smokes a lot so the EMIT screen is highly positive, which indicates marijuana usage. The sample is then sent on to the GC/MS for confirmation. The confirmation comes back negative for marijuana, but the original screen showed highly positive. Now the lab has conflicting results with a highly positive screen and negative GC/MS due to the use of Urine Luck®.

At this point the lab suspects usage of adulterant and looks for telltale signs such as acids, chromates, gluteraldehyde, nitrites, or pyridine. When no additive is detected the EMIT and GC/MS are performed again to rule out human error. When the second set of results come back similar to the first set of results, the sample is ruled unsuitable. The tester will then be asked to come back in and provide another sample. The tester can pass this test by getting the screen to be only positive and not highly positive. This is accomplished via careful preparation. Basically the individual needs to stop burning fat and lower the THCA content of their urine. The following is a list of what to do to lower THCA levels in urine:

1. Stop smoking.

2. No heavy exercise within 48 hours of test.

3. Take a vitamin B complex with each meal 48 hours before test.

4. If your stomach permits, take two aspirin with each meal.

5. Schedule test for the afternoon.

6. Urinate six to eight times before test.

7. Eat lots of proteins and carbohydrates.

8. Don't skip meals, especially breakfast (three per day).

9. Avoid foods high in sugar, fruits, and fruit juices.

10. Use the entire vial of Urine Luck.

11. Drink lots of fluids.

12. Relax.

Urine Constituents

Urinalysis is one of the most powerful diagnostic tools used in the medical field today. Hundreds of tests can be performed on an individual urine sample to determine the condition of the donor. Urine contains thousands of different types of compounds. It is literally the aqueous trash of the body. A cup of coffee has over ten thousand compounds alone. Drug testing laboratories have narrowed the choice down to two or three tests for determination of a suitable sample. If the urine sample falls out of the parameters, the sample will be labeled "too dilute, unsuitable, or adulterated" depending on which parameter is incorrect.

pH is a relative measure of acidity or basicity, with a range of 0–14. In the middle is 7.0, which is considered neutral. Acids have low pHs—usually less than 1. Bases, such as bleach, have high pHs—around 10.5. Urine samples must have a pH in the range of 4.5–9.0. Both acids and bases will destroy drug metabolites, so the labs check to see if any are present. If a chemical additive is used, it should leave the pH relatively unchanged, within the 4.5–9.0 ranges.

Specific Gravity (SG) is a fancy word for density. Simply drinking tons of water can fool a drug test. By measuring the SG a lab can detect if the donor is trying to beat a drug test by dilution. If the sample is too dilute, the SG of the urine sample will be below 1.005g/ml. A lab result like this might come back as inclusive, test not performed, or sample too dilute. It is against the law to fail an individual for providing sample(s) which are too dilute. On the flip side of the coin is high density. If a sample has a density above 1.020g/ml, then an additive has been used. It is considered proof of adulteration if the SG is at this level and it is legal to fail an individual for having a SG above 1.020g/ml.

Creatinine is a measure of kidney functions to determine how dilute or concentrated a urine sample is. The creatinine has to be below 20mg/dl for the sample to be considered too dilute. Creatinine levels above the 20mg/dl are considered acceptable. Creatinine is found in all muscle tissue and originally begins as creatine. Creatine passes through the body in two ways. First is consumption, as it is found in all types of meat. The second is production by the body. As muscles are broken down and rebuilt creatine is converted to creatinine. Creatinine in high levels is toxic, and so the kidneys filter out the creatinine from the blood and pass it on to the bladder. Creatinine extraction from the blood is at a very constant rate and the level in the urine is constant, varying only with the length between urinations. Therefore creatinine levels less than 20mg/dl indicate a bladder that is continually being emptied in an attempt to pass a drug test.Labs sometimes look at other constituents of urine with a ten-panel dipstick called a multistick. The ten tests on the multistick are:

1. Leukocytes
2. Nitrite
3. Urobilinogen
4. Protein
5. pH
6. Blood
7. Specific Gravity
8. Ketone
9. Bilirubin
10. Glucose

Adulterating Compounds/Acids

Acids were the very first type of urine adulterants used back in the early to mid 1990s. Hydrochloric and nitric acid were the most common types of acids used. The marijuana metabolite undergoes a 10–50% deterioration in an acid environment. The laboratories easily stopped the use of acid as an adulterant by simply checking the pH. Any sample with a pH of less than 4.0 was considered adulterated. The use of an acid-based additive usually left the pH 3 or less.

Chromates (Cr_2O_4) Chromates are a common compound found in vitamins and dietary aids such as Metabolife, and bodybuilding formulas. Chromates can be called several things, including chrome, chromium 6, and chromium picolinate; all of these are the same compounds under different names. The chromates give the urine an orangish color. Chromium 3 is a different species altogether and has a green color. If an individual adds chrome to a urine sample and it turns green, the chrome has been converted from chromium 6 to chromium 3, indicating the presence of a reducing sugar. This is common in diabetes individuals. In the appropriate doses, chromates are vital to the body for muscular development/toning and mental health. Older formulations of Urine Luck 5.4–5.9 contain the compounds of chromates. If an individual has too high a level of chromates in his urine,the sample may be labeled as adulterated. However, if the individual claims to be taking the dietary aids at three to four times higher than recommend dosage, the adulteration claims from chromates may be waived.

Glutaraldehyde is the compound that was used for the first formulation by Clear Choice. Because the compound is highly toxic there is no reason for it to be in urine. Labs routinely check for the compound with a multi-stick, which has a patch for aldehydes. If the Glutaraldehyde is detected, the sample is labeled adulterated and the test is not performed.

Nitrites (NO$_2$) can be found in foods such as poultry, pork, and drinking water. The body can also produce nitrites naturally, however this is usually a sign of a urinary tract infection. For this, small amounts of nitrite are permitted in the urine. Any sample with nitrites above 500mg/ml (microgram per milliliter) is consider forensically defensible as proof of adulteration. Klear and all the Urine Luck 3.0 series had nitrites in the formulations. This is why the labs continue to check for the nitrite.

Pyridine is one of the compounds found in Urine Luck 5.0–5.3. This compound can also be found in some over-the-counter medications such as Uristat and Azo-Standard. These products are used to ease the pain of a bladder infection. For this reason a tester can normally "get off" if pyridine is found in the urine. The tester must purchase medicine at the drug store and take it back to the lab. The tester can normally get a second test once he or she shows the lab that pyridine is an ingredient in these over-the-counter products.

Myths about Drug Testing

Goldenseal is a root extract available in a solid or liquid form. The root supposedly has special properties to rid the body of harmful toxins. This might be true for some toxins, but goldenseal does not rid the body of marijuana. How the false story of taking goldenseal to pass a drug test got started is not known. There have been multiple scientific studies performed to confirm goldenseal does not work at all in this capacity

Lots of people have passed drug tests after using goldenseal and swear by it. These people were probably not big pot smokers. The goldenseal did not help them out; it was the gal. of water they had to drink with goldenseal. These people passed by simple dilution of their urine sample. They would have passed the drug test anyway by just drinking the gal. of water without the goldenseal.

How to Prepare for a Marijuana Drug Test

Most people taking a drug test are concerned with marijuana because it stays in the body the longest. This is because the body stores the marijuana metabolite in the fat cells of the body. The short-term and long-term approaches to cleaning the body for a marijuana drug test are exactly opposite.

Days 0–2 before the test—Stop smoking, eat large meals, no skipping meals, no exercising, no sugars, fruits or fruit juices. This is the exact opposite of the steps given earlier above. If the marijuana is being excreted the individual will test positive. At this point the individual being tested does not want to excrete any marijuana but keep it all in his body. This is accomplished by preventing fat from burning. It is very simple; get rid of fat and fail your test. Therefore the test subject must stop the body from burning fat by eating correctly and not exercising.

Days 2–30 before the test—Stop smoking, diet and exercise. These three steps, which burn fat, also rid the body of the marijuana metabolite. The marijuana metabolites are stored in the fat cells. To keep from testing positive the marijuana has to be removed from the fat cells in the body. It is very simple; get rid of fat and get rid of marijuana. The marijuana is then excreted through the urine and bowels. However, the future test subject does not want to be excreting marijuana on the day of the test.

False Positives

False positive is a technical term for a substance, which tests positive falsely for another compound. A common example is poppy seed testing positive for opiates. This would be a false positive. This is the purpose of the confirmation step of the drug test, which utilizes the GC/MS. The GC/MS can differentiate between ibuprofen and marijuana, or poppy seeds and opiates.

Drugs of Misuse

Name	Class	Trade Name	Nickname	Detection (in days)
Marijuana	Hallucinogen	None	Pot	5–30
LSD	Hallucinogen	None	Acid	1.5–5
Phencyclidine	Hallucinogen	None	PCP, Angel Dust	14–30
MDMA	Hallucinogen	None	Ecstasy	7
Amphetamines	Stimulants	Benzedrine	Ice, crank	1–4
Methamphetamine	Stimulants	Desoxyn	Speed	1–4
Cocaine	Stimulants	None	Coke	1–6
Codeine	Analgesics*	Empirin		1–6
Morphine	Analgesics*	Roxanol	Morph	1–6
Hydocodone	Analgesics*	Vicodin	Dilles	1–6
Heroin	Analgesics*	Diacetylmor	Smack	1–6
Oxycodone	Analgesics*	Percodan	Percs	1–6
Meperdine	Analgesics*	Demerol	Demmies	1–7
Propoxypene	Analgesics*	Darvon	None	1–3
Phenobarbital	Barbiturates	Luminal	Downers	2–21
Secobarbital	Barbiturates	Seconal	Barbs, reds	2–21
Diazepam	Benzoddiaze	Valium	Downers	3–45
Alprazolam	Xanax	Xanax	Downers	3–45
Methaqualone	Methaqualone	Quaalude	Ludes	12–14

* painkillers

Drugs that Test as False Positives

Marijuana Over-the-counter NSAIDs (non-steroid anti-inflammatory drugs) such as ibuprofen, Advil, Nuprin or Pamprin.

Prescription NSAIDs anaprox, Tolectin, ifenoprofen, Lodine, Motrin, etc.

Amphetamines Over the counter remedies that contain ephedrine, psudoephedrine, propylephrine, or desoxyephedrine. These medications include Nyquil, Contac, Sudafed, and Allerest 12 hour, Tylenol Sinus Gelcaps, Vicks inhaler.

Cocaine prescription antibiotic Amoxicillin.

Opiates Emprin, Tylenol with codeine, rifampicin, prescriptions with vicodin, Percodan, percowygesic.

Barbiturates Fiorinall for tension headaches or Phenobarbital, Dilantin.

Benzodiazepines most prescription sleeping pills and anti-anxiety medications.

Drugs by Type

Narcotics	Hallucinogens	Steroids	Depressants	Stimulants
Alfentanil	Bufotenine	Dianabol	Amobarbital	Amphetamines
Cocaine	Cannabinoid	Nandrolone	Benzodiazepine	Benzedrine
Codeine	LSD		Chloral Hydrate	Butyl Nitrite
Crack Cocaine	MDA		Diazepam	Dextroamphetamine
Fentanyl	MDEA		Glutethimide	Methlyamphetamine
Heroin*	Mescaline		Meprobamate	Methylphenidate
Hydromorphone	MMDA		Methaqualone	Phenmetrazine
Ice	Phencyclidine (PCP)		Nitrous Oxide	
Meperidine	Psilocybin		Pentobarbital	
Morphine			Phenobarbital	
Nalorphine			Secobarbital	
Opium				
Oxycodone				
Propoxyphene				

*tests as an Opiate

18

Cannabis
a Crime?

Despite a growing relaxation in the enforcement of laws relating to cannabis, the majority (somewhere between 70–75%) of drugs offences relate to cannabis. By far most of these (over 90%) are simple possession charges, which can result in anything from an informal warning to a custodial sentence of several years, depending on the amount of cannabis in question, the area in the country you are in, who the arresting officer is and what the judge's personal opinions are. This inconsistency in the treatment of "cannabis criminals' is widespread and often referred to as being "justice by postcode'.

Statistics for drug-related arrests take some time to compile, and thus the effects of any recent changes in policy, official or not, will not be reflected immediately. At this time figures up to 1999 have been officially published.

Your Rights on Arrest

Please note that UKCIA who supplied us with this information can accept no responsibility for its accuracy. If you find yourself in trouble with the police seek the advice of a qualified legal practitioner as soon as possible.

When dealing with the police it's a good idea to be co-operative and polite, they can cause you hassle much easier than you can them. It's also worth noting that many of them are sympathetic to cannabis users, so not being confrontational could make all the difference. In practice you have few enforceable rights against the police: even evidence illegally obtained by them can be used in Court. However the following information may help:

Always Remember:

Don't get drawn into conversations with the police. Even apparently innocent remarks can be used against you. Keeping your mouth shut until you have spoken to a lawyer is often a good idea if you think you are in serious trouble. If the police suspect you have committed any offence, you can be arrested if you refuse to give your name and address, or if the police are not satisfied with the address you have given.

If in doubt do and say nothing until you have contacted an attorney.

If anything you ask for is refused, ask why and remember the reason given.

As soon as possible make full notes of what has happened and give them to your lawyer. These can be used as evidence in court. If you have been injured go and see a doctor as soon as possible, giving a full explanation of your injuries.

On The Street—If You Are Stopped:

Check police identity: ask to see their warrant card and remember any details. If they're in uniform remember their numbers.

If you're stopped and searched in the street, ask why. The police can stop you in any public place if they suspect you are in possession of "prohibited articles". On the street, the police can only search outer clothing such as coats, gloves etc. If the police suspect that you are in possession of illegal drugs they can take you to a police station for a more thorough search without formally arresting you. police should show evidence of identity before searching you and must keep a record of the search.

For more information on laws in the states, see NORML's (www.norml.org) state-by-state breakdown of fines, prison sentences and penalties.

If You Are Taken To A Police Station:

Don't rely on any legal advice the police offer you.

Ask if you have been arrested and if so why. Ask to see the custody officer as soon as you arrive at the police station and make sure that the starting time of your detention is correctly recorded. Remember that the reason for your arrest and detention is recorded at the top of the police custody record, as is the need for the police to ask whether you need a lawyer or relative informed. Make sure you know why you are being held. The nature of the possible charges determines your entitlements to rights at the police station.

Ask the custody officer to phone your lawyer or the public defender. Insist that a friend or relative is informed of your arrest. You have the right to have someone informed without delay unless you are being detained in connection with a "serious arrestable offence." If you are being held in connection with a serious arrestable offence, police can delay access to attorneys and relatives in specific circumstances. If they do refuse access ask why and insist that the reason is recorded on your custody sheet. Even if the police are confident that there are grounds for refusing access to a lawyer or relatives, they have to allow access before 36 hours has expired.

Ask to be charged or released. Unless you are suspected of a serious offence, you must be charged or released within 24 hours of detention and you have the right to consult an attorney at any time. Make sure that you request to see a lawyer and the time of the request is recorded by the custody officer. Whatever the police say you should NEVER sign the custody sheet saying that you don't want to see a lawyer.

In order to get bail (released from the police station before going to court) you'll probably have to satisfy the police that you have a fixed address.

If Your Home Or Workplace Is To Be Searched:

The police do not always need a warrant or your permission to enter your home to arrest someone, but in theory they should name the person sought. Searches can sometimes be conducted without a warrant, but in all cases you should ask the police to identify themselves and ask the reason of the search. You are entitled to see a copy of the search warrant.

For information and help in dealing with the police and the criminal courts in the US and UK contact:

NORML and the NORML Foundation

1600 K Street, NW, Suite 501

Washington, DC 20006-2832

Phone: (202) 483-5500 Fax: (202) 483-0057

www.norml.org

RELEASE

020 7729 9904 (24 hour help line)

388 Old Street

LONDON EC1V 9LT

www.release.org.uk

Policy Options—Decriminalization and alternatives

Is Decriminalization Desirable?

12.1.1 If decriminalization involves removing criminal penalties for possession (e.g., of less than a designated amount), but leaving supply of drugs in the hands of criminals, there would be some benefits, but many problems would remain.

(a) Benefits

(i) The move would be popular among users of drugs, reducing the levels of conflict between young people, police and society.

(ii) Removing the threat of a criminal record (and/or expunging existing criminal records for simple possession) would reduce the financial impact of an arrest on the individual and society.

(iii) The credibility of government messages among wide sections of society may increase. Our recent survey showed that the least trusted sources of drugs information were Government Ministers, the Drugs Czar, and the Police.

(iv) Society as a whole could benefit from a more tolerant climate of individual rights and responsibilities, with a less authoritarian relationship between the government and its citizens.

(b) Problems

(i) Leaving civil penalties in place for possession would not remove the "naughty" or "forbidden fruit" image of drugs, and would decrease the attractions of usage.

(ii) Civil fines would be paid by a small minority of users (those who are caught), and would therefore represent a very inefficient form of taxation.

(iii) If demand increases, the untaxed profits of drug traffickers would increase, and with this the levels of corruption and violence associated with any illegal trade.

(iv) Decriminalization would mean users still having to get their supply from a source. If the "legal" source of drug (GP, licensing) is inferior in quality to the "illegal" sources, then the criminal control of the drug trade would not be halted. To be effective the criminal element that controls the supply of drugs must be put out of business. This can be achieved by ensuring the supply of drugs is at least of a standard users are already accustomed to. In the case of cannabis the easiest solution would be to allow anyone to grow their own supply for own personal use only. This would enable relatively law abiding citizens who only smoke cannabis to avoid visiting criminal suppliers.

(v) The government would not benefit from Excise Duty revenues payable on (particularly) cannabis. Our surveys have indicated that such duties, along with reduced enforcement costs, could generate between US \$4 billion (£2 billion) and US \$2.5 billion (£5 billion) per year for the exchequer.

12.2 What are the practical alternatives?

12.2.1 *Status Quo*—No change in legislation. Public opinion is steadily moving toward support of drug law reform and some form of liberalization. Opportunities have been missed in the past (e.g. following Wooton Report and 1979 ACMD report) to reduce the criminal status of cannabis, and those failures are at least in part responsible for the levels of drug problems we face today (ten times as many drug users/arrests today as when the Misuse of Drugs Act was introduced).

12.2.2 *Reduce penalties* (reschedule cannabis to class C, Ecstasy/LSD etc. to class B)—These proposals from the Police Foundation in essence echo those of the ACMD in 1979. This would represent tinkering with the system, as the damaging effects of a criminal record for drugs on the individual and society would remain.

12.2.3 *Regulation/Licensing:* In the long term, some form of regulated supply of cannabis must be considered. The extent to which licensing could cover existing illicit preparations would depend on international agreements (i.e. for cannabis resin or herbal imported from countries where production remains illegal), although domestic production could supply the bulk of the UK cannabis market. The objective of such models would be to satisfy existing demand without creating additional demand. Different models may be appropriate for different drugs:

(a) *Prescription and dispensation from Pharmacy*—this could be appropriate for opiates, but would impact on NHS resources (GPs' time). Individual use could be regulated.

(b) *Individual licenses to possess/purchase*—Users could apply for a licence which would enable them to buy (e.g. opiates) in appropriate amounts at or near cost price.

(c) *Licenses to produce*—cannabis growers could be allowed a "duty free" surface area or lighting wattage, but could apply for licenses to produce larger amounts. Duty could be levied at quarterly intervals based on the available surface area, subject to regular inspection.

(d) *Licensed supply*

(i) Outlets such as "coffee shops" could be licensed to supply cannabis, with appropriate restrictions on advertising, age restrictions (as with alcohol or tobacco), and location (e.g. not within 1/4 mile of a school).

(ii) Alternatives would include a "club" model whereby licensed clubs could supply cannabis to their members, who would have to produce a membership card. Reciprocal agreements could allow cards to be valid in all clubs within an association.

12.2.4 *Free Market (Legalization)*—This would involve drugs being sold in normal retail outlets (e.g. supermarkets/tobacconists) without significant controls. Excise duties could be levied on producers and/or wholesalers as with tobacco or alcohol. This policy would probably lead to increased usage (particularly among middle-aged or elderly citizens), although this would also generate the highest duty revenues for government.

SO! You say. What if we get caught?

Well the whole thing is still a gray area and the sentence you get is pretty much a lottery of zip codes. Some areas will carry greater penalties than others, and the rules are constantly changing. For information on marijuana legal penalties, please see the following websites:

NORML State-by-State Laws

http://www.norml.org/index.cfm?Group_ID=4516

Yahooka

www.yahooka.com

Erowid Cannabis Vault: Legal Status

http://www.erowid.org/plants/cannabis/cannabis_law.shtml

19

What the Doctors Say

Before you are launched into a profusion of positive reports from the medical industry, I would be neglecting my duty if I didn't provide you first of all with reported negatives that have been attributed to the use of cannabis.

It has to be said that the smoking and inhalation of anything with frequency and duration can cause health problems. Although some users experience health problems from cannabis use, in most cases these are occasional and of mild severity.

Overall negative effects can include paranoia, dry mouth, respiratory problems and nervousness/racing heart. Other effects may be negative or inconvenient in certain settings or situations including reduced ability to concentrate, impaired memory, apathy, tiredness, and confusion. Side effects tend to increase with lifetime use as users age, and they often report that the anxiety-producing and uncomfortable effects increase, with the euphoria decreasing.

Contraindications

Driving while using must be avoided. While there is very little information from the various studies, of cannabis affects on driving, it is considered prudent to avoid practicing that type of activity while under the influence of any psychoactive or intoxicating substance. Treat smoking as you would alcohol, except you aren't allowed two joints as you might be allowed two pints of beer. There has to be zero tolerance. There have been studies that shown drivers who use alcohol and cannabis as a combination are far less capable than when taking either substance alone. Other studies have proven that cannabis causes impairment in driving performance, but that users often are aware of the impairment and compensate by driving more carefully.

Addiction

Of course regular participation in any enjoyable experience can become addictive, from sex to smoking. It's therefore no surprise to find that smoking cannabis can lead to psychological dependence for some people, making it hard for them to stop. It's been estimated that between 5 and 10% of people who try cannabis will become daily users at some time during their life, although most of these will have given up the habit by the age of 30 and few remain regular smokers after 40. Most people do not experience signs of physical addiction, but for regular daily users, mild to medium withdrawal symptoms occur if use is halted, generally lasting for less than a week, although they have been known to last as long as six weeks.

Long-Term Health Problems

Lung and throat problems are the main health problems that have been experienced, including coughing, reduced lung capacity and increased frequency of throat and lung infections. The results regarding possible long-term carcinogenic (cancer-causing) effects of cannabis smoking are still somewhat controversial but none the less a concern.

Poisoning

No published deaths have been confirmed from cannabis-only poisoning. However a small number of people have reported serious cannabis allergies which cause unexpectedly intense reactions, throat and lung irritation, etc.

Taking It to Heart

The heart rate increases when using cannabis, so it could potentially increase risks of heart problems in those at risk of heart disease. Although its findings were weak and based on only a small number of individuals, one study found that cannabis use increased the risk of heart attack in men over 40. In a large study of 65,000 individuals in California by Sidney et al in 1997, cannabis was not found to increase mortality rates among users under 50.

Mental Illness

Studies made of psychoactives, including cannabis, have indicated that use can precipitate neuroses or psychoses in those who are already at risk. It has also been shown that cannabis use does not appear to increase the risk of psychosis in otherwise healthy individuals.

British Medical Association Press Release 1997
BMA Report Calls for Change in Law and Development of New Cannabis-Based Medicines

In November of 1997 the British Medical Association published a major report on the therapeutic uses of cannabis. Therapeutic Uses of Cannabis drew a distinction between recreational misuse and using the drug to relieve pain. The report acknowledged that thousands of people resort to taking cannabis illegally in an attempt to ease their distressing symptoms, for example, glaucoma, muscle spasms, chronic pain and nausea. The report included moving accounts from individual patients who have used cannabis in desperation when conventional drugs failed them. However, because of the current state of the law, much of the evidence from those claiming relief is anecdotal.

The BMA report Therapeutic Uses of Cannabis examined the scientific evidence for the wider medicinal use of cannabinoid derivatives of cannabis for a range of medical problems: nausea and vomiting associated with cancer chemotherapy, muscle spasticity, pain, anorexia, epilepsy, glaucoma, bronchial asthma, mood disorders, psychiatric conditions, and hypertension. The report underpinned the policy of the BMA that certain additional cannabinoids should be legalized for wider medicinal use. It set the research agenda and identified the legal steps that needed to be taken before new treatments could be developed.

However the report also warned that cannabis contains more than 400 chemical compounds, (including more than 60 cannabinoids) some of which are potentially harmful to health. It has been estimated that smoking a cannabis cigarette (containing only herbal cannabis) leads to three times greater tar inhalation than smoking a tobacco cigarette. The levels of tar retained in the respiratory tract are also three times higher. Chronic cannabis smoking, like tobacco smoking, therefore increases the risk of cardiovascular disease, bronchitis, emphysema and probably carcinomas of the lung. Adverse effects of chronic use include suppression of ovulation in women, decreased sperm count in men, sedation, and anxiety.

Street and illicit cannabis can also contain adulterants, including pesticides, as well as naturally occurring contaminants such as microbes and fungi which can pose a risk to immuno-suppressed patients such as people with AIDS. Because cannabis contains so many different cannabinoids in varying combinations, simply smoking or eating the drug will not tell us which agents are beneficial. The report therefore recommended further research, including investigating the long-term effects of cannabinoids on chronic conditions.

To facilitate research, the BMA recommends a change in the law. It suggests that advice should be given from the World Health Organisation (WHO) to the United Nations Commission on Narcotic Drugs to reschedule certain cannabinoids under the United Nations Convention on Psychotropic Substances. The Home Office could then amend the Misuse of Drugs Act in response. If WHO feels unable to give such advice, the Government should consider changing the Misuse of Drugs Act to allow cannabinoids to be prescribed to patients with particular medical conditions whose symptoms are being inadequately controlled under present arrangements. A central registry should be kept of those patients to allow follow up of long term effects.

In November 2002 the British Lung Foundation issued their "Smoking Gun" report on the effects of cannabis on your lungs. It's my duty as a responsible author to extend this BLF report to you and uphold the spirit in which it was complied not only as a gesture to extend their works but as an echo of their intention.

Many young people will make decisions about whether they wish to use cannabis or not regardless of its legal status. We have a duty to ensure that they do so with full knowledge of the risks associated with smoking cannabis.

The Impact of Cannabis Smoking on Respiratory Health

What has been consistently missing from the public debate on the safety or otherwise of cannabis as compared to other illegal drugs is the impact of smoking cannabis on respiratory health and the possible link with nicotine addiction in the form of tobacco smoking.

This report sets out to identify existing scientific and medical research on cannabis smoking and respiratory health. It identifies what conclusions it is possible to draw from the existing evidence and highlights gaps in our knowledge which require further research.

The aim of this report is to ensure that those taking part in the debate on cannabis and those engaged in promoting health education to our young people have the fullest possible information on the medical and scientific evidence of the impact of cannabis smoking on respiratory health.

Summary of Findings and Recommendations

While there is a wealth of research into the health impact of tobacco smoking, there is relatively little on the effects of cannabis smoking.

Research investigating whether the inhalation of cannabis smoke causes damage to the lungs and airways focuses on whether this effect is independent of the effects of tobacco smoke or not. In general, die studies indicate that there is an increased negative health impact on those who smoke cannabis compared to those who do not smoke at all. When cannabis is smoked together with tobacco then the effects are additive. However, what is not clear is whether it is the addition of the cannabis or the tobacco which is more harmful or whether this is the result of the combined effects of equally harmful substances.

Studies comparing the clinical effects of habitual cannabis smokers versus non-smokers demonstrate a significantly higher prevalence of chronic and acute respiratory symptoms such as chronic cough and sputum production, wheeze and acute bronchitis episodes. 3–4 Cannabis cigarettes a day are associated with the same evidence of acute and chronic bronchitis and the same degree of damage to the bronchial mucosa as 20 or more tobacco cigarettes a day.

Cannabis smoking is likely to weaken the immune system. Infections of the lung are due to a combination of smoking-related damage to the cells lining the bronchial passage (the fine hair-like projection on these cells filter out inhaled micro-organisms) and impairment of the principal immune cells in the small air sacs caused by cannabis. The evidence concerning a possible link between cannabis smoking and Chronic Obstructive Pulmonary Disease (COPD) has not yet been conclusively established. A number of studies indicate a causal relationship between the two whereas others contradict these findings.

Research linking cannabis smoking to the development of respiratory cancer exists although there have also been conflicting findings. Not only does the tar in a cannabis cigarette contain many of the same known carcinogens as tobacco smoke but the concentrations of these are up to 50% higher in the smoke of a cannabis cigarette. It also deposits four times as much tar on the respiratory tract as an unfiltered cigarette of the same weight. Smokers of cannabis and tobacco have shown a greater increase in cellular abnormalities indicating a cumulative effect of smoking both.

The THC in cannabis has been shown to have a short term bronchodilator effect. This has lead to suggestions that THC may have therapeutic benefits in asthma. However, the noxious gases, chronic airway irritation or malignancy after long term use associated with smoking would seem likely to negate these benefits.

Recommendations

Prom a clinical perspective the main effects of smoking cannabis on the lungs are increased risk of pulmonary infections and respiratory cancers. Benzpyrene, a known constituent of the tar of cannabis cigarettes has been shown to promote alterations in one of the most common tumour suppressor genes, p.53, hence facilitating the development of respiratory cancer. Gene p.53 is thought to play a role in 75% of all lung cancers. The British Lung Foundation recommends a public health education campaign aimed at young people to ensure that they are finally aware of the increased risk of pulmonary infections and respiratory cancers associated with cannabis smoking.

The increased potency of the cannabis smoked today compared to the cannabis smoked twenty or thirty years ago suggests that earlier studies may underestimate the effects of cannabis smoking. In addition the lack of conclusive evidence concerning the link between cannabis smoking and Chronic Obstructive Pulmonary Disease (COPD) underlines the need for further research. The British Lung Foundation recommends that further research is undertaken to take into account the increased potency of today's cannabis and to establish what link (if any) there is between COPD and cannabis smoking.

Scope of This Report and Background

This report surveys the current medical and scientific research into the direct effects of smoking cannabis - both alone and in combination with tobacco on the smoker's respiratory health. The report is divided into two parts the first part outlines the constituents of cannabis, the amount of cannabis smoked and the dynamics of smoking cannabis compared with tobacco. The second part surveys the findings of the existing published research into the biological effects on respiratory health of cannabis which is smoked, both in the short-term and long-term. Full references to the individual publications are included at the end of the report. Prevalence of cannabis smoking in UK: Cannabis is the most widely consumed illegal drug to the UK by gross weight (it is estimated that 486,224kg were consumed in 1998, this is roughly the weight of 7,000 people put together). It is often smoked together with tobacco although it can also be ingested in the form of "hash cookies" or taken as cannabis oil.

Source: *Annual Report on the UK Drug Situation 2001, Drug Scope, London*

Constituents of cannabis

The smoke of the same quantity of cannabis and tobacco smoke contains the same constituents and quantities of chemicals known to be toxic to respiratory tissue as tobacco smoke, apart from nicotine. This includes carbon monoxide, bronchial irritants, tumour initiators, tumour promoters and cancer producing agents. Tar from cannabis cigarettes contains up to 50% higher concentrations of the carcinogens benzanthracenes and Benzpyrenes than tobacco smoke.

There are three main species of cannabis, Cannabis sativa, Cannabis indica and Cannabis ruderalis. The plant is also known as hemp. As a drug of abuse it is either taken in the form of herbal cannabis (marijuana) which consists of the dried leaves and female flower heads or as cannabis resin (hashish) which is the resin secreted by the leaves and flower heads and may be compressed into blocks.

Cannabis contains over 400 compounds including 60 different cannabinoids (plant derivatives unique to cannabis) the most abundant of which is tetrahydrocanabinol (THC). This accounts for the psychoactive properties of cannabis. It is highly soluble in fats and rapidly absorbed in the respiratory and gastrointestinal tract lining. The intoxicating effects depend on the way in which cannabis is taken. Blood concentrations after oral ingestion are only about 25-30% to those obtained when cannabis is smoked. About 50% of the THC in a cigarette of herbal cannabis is inhaled in the mainstream smoke, nearly all of which is absorbed through the lungs, rapidly entering the bloodstream and reaching the brain within minutes.

A greater amount of tar is inhaled from the cannabis cigarette butt rather than its tip. There is also a higher concentration of carbon monoxide and THC in the smoke from the butt end. The effect of the carbon monoxide is to produce high concentrations of carboxyhaemoglobin in the blood, which interferes with the transport of oxygen around the body. This is likely to be due to decreased filtration of insoluble particles and differential burn rates. The clinical implication of this is that smoking cannabis cigarettes down to the butt is more harmful than smoking a similar quantity of cannabis cigarettes to a longer butt length.

Other cannabinoids which interact with THC although are not actually psychoactive in themselves are cannabidiol and cannabinol. The amounts and proportions of the various cannabinoids in each plant vary from strain to strain, and can be adjusted by breeding.

Amount of Cannabis smoked

THC is present in varying concentrations in the stalks, leaves, flowers and seeds of the plant as well as the resin secreted by the female plant. This has an impact on the potency of different cannabis preparations. Furthermore, sophisticated cultivation has increased the potency of cannabis products over the last 20 years. Whereas the average cannabis cigarette of the 1960s and 1970s contained about 0.0004 oz. (10 mg) of THC today it may contain up to 0.005 oz. (150 mg) of THC, or 0.01 oz. (300 mg) if laced with hashish oil. This means that the modern cannabis smoker may be exposed to greater doses of THC than in the 1960s and 1970s, which in turn means that studies investigating the long-term effects of smoking cannabis have to be interpreted cautiously.

Dynamics of Smoking Cannabis versus Tobacco

Significant differences have been noted in the dynamics of smoking cannabis and tobacco including an approximately two-thirds larger puff volume, a one-third greater depth of inhalation and a fourfold longer breath-holding time with cannabis than with tobacco. This means that there is a greater respiratory burden of carbon monoxide and smoke particles than when smoking a singular quantity of tobacco. Similarly with tar, it has been estimated that smoking a cannabis cigarette results in a fourfold greater amount of tar inhaled and retention in the respiratory tract or one-third more tar than smoking a tobacco cigarette (due to the longer breath holding time for cannabis and differences in filtering characteristics of the two types of cigarette).

Effects of Smoking Cannabis on Respiratory Health

The British Medical Association estimates that smoking a cannabis cigarette containing only herbal cannabis leads to an approximately fivefold increase in blood carboxyhaemoglobin concentration (which is formed by carbon monoxide reacting with the oxygen carrying particle haemoglobin in red blood cells, thereby reducing the transport of oxygen).

Within minutes of smoking cannabis significant decreases in airway resistance and increases in specific airway conductance have been observed in healthy individuals, which persist for at least one hour. This is caused by THC which has subsequently been investigated for its possible therapeutic use in diseases such as asthma.

From a clinical perspective, the main effects of smoking cannabis on the lungs are pulmonary infections and respiratory cancer.

Immune Responses

Several studies indicate that smoking cannabis has a negative effect on the immune system. THC has been shown to decrease the function of several white blood cells (T cells, natural killer cells and macrophages) that help protect the lungs against micro-organisms. Alveolar macrophages in particular are important in regulating lung immunity and their central location in the lung's air sacs means that they are exposed to very large amounts of cannabis smoke.

Twice as many alveolar macrophages as normal have been found to be produced in the lungs of cannabis smokers and three times as many in cannabis & tobacco smokers. These macrophages have been found to be considerably larger and contain more ingested particles than is the case in non-smokers. They are also functionally impaired in that they are less likely to kill tumour target cells and a variety of common fungal organisms and bacteria such as Candida pseudotropicalis and Candida pseudotropicalis (can cause thrush), Legionella pneumophila (can cause pneumonia) and Staphylococcus aureus (can cause food poisoning). Macrophagal ability to produce a variety of chemicals that play a key role in the immune response to infection and malignancy has also shown to be impaired.

A decreased immune function may explain why there appears to be an association between cannabis use and opportunistic bacterial and fungal pneumonias in patients with cancer and transplant patients as well as those with human immunodeficiency virus (HIV) infection.

Inflammation

Visual inspection of the central airway of cannabis smokers has shown increased redness, swelling and mucous secretion by comparison to non-smokers. Smoking tobacco in conjunction with cannabis appears to have an additive effect. An increase in the number and size of small blood vessels and replacement of the normal ciliated surface lining cells (with hair-like projections) by mucus-secreting cells have also been observed. This may explain why cannabis smokers tend to suffer from chronic cough and phlegm as there may not be sufficient ciliated cells to remove the mucus from the airways.

Chronic Obstructive Pulmonary Disease, COPD

COPD is an umbrella term for conditions such as emphysema and chronic bronchitis. The evidence that COPD is mostly smoking related is already well established.

Currently more than 32,000 people die from COPD every year in the UK.

There is a lot of evidence that the long-term effects of habitual cannabis smoking include a significantly higher prevalence of chronic and acute respiratory symptoms such as chronic cough, chronic sputum production, wheeze and acute bronchitis episodes by comparison to non-smokers. There is evidence of a cumulative effect of smoking cannabis and tobacco in two studies although not in another.

Some studies indicate that young cannabis smokers may be at risk of developing obstructive airway disease in later life. This is supported by animal studies in which dog, monkeys and rats have been exposed to varying doses of cannabis for 12–30 months and suffered damage to the smaller airway which is a major site of injury in tobacco-related COPD as well as acute and chronic pneumonia. However, other studies contradict a causal relationship between smoking cannabis and COPD. Regular cannabis smoking has been associated with emphysema in some studies but not so in others. These studies are, however non-conclusive as they did not distinguish between smoking only cannabis and smoking cannabis together with tobacco.

They also only involved a relatively small number of participants. A further study involving rats exposed to increasing doses of cannabis for 6 months did not display any evidence of emphysema although this was the case in rats exposed to tobacco smoke.

Further research in this area is necessary to provide more conclusive results.

Respiratory cancer

More people die of lung cancer in the UK than from any other cancer —more than 34,000 people die every year in the UK.

As already mentioned, the tar from a cannabis cigarette contains many of the same (and even higher concentrations of) carcinogenic compounds found in cigarette smoke and deposits four times as much tar on the respiratory tract in comparison to an unfiltered cigarette of the same weight. This amplifies the exposure of cannabis smokers to particles that are known to be involved in the development of lung cancer.

There are a number of case studies (over 75) reporting cancers of the aerodigestive tract in young adults with a history of cannabis use which are rare in adults under the age of 60 although the exact cause of these cancers is not dearly identifiable as many of the cases also used alcohol and tobacco. A retrospective study undertaken in the United States did not find a link between smoking cannabis and tobacco related cancers but it has been suggested that the time span investigated may not have been sufficient to study the long-term effects. There is clearly a need for more epidemiological research in this area.

As it is, the development of cancer is a multi-step process comprised of sequential alterations in genomic DNA (the genetic material contained in cells), which are promoted and/or interact with environmental and genetic factors. It is therefore often not clear what the exact cause of a particular cancer may be.

Research suggests that cannabis might contribute to cancer by manipulating the genetic makeup of cells. For lung cells to transform into cancerous cells, a specific combination of genes that regulate cell growth must be activated (in the case of oncogenes) and/or mutate (in the case of tumour suppressor genes). THC has been shown to increase the production of a chemical particle (CYP1A1) that is responsible for causing benzpyrene (a constituent of cannabis smoke) to promote alterations in one of the most common tumour suppressor genes, P53 thereby facilitating the development of respiratory cancer. The gene P53 is thought to play a role in 75% of all lung cancers and has been found to be expressed in 11% of individuals who smoke cannabis and tobacco. Other studies looking at the effect of tar in cannabis smoke on animals also indicate a correlation between cannabis and respiratory cancer.

An increase in cellular abnormalities has also been observed in cannabis smokers by comparison to nonsmokers. Abnormalities include an increase in the production of mucus producing cells (goblet cells) and reserve cells, transformation of ciliated cells into cells that resemble skin (squamous metaplasia), an accumulation of inflammatory cells and abnormalities in the cell nuclei. Nuclear alterations and squamous metaplasia have been described as precursors to the development of lung cancer in tobacco smokers. In addition, smokers of cannabis and tobacco have shown a greater increase in cellular abnormalities indicating an additive effect.

Oral soft tissues

The effects of tobacco smoking on oral soft tissues have been well documented but there is little data available on the effects of cannabis smoking. However, there are some case reports that heavy cannabis use is associated with cancer of the tongue, larynx and lung.

Other lung conditions

There have been isolated reports of spontaneous pneumothorax (breaches of the lungs causing gas in the lung cavity leading to compression of the lungs) and pneumomediasdnum (breaches of the lungs causing gas in the cavities of the respiratory tract) associated temporally with the use of cannabis which are thought to be caused by deep inhalation of cannabis smoke to enhance absorption of THC and hence the intoxication caused by it. Deep inhalation coupled with direct pulmonary toxicity from components in cannabis in susceptible smokers has also been implicated with the formation of large lung bullae (watery blisters) in the upper respiratory area.

Contamination of cannabis
There has been a report of chronic cannabis smoking leading to necrotising pulmonary granulomata (these are changes in the lungs at cellular level which may prevent the lungs from working as they should) as a result of possible fungal contamination of cannabis.

Health care utilization by cannabis smokers
This has been assessed in an epidemiological study in which cannabis smokers who had never smoked tobacco were compared with non-smokers. Frequent cannabis smokers showed a slight increase in outpatient visits for respiratory and other illnesses compared with non-smokers as well as a small increased risk of hospitalisation.

Potential therapeutic benefits
The bronchodilator effects of THC in cannabis have also been found in the case of asthmatics with mild to moderate airway obstruction although not to the same extent as in healthy people. This has led to suggestions that THC might have therapeutic benefits in asthma. However, the noxious gases, chronic airway irritation or malignancy after long-term use associated with smoking would seem likely to negate these benefits over the long term. Oral intake of THC has also shown to cause unwanted side-effects such as central nervous system intoxication and an excessive increase in heart rate. Furthermore, tolerance to the bronchodilator effects of THC has been demonstrated after several weeks of use.

   The full report and reference to the source of information that helped compile this report is available on the British Lung Foundation Website at *www.britishlungfoundation.org*

Medicinal Claims

It is claimed cannabis can help alleviate the following symptoms:

· Adult ADD	· Aggressive Disorders	· AIDS
· Alcoholism	· Alzheimers disease	· Asthma
· Cancer	· Chemotherapy	· Chronic Pain
· Crohn's Disease	· Depression	· Diabetic Gastroparesis
· Dystonia	· Epilepsy	· Glaucoma
· Insomnia	· Labor Pains	· Menstrual cramps
· Migraine	· Multiple Sclerosis	· Paraplegia
· Phantom limb pain	· PMT	· Pruritis
· Psuedotumour Cerebri	· PTSD Quadriplegia	· Rheumatic diseases
· Schizophrenia	· Severe nausea	· Systemic Sclerosis
· Tinnitus	· Tumors	

More symptoms cannabis may help with AIDS

(Aquired Immunodeficiency Syndrome)

Antiviral drugs, of which the best known is AZT, are used to attack HIV. Unfortunately, AZT suppresses the production of red blood cells, decreases the number of white blood cells, and has many damaging effects on the digestive system. It sometimes causes severe nausea that heightens the danger of semi-starvation for patients who are already losing weight because of the illness. About 20% of AIDS patients develop an infectious disease of the eye that can cause blindness. A drug called Foscavir is used to treat it, but this too has the side effect of nausea. The anti-emetic properties of cannabis indicate that it is likely to be useful in treating the nausea caused by the disease and these other medications.

Human Immunodeficiency Virus (HIV) is contracted by the exchange of body fluids with an infected person. Once thought to be limited to intravenous drug users and gay men, it is increasingly present in the heterosexual population as well. Additionally, some haemophiliacs are HIV-positive after receiving tainted blood products prior to routine screening being introduced. People with the virus usually go on to contract Aquired Immuno-deficiency Syndrome (AIDS). The patient's diagnosis changes when either their T-cell count (the number of healthy immune cells the patient has) falls below 200 (normal range is 800–1200) or they contract one of the 30 separate AIDS diseases. These are mostly common "opportunistic infections" that prey on patients with AIDS suffer from "wasting syndrome", which is defined by the (US) Centers for Disease Control as "the involuntary loss of more than 10% of baseline average body weight in the presence of diarrhoea or fever of more than 30 days that is not attributable to other disease processes". This can occur by either starvation or cachexia, and chances of survival decrease significantly for the patient if as little as 5% of their body weight is lost. Existing therapy for wasting syndrome is the use of appetite stimulants (such as megestrol acetate) but few medications have proven successful. Cannabis too is an appetite stimulant (as can be seen in the "munchies" that recreational users often get).

In America, oral synthetic THC is available medically, under the trademark Marinol. Its license includes its usage as an appetite stimulant in AIDS patients. An amendment to the Misuse Of Drugs Regulations in 1995 means that it can be prescribed on a named-patient basis in the UK as well, however in practice it is not available, perhaps due to the large amount of administration, regulation and paperwork needed to be done in order to use it medically.

Some concern has been shown as it seems possible that cannabis may suppress the immune system. However, it is not known whether this occurs in humans at the required dosages. If immuno-suppression occurs however, it does not seem severe enough to preclude the use of cannabis as a medicine. Certainly there is no evidence that cannabis use increases the rate of progression to AIDS from HIV-positive patients. All in all, from both research and anecdotal evidence, cannabis seems to reduce any nausea, appetite suppression and physical pain that can come from either the disease itself, or its currently-prescribed medications.

Cancer Chemotherapy

The drugs used to treat cancer are among the most powerful, and most toxic, chemicals used in medicine. They kill both cancer cells and healthy cells, producing extremely unpleasant and dangerous side effects. The most common is days or weeks of vomiting, retching, and nausea after each treatment. Feeling loss of control can be highly depressing, and patients find it difficult to eat anything, losing weight and strength. Patients may find it more difficult to sustain the will to live, and some may chose to discontinue treatment, preferring death.

Cannabis can be used as an antiemetic, a drug which relieves nausea and allows patients to eat and live normally. Despite great advances in the last few years of antiemetic research, cannabis is safer, cheaper and often more effective than standard synthetic antiemetics. Smoking cannabis can be more effective than taking it (or its synthetic derivatives such as Marinol) orally as patients find it difficult to keep anything down long enough for it to have an effect. Smoking cannabis produces an immediate effect, and patients find it easier to control the dosage. Additionally the euphoric properties act as an anti-depressant, and the hunger and enjoyment of food properties ("the munchies') make weight gain easy, and these increase the chances of recovery.

The method by which chemotherapy generates nausea and vomiting is not entirely certain, although studies point to it being caused by receptor stimulation in the central nervous system or gastrointestinal tract. However, cannabis as an antiemetic seems to work via a different mechanism than the currently-used antiemetic drugs in this field (such as corticosteroids). It is therefore worthy of investigation whether a combination of cannabinoids and existing therapies may benefit the patient more than either of the two taken separately. It also suggests that patients who do not respond well to traditional antiemetic medications may find greater benefit with cannabis-based drugs.

A relatively large number of studies have been done on the anti emetic properties of cannabis in regard to the negative effects of chemotherapy. Almost invariably cannabis (and some of its constituent cannabinoids) have been found effective. As a result of this, in 1985 the US FDA licenced synthetic THC (Dronabinol) for these symptoms. In the UK however it is not licensed in this way. It is actually possible to prescribe Dronabinol to patients in the UK, but only on an individual basis. This is very rarely done, perhaps not surprisingly given the large amount of administrative obstacles that need to be overcome.

However, in 1982 Nabilone (an analogue of delta-9-THC) was licensed in the UK to allow it to be prescribed for nausea following chemotherapy, as long as other treatment was ineffective and that it was solely used within a hospital environment.

In terms of efficacy, cannabis has several competitors as an antiemetic. However, the Institute of Medicine's 1999 report summed it up nicely when it stated that *"the critical issue is not whether marijuana or cannabinoid drugs might be superior to the new drugs, but rather whether there is a group of patients who might obtain added or better relief from marijuana or cannabinoid drugs"*.

Both scientific research and testimonies of currently-criminalised users seem to state that this group of patients does indeed exist.

The treatment of nausea and vomiting is not the only way in which cannabis can help cancer sufferers. Both the analgesic (pain-relieving) and appetite-stimulating qualities of cannabis can make a patient's life both longer and more bearable.

Chronic Pain

The most frequent complaint that patients look for medical help with is pain. There are several different types of pain, and unfortunately none of the currently-prescribed pharmacological treatments for pain work completely for certain types. A particular example is that of pain caused by damaged nerves (such as that which causes phantom limb pain), which does not respond well to existing medications.

Severe chronic pain is usually treated with opiates, but these are addictive, and tolerance develops so that the dose has to be increased. The risk of severe side effects such as nausea is great, and additionally the user feels drugged, and finds it difficult to function properly. Family life may suffer as patients find it hard to relate to other people, and even reading to children is difficult. Synthetic analgesics are non-addictive but they are not powerful enough.

Cannabis has fewer side effects than other analgesics, and users report it "rounds off" the pain quickly after smoking. An Institute of Medicine report contains a minimal list of 5 situations in which cannabis-based medicines are of use in treating pain:

There are medical conditions or patients in which they are more effective than any currently available medication.

They have a broad clinical spectrum of efficacy and a unique side effect profile that differs from other analgesics.

They have synergistic interactions with other analgesics.

They exhibit "side effects" which are considered useful in certain clinical situations.

Their efficacy is enhanced in patients who have developed tolerance to opioids.

Some people have used cannabis to control pain for 20 years or more, and many report that they were able to kick their addiction to opiates with small amounts of cannabis. One strange fact is that more experienced users get a greater pain-relieving effect from cannabis than novices. Experienced users also are able to function normally and ignore the psychoactive effects. Cannabis may be better at controlling the different types of pain.

Cannabis has had a long history of use as an analgesic, and was widely used in 19th century Britain, including in the royal household. Dr. J. Russell Reynolds, Fellow of the Royal Society and Physician to Queen Victoria reported in the Lancet in 1890 that he had been prescribing cannabis for 30 years and considered it "one of the most valuable medicines we possess". According to Reynolds Indian hemp remained effective as an analgesic for months and even years without an increase in the dose.

It seems that cannabis shares some method of action with opioids, but the mechanism with which it accomplishes its analgesic effects differs. This indicates that they may produce an additive effect when used in conjunction with current medicines. In addition they might provide help to patients who do not react satisfactorily to other treatments. Much anecdotal evidence seems to indicate that this is the case.

Indeed, the British Medical Association has gone on record as stating that "the prescription of Nabilone, THC and other cannabinoids ... should be permitted for patients with intractable pain". Other official bodies have found similar results. A House of Lords report summed up the situation stating that "there is scientific evidence that cannabinoids possess pain relieving properties, and some clinical evidence to support their medical use in this indication". In a press conference on October 26th 1997, the US Society for Neuroscience claimed that "substances similar to or derived from marijuana ... could benefit the more than 97 million Americans who experience some form of pain each year."

Epilepsy

Epilepsy is a neurological condition, which affects approximately 1 in 100 people. Depending on how wide spread in the brain the neurological disturbance is (the focus), there are a range of possible seizures from lapses in consciousness (absence) or convulsions (Grand Mal) to grimacing or repetitive movements (temporal) to just odd sensations (auras). Epilepsy is as individual as the people who have it and everyone has their own patterns of seizures. There are sometimes triggers for seizures such as sleep loss, low blood sugar, stress or even boredom. Some common causes of epilepsy include head trauma, birth injury, hormonal imbalances, and viral attacks.

Some kinds of epilepsy can be well controlled by anti-convulsant drugs, but a few forms do not react well to these. Anti-convulsant drugs have potentially serious side-effects, including bone softening, reduced production of red blood cells, swelling of the gums, and emotional disturbances. Other occasional effects include uncontrollable rapid eye movements, loss of motor co-ordination, coma and even death. In addition, these medications are far from ideal in that they only completely stop seizures in about 60% of patients.

Cannabis has long been known to have anti-convulsant properties, and these have been investigated from the 19th century. Large amounts of anecdotal reports and 1-patient case studies indicate the assistance of cannabis in controlling seizures. Cannabis analogues have been shown to prevent seizures when given in combination with prescription drugs. Patients report that they can wean themselves off prescription drugs, and still not experience seizures if they have a regular supply of cannabis.

Some interest has been shown in the use of cannabidiol (a cannabinoid) in treatment. A small amount of data is available about this, and cannabidiol has little or none of the psychoactive side-effects that treatment with cannabis (or THC) could induce. There seems to be no plans to make a great effort to concentrate on cannabis research in the field of epilepsy at present. The British Medical Association has however stated that it may possibly prove useful as an "adjunctive therapy" for patients who cannot be kept satisfactorily free of seizures on current medications. Likewise, the National Institutes of Health workshop considered that this is "an area of potential value", based largely on animal research showing anticonvulsant effects.

Glaucoma

The human eyeball is filled with fluid which exerts pressure to keep the eyeball spherical. Glaucoma is a condition where the channels through which the fluid flows gradually become blocked, and the intraocular pressure (IOP) gradually increases causing increasing damage to the optic nerve and gradual deterioration of vision. Glaucoma is the second-largest cause of blindness, and affects 1.5% of 50-year-olds and 5% of 70-year-olds.

Standard treatments have unpleasant or dangerous side effects, and have little effect on intraocular pressures in end-stage glaucoma. Cannabis however lowers intraocular pressures dramatically, with none of the serious side effects. Patients' who find that standard medicines do not help their condition, report that smoking cannabis quickly restores their vision. Many long-term glaucoma patients have successfully maintained their sight using cannabis for 20 or 25 years, and avoided the gradual painful deterioration to blindness that is otherwise inevitable.

However older generations, who are most at risk of glaucoma, do not appreciate the euphoric side effects of smoked or ingested cannabis. There is also concern about the effects on the cardio-vascular system. These disadvantages are especially significant when one takes into account that a dose of cannabis needs to be taken about every 4 hours for the full benefits to occur.

There is hope that a cannabis-containing eyedrop could be developed in the future which would have no side effects but this is made difficult since cannabinoids are not naturally water soluble. However, animal experiments have taken place using THC dissolved in oil to aid its solubility, which have shown benefits without any of the afore-mentioned side-effects.

Whilst cannabinoids are known to lower IOP it is not currently known how they achieve this. There have been no conclusive tests to determine the mechanism of action, or even if the effect is achieved by brain-receptor interaction (as is the psychoactivity of cannabis). If the effect is achieved through CB2 receptors, then more specific cannabis-based medications could be developed that do not have any unwanted effect on the Central Nervous System. It is also of course possible that the medical effects work through an entirely different route and are not receptor-based. The uncertainty of cannabis' course of action in lowering IOP implies that it is also unknown whether or not it works in the same way as current medications do. If the mechanism of action differs from existing therapies then it is likely to be able to be used with other medications to provide additional benefits that wouldn't be seen if either medication was taken separately.

Several synthetic cannabinoids, including Nabilone, have been tested for the treatment of glaucoma with differing results in terms of efficacy to the condition and side-effects. Synthesised and isolated cannabinoids seem worthy of further investigation. It is feasible that future research could lead to the development of a drug based on cannabis which has fewer side effects and doesn't require such frequent dosing than THC alone. In addition, reducing IOP is not necessarily the only way to help glaucoma sufferers. More direct action on blood flow and neural protection may be of benefit. Researchers have studied a synthetic cannabinoid which is thought to provide some degree of neural protection.

Despite the possible drawbacks, one should be reminded that using cannabis evidently does some glaucoma sufferers a lot of good. 2 out of the 8 patients who are legally permitted to use cannabis medicinally in the US have used government-supplied cannabis for over 10 years to maintain their sight. It seems cruel to prohibit and, indeed, punish the huge numbers of glaucoma sufferers that could be helped by cannabis. Following a review of existing research, the Australian National Task Force on Cannabis concluded that it would not be desirable to criminalise such users.

Ironically, the discovery that cannabis lowers intraocular pressure was made accidentally during a police experiment. They were trying to discover if cannabis caused pupil dilation in users so that they could detect and arrest them more easily!

Morning Sickness, Menstrual pain and Labor Pains

One of the biggest medical uses of cannabis in the 19th century was for the treatment of menstrual cramps and reduction of labor pain. Queen Victoria was prescribed cannabis for this reason by her physician J.R. Reynolds. Yet there is nothing mentioned in 20th century medical literature. Possibly we have a such a fear of the unborn child being harmed by its mother's drug taking that any research on this subject would leave the researcher open to attack. However studies in populations that use cannabis socially (Costa Rica and Jamaica) have shown that there is no negative effect on the unborn child.

The studies that do show a negative effect need to be checked to make sure that it is not some other factor such as poverty that causes the effect. Also, most studies concentrate on people that take cannabis by smoking it. One must be careful to separate the effects of smoking from those intrinsic to cannabis. As well as the various tars and other by-products of smoking, smoking leads the user to inhale more carbon monoxide than they would otherwise. This reduces the ability of blood to transport the necessary oxygen to the foetus. As a result of these issues, several studies regarding cannabis have produced a result showing similar effects to those of tobacco smokers.

Despite the controversy, many women have experimented with cannabis, and have found that it does control menstrual cramps, makes labor quicker and less painful and relieves the nausea (morning sickness) associated with pregnancy. If severe nausea is reducing the mother's food intake, then the child may be harmed by not taking cannabis. Very little scientific research has been done on the subject of treating menstrual cramps, morning sickness and labor pain with cannabis. The analgesic and anti-emetic effects of cannabis discussed elsewhere show at least a potential in solving some of the problems women experience as a result of these problems.

Migraine

A migraine is a severe headache that lasts for hours or days, often accompanied by disturbance of vision and nausea and vomiting. The attacks usually re-occur and can be brought on by stress, certain types of food, bright lights, loud noise and even strong smells. About 20% of the population has experienced a migraine attack and women are more likely to experience them. A person's first attack usually happens before age 20, and rarely after age 50.

Drugs can either be used to prevent long-term reoccurrence, to cut short attacks, or for pain relief once an attack has started. 10–20% of sufferers get no relief from these drugs and many more get incomplete relief or suffer serious side effects.

Cannabis was highly regarded as a treatment for migraine in the 19th century. Dr J.B. Mattison wrote in 1891 that the treating migraine was the most important use of cannabis. Reviewing his own and earlier physicians' experiences, he concluded that cannabis not only blocks the pain, but prevents attacks. In 1913 William Osler expressed his agreement, saying that cannabis was probably the most satisfactory remedy for migraine. Yet there is little mention of the effect of cannabis on migraine in 20th century medical literature.

Individuals have experimented with cannabis however. They report that smoking a little amount of cannabis just as the early-warning signs of an attack (such as flickering vision) appear will prevent the attack from continuing. This may just be another analgesic effect of cannabis (combined with its anti-nausea effect), or it may be actually affecting the unknown biochemistry of the migraine in some manner.

Multiple Sclerosis

In the condition known as MS the normal functioning of the nerves in the brain and spinal cord is disrupted, probably caused by abnormal activity in the immune system. Debilitating attacks, which last for weeks, come and go unpredictably, with gradual deterioration and eventual disability. Because the central nervous system controls the entire body, the effects may appear anywhere. Common symptoms include tingling, numbness, impaired vision, difficulty in speaking, painful muscle spasms, loss of co-ordination and balance, fatigue, weakness or paralysis, loss of bladder control, urinary tract infections, constipation, skin ulcerations and severe depression.

There is no known effective treatment. Almost all MS patients experience some degree of spasticity, including stiffness, muscle spasms, cramps or muscle pain. The standard drugs used to treat the muscle spasms are addictive, have severe short-term side effects and worryingly damaging long-term side effects. Many MS sufferers find that they don't even work.

Animal studies have shown that cannabinoid receptors are densely populated in the areas of the brain which control movement, which suggests that cannabis may have anti-spastic effects. It seems indeed that cannabis has a startling and profound effect on the symptoms of MS. It stops muscle spasms, reduces tremors, restores balance, restores bladder control and restores speech and eyesight. Many wheelchair-bound patients report that they can walk unaided when they have smoked cannabis. Patients also report that they find smoked herbal cannabis better at controlling their symptoms than synthetic derivatives. It is now thought that cannabis may even retard the progression of the disease.

A certain degree of efficacy can be shown purely in the huge amounts of anecdotal evidence that abound. A House of Lords report states that the Multiple Sclerosis Society (consisting of approximately 35000 MS-suffering patients) estimates that as many as 4% of their population already use cannabis for the relief of their symptoms despite the considerable legal and health risks associated with the seemingly inhumane current prohibition of cannabis for any condition. The chairman of the committee went on to state that "we have seen enough evidence to convince us that a doctor might legitimately want to prescribe cannabis to relieve ... the symptoms of multiple sclerosis and that the criminal law ought not to stand in the way.'

Many of the witnesses for that report shared the British Medical Association's view that "A high priority should be given to carefully controlled trials of cannabinoids in patients with chronic spastic disorders". Indeed, at the current time a BMA report requests that the synthetic cannabinoids Nabilone and Dronabinol are officially licensed for use in MS and other spastic disorders.

Medical Grade Cannabis

Cannabis has been known for several thousands years in herbal medicine. Its active substances are the cannabinoids, especially tetrahydrocannabinol (THC). Over the years, Cannabis Sativa as the herb is officially known, has been claimed to increase the appetite, relax the muscles, sharpen the mind, improve mood, have a sedative effect, ease fear, and combat pain and nausea. (Health Council of the Netherlands. Standing Committee on Medicine. Marihuana as Medicine. Rijswijk: Health Council of the Netherlands, 1996; publication no. 1996/21).

Maripharm has developed Medical Grade Cannabis (MGC). All standards which are used for testing "herbal drug" are being met. The product is standardised and sterilised. The quality control takes in Maripharm's laboratory, but is also monitored by random checks carried out by other laboratories (see J. Khodabaks & O. Engelsma,

The standardised Medical Grade Marijuana plant, Proceedings Symposium International Cannabinoid Research Society, 1998). Medical Grade Cannabis is already applied to several syndromes such as those connected with cancer (patients undergoing chemotherapy), MS, glaucoma, chronic pain and migraine.

At present, Maripharm supplies 600 Dutch pharmacies with Medical Grade Cannabis. Thus, patients can be provided with the herb, on prescription by their physician. At the time, MGM has acquired a so-called KNMP-tax number, which means that, in principle, compensation by health insurance is possible. All this does not mean, however, that MGM has acquired an adequate legal status. Until now, MGM is tolerated in the Netherlands, in the same way in which, use of cannabis for recreational purpose is tolerated. Unfortunately, its pseudolegal status hinders MGM's full therapeutic potential and for several reasons patients are unable to obtain cannabis or they have to depend on "alternative" supply thus running the risk of getting polluted cannabis. Compared to the most other countries, however, the possibilities for Dutch patients to acquire cannabis for therapeutic purposes may be called adequate.

20

Cannabis in Religions

Far from being forbidden, cannabis has historically had an important and sacred role in spiritual traditions around the world, some extending to the present. In this chapter we'll look at some of these, and examine sacred texts that may point to a more exalted role for the herb.

Marijuana Worldwide

The BANTUS (Africa) had sacred Dagga Cults. These are societies that restricted cannabis use to ruling men. In addition to revering it as a religious sacrament, the Pygmies, Zulus and Hottentots all found it an indispensable medication for cramps, epilepsy and gout. Their Dagga cults believed Holy Cannabis was brought to the earth by the gods, in particular from the Two Star Dog system that we call Sirius A and B. Dagga literally means "cannabis." The surviving Indo-European word for the plant can also be read as "canna," "reed" and "bi," or "two" as well as "canna," as in "canine," and "bis," meaning "two"—"Two dogs." (*Emperor Wears No Clothes*)

With offerings of devotion, ships from the isles will meet to pour the wealth of the nations and bring tribute to his feet. The Coptic Church believes fully the teachings of the Bible, and as such we have our daily obligations, and offer our sacrifices, made by fire unto our God with chants and Psalms and spiritual hymns, lifting up holy hands and making melody in our hearts.

Herb (marijuana) is a Godly creation from the beginning of the world. It is known as the weed of wisdom, angel's food, the tree of life and even the "Wicked Old Ganja Tree." Its purpose in creation is as a fiery sacrifice to be offered to our Redeemer during obligations. The political worldwide organizations have framed mischief on it and called it drugs. To show that it is not a dangerous drug, let me inform my readers that it is used as food for mankind, and as a medicinal cure for diverse diseases. Ganja is not for commerce; yet because of the oppression of the people, it was raised up as the only liberator of the people, and the only peacemaker among the entire generation. Ganja is the sacramental rights of every man worldwide and any law against it is only the organized conspiracy of the United Nations and the political governments who assist in maintaining this conspiracy. — Walter Wells, Elder Priest of the Ethiopian Zion Coptic Church of Jamaica, West Indies

Marijuana has played a significant role in the religions and cultures of Africa, the Middle East, India, and China. Richard E. Schultes, a prominent researcher in the field of psychoactive plants, says in his article, "Man and Marijuana":

...that early man experimented with all plant materials that he could chew and could not have avoided discovering the properties of cannabis (marijuana), for in his quest for seeds and oil, he certainly ate the sticky tops of the plant. Upon eating hemp the euphoric, ecstatic and hallucinatory aspects may have introduced man to another worldly plane from which emerged religious beliefs, perhaps even the concept of deity. The plant became accepted as a special gift of the gods, a sacred medium for communion with the spiritual world and as such it has remained in some cultures to the present.

The effects of marijuana were proof to the ancients that the spirit and power of the god(s) existed in this plant and that it was literally a messenger (angel) or actually the Flesh and Blood and/or Bread of the god(s) and was and continues to be a holy sacrament. Considered to be sacred, marijuana has been used in religious worship from before recorded history.

According to William A. Embolden in his book *Ritual Use of Cannabis Sativa L,* (p. 235):

Shamanistic traditions of great antiquity in Asia and the Near East have as one of their most important elements the attempt to find God without a vale of tears; that cannabis played a role in this, at least in some areas, is born out in the philology surrounding the ritualistic use of the plant. Whereas Western religious traditions generally stress sin, repentance, and mortification of the flesh, certain older non-Western religious cults seem to have employed cannabis as a euphoriant, which allowed the participant a joyous path to the Ultimate; hence such appellations as "heavenly guide."

According to *Licit and Illicit Drugs* by the Consumer Union, (pp. 397–398):

Ashurbanipal lived about 650 B.C., but the cuneiform descriptions of marijuana in his library "are generally regarded as obvious copies of much older texts." Says Dr. Robert P. Walton, an American physician and authority on marijuana, "This evidence serves to project the origin of hashish back to the earliest beginnings of history."

The Use of Marijuana as Incense

According to the *Encyclopaedia Britannica*'s discussion of Pharmacological Cults, "...the ceremonial use of incense in contemporary ritual is most likely a relic of the time when the psychoactive properties of incense brought the ancient worshipper in touch with supernatural forces."

In the temples of the ancient world, the main sacrifice was the inhalation of incense. Incense is defined as the perfume or smoke from spices and gums when burned in celebrating religious rites or as an offering to a deity. Bronze and gold incense burners were cast very early in history and their forms were often inspired by cosmological themes representing the harmonious nature of the universe.

The following piece was taken from *Licit and Illicit Drugs,* (p. 31):

"In the Judaic world, the vapors from burnt spices and aromatic gums were considered part of the pleasurable act of worship. In Proverbs (27:9) it is said that "Ointment and perfumes rejoice the heart.' Perfumes were widely used in Egyptian worship. Stone altars have been unearthed in Babylon and Palestine, which have been used for burning incense made of aromatic wood and spices. While the casual readers today may interpret such practices as mere satisfaction of the desire for pleasant odors, this is almost certainly an error; in many or most cases, a psychoactive drug was being inhaled. In the islands of the Mediterranean 2,500 years ago and in Africa hundreds of years ago, for example, leaves and flowers of a particular plant were often thrown upon bonfires and the smoke inhaled; the plant was marijuana." — (Edward Preble and

Gabriel V. Laurey, "Plastic Cement: The Ten Cent Hallucinogen," *International Journal of the Addictions,* 2 (Fall 2967): 271–272.)

The earliest civilizations of Mesopotamia brewed intoxicating beer of barley more than 5,000 years ago; is it too much to assume that even earlier cultures experienced euphoria, accidentally or deliberately, through inhalation of the resinous smoke of Cannabis? — *Ritual Use of Cannabis Sativa L,* (p. 216.)

It is said that the Assyrians used hemp (marijuana) as incense in the seventh or eighth century before Christ and called it "Qunubu," a term apparently borrowed from an old East Iranian word "Konaba," the same as the Scythian name "cannabis." — *Plants of the Gods: Origin of Hallucinogenic Use,* by Richard E. Schultes and Albert Hofmann

It is recorded that the Chinese Taoist recommended the addition of cannabis to their incense burners in the 1st century as a means of achieving immortality. — *Marijuana, the First Twelve Thousand Years* by Earnest Abel, (p. 5)

There is a classic Greek term, cannabeizein, which means to smoke cannabis. Cannabeizein frequently took the form of inhaling vapours from an incense burner in which these resins were mixed with other resins, such as myrrh, balsam, frankincense, and perfumes. — *Ritual Use of Cannabis Sativa L*

Herodotus in the fifth century B.C. observed the Scythians throwing hemp on heated stone to create smoke and observed them inhaling this smoke. Although he does not identify them, Herodotus states that when they "have parties and sit around a fire, they throw some of it into the flames. As it burns, it smokes like incense, and the smell of it makes them drunk, just as wine does us. As more fruit is thrown on, they get more and more intoxicated until finally they jump up and start dancing and singing." — (Herodotus, *Histories* 1.202.)

Evidence Indicating Cannabis of Semitic Origin

The name *cannabis* is generally thought to be of Scythian origin. Sula Benet in *Cannabis and Culture* argues that it has a much earlier origin in Semitic languages like Hebrew, occurring several times in the Old Testament. He states that in Exodus 30:23, God commands Moses to make a holy anointing oil of myrrh, sweet cinnamon, kaneh bosm, and kassia. He goes on to say that the term *kaneh bosm* is also rendered in the traditional Hebrew as *kannabos* or *kannabus* and that the root "kan" in this construction means "reed" or "hemp", while "bosm" means "aromatic." Benet states that in the earliest Greek translations of the Old Testament, "kan" was rendered as "reed," leading to such erroneous English translations as "sweet calamus" (Exodus 30:23), "sweet cane" (Isaiah 43:24, Jeremiah 6:20) and "calamus" (Ezekiel 27:19, Song of Songs 4:14). Benet argues from the linguistic evidence that cannabis was known in Old Testament times at least for its aromatic properties and that the word for it passed from the Semitic language to the Scythians, i.e., the Ashkenaz of the Old Testament.

Sara Benetowa of the Institute of Anthropological Sciences in Warsaw is quoted in *The Book of Grass* as saying:

> The astonishing resemblance between the Semitic "kanbos" and the Scythian "cannabis" leads me to suppose that the Scythian word was of Semitic origin. These etymological discussions run parallel to arguments drawn from history. The Iranian Scythians were probably related to the Medes, who were neighbors of the Semites and could easily have assimilated the word for hemp. The Semites could also have spread the word during their migrations through Asia Minor.
>
> Taking into account the matriarchal element of Semitic culture, one is led to believe that Asia Minor was the original point of expansion for both the society based on the matriarchal circle and the mass use of hashish.

The Ancient Israelites were a Semitic people. Abraham, the father of the Israelite nation, came from Ur, a city of Babylonia located in Mesopotamia. The Israelites migrated throughout Asia Minor and could easily have spread the religious use of marijuana.

The Israelite Use of Incense

It was said that Moses, at the direction of Almighty God, first brought the use of incense to public worship, and that the other nations of antiquity copied the practice from him. It was, however, a practice that began with Adam. The Book of Jubilees, an Apocryphal book, (the Apocrypha was considered canonical by the early church and is considered so to this day by the Ethiopian Zion Coptic Church) states that "on the day when Adam went forth from the Garden of Eden, he offered as a sweet savor an offering of frankincense, galbanum, and stacte, and spices, in the morning with the rising of the sun, from the day when he covered his shame." And of Enoch we read that "he burnt the incense of the sanctuary, even sweet spices, acceptable before the Lord, on the Mount."

Incense was assigned miraculous powers by the Israelites. It was burned in golden bowls or cauldrons placed on or beside the altar. It was also burned in handheld censers. In the Blessing of Moses, a poem belonging to the Northern Kingdom of Israel, and written about 760 B.C., the sacrificial smoke is offered to the God of Israel: "Let them teach Jacob thy judgments, and Israel thy law; Let them offer sacrificial smoke to thy nostrils, and whole burnt sacrifice upon thy altar."

Throughout the Bible the ancient patriarchs were brought into communion with God through smoking incense, and at Mt. Sinai God talked to Moses out of a bush that burned with fire (Exodus 3:1–12). After Moses brought the Israelite people out of Egypt he returned to Mt. Sinai, at which time God made a covenant with him in which the Ten Commandments were revealed. Exodus 19:8 describes the conditions at the time of this covenant: "And Mount Sinai was altogether on smoke, because the Lord descended upon it in fire: and the smoke thereof ascended as smoke of a furnace, and the whole mount quaked greatly."

The mysterious smoke mentioned in the covenant on Mt. Sinai is also referred to as a cloud: "And Moses went up into the mount, and a cloud covered the mount. 16 And the glory of the Lord abode upon Mount Sinai, and the cloud covered it six days: and the seventh day he called unto Moses out of the midst of the cloud." (Exodus 24:15–16)

Scriptures make it abundantly clear that the clouds and the smoke are related to the burning of incense. Exodus 40:26 describes Moses burning incense, a cloud covering the tent of the congregation, and the glory of the Lord filling the tabernacle. Leviticus 16:2–13 describes how God appeared in a cloud and refers to it as the clouds of incense. Numbers 16:17–19 describes how every man of the congregation had a censer full of burning incense and that the glory of the Lord appeared unto all the congregation. Isaiah 6:4 describes how Ezekial saw God in a smoke-filled inner court. Numbers 11:25 describes how God was revealed to Moses and the seventy elders in a cloud; that the spirit rested upon them and that they prophesied and ceased not.

The Book of Grass, by George Andrews and Simon Vinkenoog, includes a section on Ancient Scythia and Iran by Mircea Eliade, one of the foremost experts on the history of religions. On pages 11 and 12 is the following:

> "One document appears to indicate the existence of a Getic shamanism: It is Straho's account of the Myssian KAPNOBATAI, a name that has been translated, by analogy with Aristophanes' AEROBATES, as "those who walk in clouds'; but it should be translated as "those who walk in smoke'! Presumably the smoke is hemp smoke, a rudimentary means of ecstasy known to both the Thracians and the Scythians ..."

This passage should be carefully noted. Biblical passages make it abundantly clear that the ancient Isrealites also walked in clouds and in smoke. In fact it was in the clouds of smoke that God was revealed to the ancient Israelites. The words "smoke" and "smoking" appear fifty times in the King James Version of the Bible and two separate times the Bible says of the Lord, "There went up a smoke out of his nostrils." (II Samuel 22:9, Psalms 18:8) There are numerous other places in the Bible that mention the burning of incense, the mysterious cloud, and smoke. This common thread is found throughout the Bible, including the New Testament.

St. Matthew 24:30: "And then shall appear the sign of the Son of Man in heaven: and then shall all the tribes of the Earth mourne and they shall see the Son of Man coming in the clouds of heaven, with power and great glory."

Revelations 1:7: "Behold, he cometh with clouds; and every eye shall see him, and they also which pierced him: and all the kindreds of the earth shall wail because of him. Even so, Amen."

Revelations 8:3-4: "And another angel came and stood at the altar, having a golden censer: and there was given unto him much incense, that he should offer it with the prayers of all saints upon the golden altar which was before the throne. 4 And the smoke of the incense, which came with the prayers of the saints, ascended up before God out of the Angel's hand."

Revelations 15:8: "And the temple was filled with smoke from the glory of God, and from his power."

The Symbolism of Fire in the Ancient World

The word "fire" is mentioned several hundred times in the King James Version of the Bible. The sacrifice of the Lord is made by fire (Exodus 29:18, 25; Leviticus

2:10–11; Leviticus 6:13; Numbers 28:6; Deuteronomy 4:33; Joshua 13:14; I Samuel 2:28; II Chronicles 2:4; Isaiah 24:15; Matthew 3:11; Luke 1:9; Revelations 8:4–5).

Abraham, the father of the Israelite nation, came from Ur which was a city of Ancient Sumer in South Babylonia. For the Babylonians, fire was essential to sacrifice and all oblations were conveyed to the gods by the fire god Girru-Nusku, whose presence as an intermediary between the gods and man was indispensable. Girru-Nusku, as the messenger of the gods, bore the essence of the offerings upward to them in the smoke of sacrificial fire.

At Babylon: "The glorious gods smell the incense, noble food of heaven; pure wine which no hand has touched do they enjoy." (L. Jeremias, in *Encyclopedia Biblica*, IV, 4119, quoting Rawlinson, *Cuneif. Inscrip.*, IV, 19 (59).)

The most important of the ancient Indian gods was Agni, the god of fire, who like the Babylonian god Girru-Nusku, acted as a messenger between men and the gods. The fire (Agni) upon the altar was regarded as a messenger, their invoker.

"... For thou, O sage, goest wisely between these two creations like a friendly messenger between two hamlets."

According to the *Encyclopaedia Britannica*'s discussion of mysticism:

The Vedas (Hindu sacred writings) are hymns to the mystic fire and the inner sense of sacrifice, burning forever on the "altar Mind." Hence the abundance of solar and fire images: birds of fire, the fire of the sun, and the isles of fire. The symbol system of the world's religions and mysticisms are profound illuminations of the human-divine mystery. Be it the cave of the heart or the lotus of the heart, "the dwelling place of that which is the Essence of the Universe," "the third eye," or "the eye of wisdom"—the symbols all refer back to wisdom entering the aspiring soul on its way to progressive self-understanding. "I saw the Lord with the Eye of the Heart. I said, "Who art thou?" and he answered, "Thou."

The ancient Indian mystics said:

...that in the ecstasy of bhang (marijuana) the spark of the Eternal in man turns into light the murkiness of matter or illusion and the self is lost in the central soul fire. Raising man out of himself and above mean individual worries, bhang makes him one with the divine force of nature and the mystery "I am he" grew plain. —from the *Indian Hemp Drugs Commission Report* written at the turn of the twentieth century

The concept of spiritual or inner light was found throughout the ancient world. As we shall see that spiritual light was directly related to the burning of incense. According to Lucie Lamy in *Egyptian Mysteries,* (p. 24):

> The Pharaonic word for light is akh. This word, often translated as "transfigured," designated transcendental light as well as all aspects of physical light; and in the funerary text it denotes the state of ultimate sublimation.
>
> The word akh, first of all, is written with a glyph showing a crested ibis, ibis comata. This bird—the name of which was also akh—lived in the southern part of the Arabian side of the Red Sea (near Al Qunfidhah) and migrated to Abyssinia (Ethiopia) during the winter. Both these places are near the regions from which sacred incense came, and were called the "Divine Land." The bird's crest, together with its dark green plumage shot with glittering metallic specks justifies the meanings "to shine," "to be resplendent," "to irradiate." of the root akh in the hieroglyphic writing.
>
> Akh indeed expresses all notions of light, both literally and figuratively, from the Light which comes forth from Darkness to the transcendental light of transfiguration. It is also used to designate the "third eye," the ureaeus, related in old tradition to the pineal body and to the spirit.

The sacred cloud of incense was instrumental in the transfiguration of Christ. Note that Ethiopia was referred to as the "Divine Land" and that it was the source for the sacred incense. The ancients also referred to Ethiopia as the "Land of God." The ancient Egyptians believed that they had received their divinities from Ethiopia and have always held to the ancient and honoured tradition of their southern origin. Ethiopia is so important in ancient history that it is mentioned as being in the Garden of Eden (Genesis 2:12).

The ancient Greek historian Diodorus Siculus wrote:

> The Ethiopians conceived themselves to be of greater antiquity than any other nation; and it is probable that, born under the sun's path, its warmth

may have ripened them earlier than other men. They supposed themselves to be the inventors of worship, of festivals, of solemn assemblies, of sacrifice, and every religious practice.

Marijuana as the Christian Sacrament

According to Jack Herer in *The Emperor Wears No Clothes or Everything You Wanted to Know About Marijuana But Were Not Taught in School,* "The Essenes, a kabalistic priest/prophet/healer sect of Judaism dating back to the era of the Dead Sea Scrolls, used hemp, as did the Theraputea of Egypt, from where we get the term "therapeutic.""

The Theraputea of Egypt were Jewish ascetics that dwelt near Alexandria and were described by Philo (first century B.C.) as devoted to contemplation and meditation. Alexandria is where St. Mark is traditionally held to have established the Coptic Church in 45 A.D. The Coptic Church has been neglected by Western scholars despite its historical significance. This has been due to the various biases and interest of the Catholic Church, which claimed Christianity for its own. The result is that for the Coptic Church there is very little history. It is, however, assumed that the Coptic religious services have their roots in the earliest layers of Christian ritual in Jerusalem and it is known that the Coptic Church is of ancient origin going back to the time of the first Christian communities and even before.

Tradition states that the term "Coptic" was derived from "Kuftaim," son of Mizraim, a grandchild of Noah who first settled in the Nile valley, in the neighborhood of Thebes, the ancient capital of Egypt. At one time Thebes was the greatest city in the world and history records that by 2200 B.C. the whole of Egypt was united under a Theban prince. The splendor of Thebes was known to Homer, who called it "the city with a hundred gates." (Richard Schultes states that in ancient Thebes marijuana was made into a drink.)

According to E.A. Wallis Budge in *The Divine Origin of the Herbalist,* (p. 79), "The Copts, that is to say the Egyptians who accepted the teachings of St. Mark in the first century of our era, and embraced Christianity, seem to have eschewed medical science as taught by the physicians of the famous School of Medicine of Alexandria, and to have been content with the methods of healing employed by their ancestors."

The Essenes were an ascetic sect closely related to the Theraputea that had established a monastic order in the desert outside of Palestine and were known as spiritual healers. It has been suggested that both John the Baptist and Jesus may have been of the Essene sect as they were both heavily dependent on Essene teachings. The scriptures make no mention of the life of Jesus from the ages of 13 to 30. Certain theologians speculate that Jesus was being initiated by the Essenes, the last fraternity to keep alive the ancient traditions of the prophets.

Every prophet, however great, must be initiated. His higher self must be awakened and made conscious so that his mission can be fulfilled. Among the Essenes, ritual lustrations preceded most liturgical rites, the most important one of which was participation in a sacred meal—an anticipation of the Messianic banquet.

Throughout the ancient world sacrifice was a sacramental communal meal involving the idea of the god as a participant in the meal or as identical with the food consumed. The communion sacrifice was one in which the deity indwells the oblation so that the worshippers actually consume the divine. The original motive of sacrifice was an effort toward communion among the members of a group, on one hand, and between them and their god on the other. At its best, sacrifice was a "sacrament" and in one form or another life itself.

The central focus of the early Christian church was the Eucharist or the "body and blood" of the Lord. This was interpreted as a fellowship meal with the resurrected Christ. In meeting the Resurrected One in the Eucharist meal the Christian community had the expectation of the Kingdom of God and salvation.

Christ communicated life to his disciples through the Eucharist or Christian sacrament. Christ said in describing the sacrament, "Take, eat, this is my body, this is my blood. Do this as often as you will in remembrance of me." (I Corinthians 11:24–25)

Baptism is defined as the Christian sacrament used in purification and the spiritual rebirth of the individual. I Corinthians 10:1 makes it clear that the smoking cloud of incense was directly related to baptism.

I Corinthians 10:1–3: "Moreover, brethren, I would not that ye should be ignorant, how that our fathers were under the cloud, and all passed through the sea; 2 And were all baptized unto Moses in the Cloud and in the sea; 3 And did all eat the same spiritual meat: for they drank of that Spiritual Rock that followed them: and that Rock was Christ."

In the Biblical story of Creation, God said, "Behold, I have given you every herb bearing seed and to you it will be for meat." (Genesis 1:29) Marijuana is technically an herb and was considered a spiritual meat in the ancient world. From this passage in Corinthians we see that the spiritual cloud resulting from the burning of incense was instrumental in the baptism of the Israelites. This baptism is also compared to the "eating and drinking" of the spirit of Christ.

Spirit is defined as the active essence of the Deity serving as an invisible and life-giving or inspiring power in motion. Scripture makes it abundantly clear that the sacrificial cloud or smoke contained the Spirit of God (Christ) and was instrumental in inspiring, sanctifying, and purifying the patriarchs.

In Numbers 11:25 the cloud results in the Spirit resting upon Moses and the 70 elders. This passage indicates that they prophesied ecstatically. "Prophesy" is defined as follows: to utter or announce by or as if by divine inspiration; to speak for God or a deity; to give instruction in religious matters. Throughout the Holy Bible prophets of God spake as they were moved by the Holy Spirit. The smoking burning cloud of incense contained the spirit and was instrumental in bringing about the spiritual revelations of the prophets. In the ancient world marijuana was used to reveal the future. The virtues of marijuana include speech-giving and inspiration of mental powers.

"Psychoactive" is defined as effecting the mind or behavior. When we of the Ethiopian Zion Coptic Church think of mind or behavior we think of that inward essence or element that makes up the individual. This is the person's spirit. We are all spiritual beings. It is just as important to keep the spiritual part of a person healthy as it is to keep the physical body healthy and in fact they are related— hence marijuana and its relationship to spiritual food.

In the Apocrypha (Book of Jubilees), chapter 10, God tells an angel to teach Noah the medicines that heal and protect from evil spirits. Surely God taught Noah about marijuana. In the ancient world marijuana played an important role in purification and protecting from evil influences.

Note the following concerning the transfiguration of Christ:

"And after six days Jesus taketh Peter, James, and John his brother, and bringeth them up into a high mountain apart. 2 And he was transfigured before them: and his face did shine as the sun, and his raiment was white as light. 3 And, behold, there appeared unto them Moses and Elias talking with him. 4 Then answered Peter, and said unto Jesus, Lord, it is good for us to be here: if thou wilt, let us make here three tabernacles; one for thee, one for Moses, and one for Elias. 5 When yet he spake, behold a bright cloud overshadowed them; and behold a voice out of the cloud, which said, This is my beloved Son, in whom I am well pleased; hear ye him." — (St. Matthew 17:1–5)

In *The Bible Dictionary* (p. 898), John McKenzie says of the transfiguration that the cloud and the formula of the utterance of the Father are derived from the baptism of Jesus. He says that the change described in the appearance of Jesus suggests the change which is implied in the resurrection narratives.

Some synonyms for or words associated with transfiguration are transformation, metamorphosis, transubstantiation. These terms imply the change that accompanies resurrection or deification. Across the world, legends of godlike men who manage to rise in a state of perfection go back to an era before human beings had cast away from the divine source. Hence the gods were beings that once were men, and the actual race of men will in time become gods. Christ revealed this to the people of his day when he told them to whom the word of God came: "Ye are gods." (St. John 10:34)

St. Matthew 17:2 says that during the transfiguration of Christ, his face did shine as the sun. The face of Moses also shone when he returned from the cloud on Mt. Sinai (Exodus 30:34). The shining countenances are the result of their resurrections, of their being spiritually illumined in the cloud of smoking incense.

Most people are under the impression that Christ baptized with water. As you can see from the following account of John the Baptist this isn't so. John the Baptist baptized with water and Christ baptized with fire: "I indeed baptize you with water into repentance: but he that cometh after me is mightier than I, whose shoes I am not worthy to bear; he shall baptize you with the Holy Spirit and with fire." (St. Matthew 3:11)

It is only logical that this baptism with the Holy Spirit and with fire is related to the baptism of Christ in the burning, smoking cloud of incense and to the baptism of the patriarchs in which the patriarchs did all eat of the same spiritual meal (incense). In its discussion of the Holy Spirit, the *Encyclopaedia Britannica* states that Christian writers have seen in various references to the Spirit of Yahweh in the Old Testament an anticipation of the doctrine of the Holy Spirit. It also says that the Holy Spirit is viewed as the main agent of man's restoration to his original natural state through communion in Christ's body and, thus, as the principle of life in the Christian community.

The patriarchs were recipients of a revelation coming directly from the Spirit (incense) and this was expressed in the heightening and enlargement of their consciousness. It is clear from scripture that this spiritual dimension was also evident in the life of Jesus, in whom the experience of the Hebrew prophets was renewed. Through the Eucharist Christ passed this spiritual dimension on to his apostles. One of the apostles even makes mention in Philippians 4:18 of a sweet-smelling sacrifice that is well pleasing to God.

Christ compares this baptism to the drinking of a cup.

> But Jesus said unto them, Ye know not what ye ask: can ye drink of the cup that I drink of? and be baptized with the baptism that I am baptized with? — (St. Mark 10:38)

This cup is referred to as the cup of salvation in Psalms 116:12:

> What shall I render unto the Lord for all his benefits toward me? I will take the cup of salvation and call upon the name of the Lord.

It is called the cup of blessing in connection with the Eucharist.

> The cup of blessing which we bless, is it not the communion of the blood and the body of Christ? 17 For we being many are one bread, and one body; for we are all partakers of one bread. — (1 Corinthians 10:16)

Here we see a connection between the cup of blessing and the communion of the blood of Christ. Blood is the life-giving substance of the living being. Christ communicated life to his disciples through the Eucharist or Christian sacrament.

In I Corinthians 10:16 we note the mention of bread as the communion of the body of Christ and that we are all partakers of one bread. This is the spiritual bread or food used by Christ and his disciples. (A synonym for the Eucharist or the Body and Blood of the Lord is the bread of life.) It is interesting to note that the finest marijuana in Jamaica is called Lamb's Bread.

> For by one Spirit are we all baptized into one body, whether we be Jew or Gentiles, whether we be bond or free; and have all been made to drink into one Spirit. — (1 Corinthians 12:13)

> After the same manner also he took the cup, when he had supped, saying, This cup is the New Testament in my blood: this do ye, as oft as ye drink it, in

remembrance of me. 26 For as often as ye eat this bread and drink this cup, ye do shew the Lord's death till he come. — (1 Corinthians 11:25)

If these passages are compared to 1 Corinthians 10:1–4, it is plain that the "eating of one bread" is the same as the patriarchs "eating the same spiritual meat" and the "drinking of one Spirit" (the cup) is the same as the patriarchs "drinking of the Spiritual Rock that followed them: and that Rock was Christ." By making this comparison we see that the terminology of the Eucharist is directly related to the smoking cloud of incense used in the baptism of Christ and the patriarchs.

It is interesting to note that smoking was referred to as "eating" or "drinking" by the early American Indians. In *Hallucinogen and Culture* Peter J. Furst states:

Considering its enormous geographic spread in the Americas at the time of European discovery, as well as the probable age of stone tobacco pipes in California, the inhaling (often called "drinking" or "eating") of tobacco smoke by the Shaman, as a corollary to therapeutic fumigation and the feeding of the gods with smoke, must also be of considerable antiquity.

In *Licit and Illicit Drugs* (p. 209), the following is quoted:

"Columbus and other early explorers who followed him were amazed to meet Indians who carried rolls of dried leaves that they set afire—and who then "drank the smoke" that emerged from the rolls. Other Indians carried pipes in which they burned the same leaves, and from which they similarly "drank the smoke."

The *Encyclopedia Britannica* states in the section on sacrifice that the interpretation of sacrifice and particularly of the Eucharist as sacrifice has varied greatly within the different Christian traditions because the sacrificial terminology in which the Eucharist was originally described became foreign to Christian thinkers.

We of the Ethiopian Zion Coptic Church declare that the true understanding of the Eucharist has been passed down from generation to generation so that we are able to give an accurate interpretation of the sacrificial terminology used to describe the Eucharist. We have shown, using history and Biblical passages, that this terminology is directly related to burning and smoking incense. We have shown that the "eating" or "drinking" contained in the terminology concerning the Eucharist is associated with the inhalation of smoke. We have shown that marijuana was used as incense and that it was the number one spiritual plant of the ancient world.

We of the Ethiopian Zion Coptic Church declare that the cup that Christ baptized his disciples with in the baptism of the Holy Spirit and fire was in fact a pipe or chillum in which marijuana was smoked. This is a bottomless cup and as soon as it is emptied it is filled again and passed in a circle. Like the pipe of the ancient North American Indians, this cup was a portable altar.

Christ was the Father of the doctrine of the Eucharist which is the communion that Jesus gave his brethren. Jesus taught that the communion is his body and blood. Jesus was not speaking of His physical body and blood. He was speaking of His spiritual body and spiritual blood that was the communion of his holy church. The supper that Jesus celebrated with his disciples "on the night that he was betrayed" (1 Corinthians 11:23) inaugurated the heavenly meal that was to be continued.

> For I have received of the Lord that which also I delivered unto you, that the Lord Jesus the same night in which he was betrayed took bread: 24 And when he had given thanks, he brake it and said, Take, eat, this is my body, which is broken for you; this do in remembrance of me. 25 After the same manner also he took the cup, which he had supped, saying, This cup is the new testament in my blood; this do ye, as oft as ye drink it, in remembrance of me. 26 For as often as ye eat this bread, and drink of this cup, ye do shew the Lord's death till he come. 27 Wherefore whosoever shall eat of this bread, and drink of this cup of the Lord unworthily, shall be guilty of the body and blood of the Lord. 28 But let a man examine himself, and let him eat of the bread, and drink of that cup. 29 For he that eateth and drinketh unworthily, eateth and drinketh damnation to himself, not discerning the Lord's body. — (1 Corinthians 11:23–29)

Christ said, "Do this in remembrance of me." Here the original unity of man with God is restored. In general the reception of the Holy Spirit is connected with the actual realization, the inward experiencing of God.

Marijuana has been referred to as a mild euphoric (the producer of a feeling of well-being) that produces a profound religious experience of a mystical and transcendental nature. This religious experience is said to be brought about by the stirring of deeply buried, unconscious sensitivities so that one experiences ultimate reality or the divine and confirms the feeling of the worshipper that he has been in the presence of God and has assimilated some of His powers.

To be lifted above sense to behold the beatific vision and become "incorporate" in God is the end sought in ecstasy. The priest or mystic in enthusiasm or ecstasy enjoys the beatific vision by entering into communion with God and by undergoing deification. The experience of ecstasy, according to Mircea Eliade, one of the foremost authorities on religion, is a timeless primary phenomenon. Psychological experiences of rapture, he continues, are fundamental to the human condition and hence known to the whole of archaic humanity. (Some of the synonyms of rapture are bliss, beatitude, transport, exaltation.)

Baudelaire, a member of the *Club Des Hashichins* (Hashish Club) founded in Paris around 1835, and author of *Artificial Paradises* states the following about hashish (the unadulterated resin from the flowering tops of the female hemp plant):

> One will find in hashish nothing miraculous, absolutely nothing but an exaggeration of the natural. The brain and organisms on which hashish operates will produce only the normal phenomena peculiar to that individual—increased, admittedly, in number and force, but always faithful to the original. A man will never escape from his destined physical and moral temperament: hashish will be a mirror of his impression and private thoughts—a magnifying mirror, it is true, but only a mirror.

He cautions that the user must be in the right frame of mind to take hashish, for just as it exaggerates the natural behavior of the individual, so too does hashish intensify the user's immediate feelings. Baudelaire describes three successive phases a hashish user will pass through. He says the final stage is marked by a feeling of calmness, in which time and space have no meaning, and there is a sense that one has transcended matter. He says that in this state, one final supreme thought breaks into consciousness: "I have become God."

Realization of one's union with God is necessary in understanding the true Christian sacrament. The understanding of man's relationship to God and God's relationship to man (God in man and man in God) was quite prevalent in the ancient world, particularly among the religions that utilized marijuana as part of their religious practice.

Said the great Hindu sage, Manu: "He who in his own soul perceives the Supreme Soul in all beings and acquires equanimity toward them all, attains the highest bliss." To recognize oneness of self with God was contained in all the teachings of Gautama Buddha. In the Liturgy of Mithra (the Persian god of light and truth) the suppliant prays "abide with me in my soul; leave me not...that I may be initiated and the Holy Spirit may breathe within me." The communion became so intimate as to pass into identity: "I am thou and thou art I." Athanasius, a theologian, ecclesiastical statesman, and Egyptian national leader who was closely tied to the Coptic Church in Egypt said, "Even we may become gods walking in the flesh," and "God became man that man might become God."

Western theology (Catholic and Protestant) teaches that the spirit created matter but remained aloof from it. In Hinduism and other Eastern religions, the spirit is the inside, the matter is the outside; the two are inseparable. Eastern theologians have rightly perceived that the God one worships must posses all the aspects of his worshipper's nature as well as his own divine nature. Otherwise, how can he create beings whose nature is entirely foreign to his own? What, then, would be the meaning of the Biblical phrase: "God made man in his own image"?

The fact that modern Christendom has no sense of union with God has led to numerous churches without the understanding for building a Christian culture and kingdom to replace the confusion of modern politics. This understanding was not lacking in the ancient church and was a major source of enthusiasm for the prophets of old. In fact, the power of the early church was manifested due to this understanding of the spirit of God dwelling in man, the temple of God. To the ancient prophets it was not a God above, nor a God over yonder, but a God within. "Be still and know that I am God"—for the visionaries and mystics of every time and place, this has been the first and greatest of the commandments.

In 1 Corinthians 11:28 Christ said, "Let a man examine himself, and so let him eat of the bread, and drink of the cup." Probably the most relevant study to date about what might be considered typical marijuana experience, Dr. Charles Tart's "On Being Stoned: A Psychological Study of Marijuana Intoxication," concludes that marijuana gives spontaneous insights into self.

The sacrament of marijuana is declared by Christ himself and can be understood only when a person partakes of the natural divine herb. The fact is communion of Jesus cannot be disputed or be destroyed. Marijuana is the new wine divine and cannot be compared to the old wine, which is alcohol. Jesus rejected the old wine and glorified the "new wine" at the wedding feast of Cana. Cana is a linguistic derivation of the present-day cannabis and so it is. (Some Biblical scholars—

and there is a certain amount of support in early tradition of the view—have looked upon the miracle of Cana as a sign of the Eucharist.)

Note the references to new wine in the Bible:

Thus saith the Lord, As the new wine is found in the cluster, and one saith, Destroy it not; for a blessing is in it; so will I do for my servant's sake. — (Isaiah 65:8)

Others mocking said, "These men are full of new wine." — (Acts 2:13)

Isaiah 65:8, noted above, declares that the new wine is found in the cluster and that a blessing is in it. When one mentions clusters, one thinks of clusters of grapes. *Webster's New Riverside Dictionary* defines marijuana thus: "1. Hemp 2. The dried flower clusters and leaves of the hemp plant, esp. when taken to induce euphoria."

The *Encyclopaedia Britannica* says the following about hemp: "Seed producing flowers form elongate, spike like clusters growing on the pistil late, or female plants; pollen producing flowers form many branched clusters or staminate, on male plants." Here and in *Webster's,* marijuana fits the description of the new wine and as history has shown a blessing is in it.

Baudelaire said the following about the effects of hashish:

This marvellous experience often occurs as if it was the effect of superior and invisible power acting on the person from without... This delightful and singular state...gives no advance warning. It is as unexpected as a ghost, an intermittent haunting from which we must draw, if we are wise, the certainty of a better existence. This acuteness of thought, this enthusiasm of the senses and the spirit must have appeared to man through the ages as the first blessing.

In the books of Acts the apostles were accused of being full of new wine. Acts 2:13 was the time of Pentecost when the Holy Spirit descended upon the apostles. Numerous outpourings of the Spirit are mentioned in the Acts of the apostles in which healing, prophesy, and the expelling of demons are particularly associated with the activity of the Spirit. Incense (marijuana) was used by the ancients for healing, prophesy, and the expelling of demons.

When Christ ascended into heaven in the cloud (Acts 1:9–11) he sent his disciples the Holy Spirit with the "gift of tongues" (Acts 2:3) and there appeared unto them cloven tongues like as a fire, and it sat upon each of them, and they were filled with the Holy Spirit and were given the power to prophesy or witness. (Marijuana has been credited with speech giving and inspiration of mental powers.)

The first two gifts of the Holy Spirit are traditionally said to be wisdom and understanding, which no doubt are the two things most needed by the human race. In Jamaica today marijuana is referred to as the "weed of wisdom" and is reputed to be the plant that grew on Solomon's grave, a man known for his great wisdom. Marijuana expands consciousness and enhances the capacity for mystical and creative inspiration.

In Acts 2:3, fire speaks figuratively of the Holy Spirit. Fire was also a means by which to transport a saint to heaven.

And it came to pass, as they still went on, and talked, that, behold, there appeared a chariot of fire, and horses of fire, and parted asunder; and Elijah went up by a whirlwind into heaven. — (2 Kings 2:11)

Recent writers have speculated that this passage was in reference to flying saucers. That is because they look at this passage physically. This ascension of Elijah, like the ascension of Christ in the cloud into heaven, is the "withdrawal" from the external or physical world, to the inmost reality of all. This can be referred to as ecstasy, rapture, or transport and is a result of the Holy Spirit. Ecstasy, rapture, or transport all designate a feeling or state of intense, often extreme mental and emotional exaltation. Rapture is defined as ecstatic joy or delight; joyful ecstasy. Some of the synonyms of rapture are bliss, beatitude, transport, and exultation. The true rapture is therefore one in which one is spiritually transported to the heavens. Don't expect to float up into the sky.

Marijuana, as history has shown, is the catalyst used to achieve the spiritual journey into the heavens. That is why in India it was referred to as the Heavenly-Guide, the Poor Man's Heaven, and the Sky-flier. That is why Professor Mircea Eliade, perhaps the foremost authority on the history of religion, suggested that Zoroaster may have caused hemp to bridge the metaphysical gap between heaven and earth.

The dictionary definition of marijuana above refers to the inducing of euphoria. Euphoria is defined by the same dictionary as great happiness or bliss. (In India, marijuana has been referred to as the joy-giver and the soother of grief.)

Bliss is defined as the ecstasy of salvation, spiritual joy. Some of the synonyms of bliss are beatitude, transport, rapture, ecstasy, paradise, heaven.

Throughout the ancient world there is mention of "magical flight," "ascent to heaven," and "mystical journey." All these mythological and folk traditions have their point of departure in an ideology and technique of ecstasy that implies "journey in spirit."

The pilgrimage from earth to heaven is not a journey to some other place or some other time, but a journey within. One must realize that "death," through which we must pass before God can be seen, does not lie ahead of us in time. Rather it is now that we have a man of sin within us that must be killed and a new man free from sin that must be born. This is actualized in baptism and the sacramental life in the church. "For as many of you as have been baptized into Christ have put on Christ." (Galatians 3:27) The effect of baptism is spiritual regeneration or rebirth, whereby one is "en-Christened," involving both union with Christ and remission of sins. In Titus 3:5 baptism is the "bath of regeneration" accompanying renewal by the Spirit. Some of the synonyms of regeneration are beatification, conversion, sanctification, salvation, inspiration, bread of life, Body and Blood of Christ.

Again, Sara Benetowa, quoted in *The Book of Grass*:

> "By comparing the old Slavic word "Kepati' and the Russian "Kupati' with the Scythian "cannabis' Shrader developed and justified Meringer's supposition that there is a link between the Scythian baths and Russian vapour baths. In the entire Orient even today to "go to the bath' means not only to accomplish an act of purification and enjoy a pleasure, but also to fulfil the divine law. Vambery calls "bath' any club in which the members play checkers, drink coffee, and smoke hashish or tobacco."

St. Matthew's account of the institution of the Eucharist attaches to the Eucharist cup these words: "Drink of it, all of, for this is the blood of the covenant, which is poured out for many for the remission of sins." (St. Matthew 26:27). Drinking the sacramental cup therefore serves like baptism (Acts 2:38), where Peter said unto them, "Repent, and be baptized every one of you in the name of Jesus Christ for the remission of sins, and ye shall receive the gift of the Holy Spirit." We of the Ethiopian Zion Coptic Church declare a three-part doctrine of the Holy Herb, the Holy Word, and the Holy Man (Woman).

The present and future benefits to the individual communicant have their importance given them by Jesus, who said, "He who eats my flesh and drinks my blood has eternal life, and I will raise them up at the last day." (John 6:54) As such we must see that the divine person who is active in creation, in renewal, and in human rebirth and resurrection, is also active in the Eucharist.

There was a profound change in America when marijuana smoking started on a large scale in the late 1960s. A large number of people resisted the draft, resisted the war...started letting their hair and beards grow...became interested in natural foods, the ecology and the environment. What we really saw was the awakening of our generation to the beginning of Christian mentality through marijuana smoking. The earmarks of this mentality are: I don't want to go to war; I really don't want to be part of the political-military-economic fiasco you call society.

Like the Indian's Hemp Drug Commission three quarters of a century earlier, the Canadian Le Dain Commission conducted an inquiry into the use of marijuana. On page 156 of their report is the following:

In the case of cannabis, the positive points which are claimed for it include the following: It is a relaxant; it is disinhibiting; it increases self-confidence and the feeling of creativity (whether justified by creative results or not); it increases sensual awareness and appreciation; it facilitates self acceptance and in this way makes it easier to accept others; it serves a sacramental function in promoting a sense of spiritual community among users; it is a shared pleasure; because it is illicit and the object of strong disapproval from those who are, by and large, opposed to social change, it is a symbol of protest and a means of strengthening the sense of identity among those who are strongly critical of certain aspects of our society and value structure today."

On page 144 of the Report, marijuana is associated with peace:

In our conversation with [students and young people] they have frequently contrasted marijuana and alcohol effects to describe the former as a drug of peace, a drug that reduces tendencies to aggression while suggesting that the latter drug produces hostile, aggressive behavior. Thus marijuana is seen as particularly appropriate to a generation that emphasizes peace and is, in many ways, anticompetitive.

An article by G. S. Chopra entitled "Man and Marijuana" deals with Human Experiments. One hundred persons with an established marijuana smoking habit smoked marijuana. They described the symptoms as follows: "I have done things today which I usually dislike but which I rather enjoyed doing today." "Nothing seemed impossible to accomplish." "I assumed a cool and composed attitude and forgot all mental worries." "I behaved in a childish and foolish manner." "It relieves sense of fatigue and gives rise to feelings of happiness." "I feel like laughing." "My head is dizzy." "I feel like taking more food." "The world is gay around me." "I feel inclined to work." "I am a friend to all and have no enemy in the world."

According to the *Encyclopaedia Britannica,* in its discussion of Roman Catholicism:

> To understand the meaning and use of the Eucharist we must see it as an act of universal worship, of cooperation, of association else it loses the greater part of its significance. Neither in Roman Catholic nor in Protestant Eucharistic practice does the sacrament retain much of the symbolism of Christian unity, which clearly it has. Originally, the symbolism was that of a community meal, an accepted social symbol of community throughout the whole of human culture.

Marijuana has been used as a sacrifice, a sacrament, a ritual fumigant (incense), a goodwill offering, and as a means of communing with the divine spirit. It has been used to seal treaties; friendships; solemn, binding agreements; and to legitimize covenants. It has been used as a traditional defence against evil and in purification. It has been used in divinations (1. the art or practice that seeks to foresee or foretell future events or discover hidden knowledge; 2. unusual insight; intuitive perception.) It has been used in remembrance of the dead and praised for its medicinal properties.

Most Christians agree that participation in the Eucharist is supposed to enhance and deepen communion of believers not only with Christ but also with one another. We must therefore ask the question, "What substance did the ancients use as a community meal to facilitate communion with the Lord?" The answer to that question is marijuana. Hemp as originally used in religious ritual, temple activities, and tribal rites, involved groups of worshippers rather than the solitary individual. The pleasurable psychoactive effects were then, as now, communal experiences.

Practically every major religion and culture of the ancient world utilized marijuana as part of their religious observance. Marijuana was the ambrosia of the ancient world. It was the food, drink, and perfume of the gods. It was used by the Africans, the Egyptians, the Assyrians, the Asians, the Europeans, and possibly the Indians of the Americas. Would it be too much to suggest that the ancient Israelites also utilized marijuana?

The following information was taken from the most authoritative books dealing with the history of marijuana.

Marijuana in Historical Cultures
Marijuana in India

In Indian tradition marijuana is associated with immortality; in Hindu mythology Amrita means immortality; also, the ambrosial drink which produced it. There is a complex myth of the churning of the Ocean of Milk by the gods, their joint act of creation. They were in search of Amrita, the elixir of eternal life. When the gods, helped by demons, churned the ocean to obtain Amrita, one of the resulting nectars was cannabis. After churning the ocean, the demons attempted to gain control of Amrita (marijuana), but the gods were able to prevent this seizure, giving cannabis the name Vijaya ("victory") to commemorate their success.

Other ancient Indian names for marijuana were "sacred grass," "hero leaved," "joy," "rejoicer," "desired in the three worlds," "gods' food," "fountain of pleasures," and "Shiva's plant." Early Indian legends maintained that the angel of mankind lived in the leaves of the marijuana plant. It was so sacred that it was reputed to deter evil and cleanse its user of sin. In Hindu mythology hemp is a holy plant given to man for the "welfare of mankind" and is considered to be one of the divine nectars able to give man anything from good health, to long life, to visions of the gods. Nectar is defined as the fabled drink of the gods.

Tradition maintains that when nectar or Amrita dropped from heaven, cannabis sprouted from it. In India hemp is made into a drink and is reputed to be the favorite drink of Indra (the King of Indian gods.) Tradition maintains that the god Indra gave marijuana to the people so that they might attain elevated states of consciousness, delight in worldly joy, and enjoy freedom from fear. According to Hindu legends, Shiva The Supreme God of many Hindu sects, had some family squabble and went off to the fields. He sat under a hemp plant so as to be sheltered from the heat of the sun and happened to eat some of its leaves. He felt so refreshed from the hemp plant that it became his favorite food, and that is how he got his title, the Lord of Bhang.

Cannabis is mentioned as a medicinal and magical plant as well as a "sacred grass" in the Atharva Veda (dated 2000–1400 B.C.) It also calls hemp one of the five kingdoms of herbs that release us from anxiety, and refers to hemp as a "source of happiness," "joy-giver" and "liberator." Although the holy books, the Shastras, forbid the worship of the plant, it has been venerated and used as a sacrifice to the deities. Indian tradition, writing, and belief is that Siddhartha (the Buddha), used and ate nothing but hemp and its seeds for six years prior to announcing (discovering) his truths and becoming the Buddha.

Cannabis held a preeminent place in the Tantric religion that evolved in Tibet in the seventh century A.D. Tantrism was a religion based on fear of demons. To combat the demonic threat to the world, the people sought protection in plants such as cannabis, which were set afire to overcome evil forces.

In the tenth century A.D. hemp was extolled as indracanna, the "food of the gods." A fifteenth-century document refers to cannabis as "light-hearted" and "joy-full," and claimed that among its virtues are "astringency," "heat," "speech-giving," "inspiration of mental powers," "excitability" and the capacity to "remove wind and phlegm."

Today in the Tantric Buddhism of the Himalayas of Tibet, cannabis plays a very significant role in the meditative ritual to facilitate deep meditation and height-en awareness. In modern India it is taken at Hindu and Sikh temples and Mohammedan shrines. Among fakirs (Hindu ascetics) bhang is viewed as the giver of long life and a means of communion with the divine spirit. Like his Hindu broth-er, the Musalman fakir reveres bhang as the lengthener of life and the freer from the bonds of self.

At the turn of the twentieth century, the Indian Hemp Drugs Commission set up to study the use of hemp in India reported the following:

It is inevitable that temperaments would be found to whom the quickening spirit of bhang is the spirit of freedom and knowledge. In the ecstasy of bhang the spark of the Eternal in man turns into the light the murkiness of matter... Bhang is the Joy-giver, the Sky-filler, the Heavenly- Guide, the Poor Man's Heaven. The Soother of Grief... No god or man is as good as the religious drinker of bhang... The supporting power of bhang has brought many a Hindu family safe through the miseries of famine. To forbid or even seriously restrict the use of so gracious an herb as the hemp would cause widespread suffering and annoyance and to large bands of worshipped ascetics, deep-seated anger. It would rob the people of a solace on discomfort, of a cure in sickness, of a guardian whose gracious protection saves them from the attacks of evil influences.

Marijuana in China

Hemp was so highly regarded in ancient China that the Chinese called their country "the land of mulberry and hemp." Hemp was a symbol of power over evil and in emperor Shen Nung's pharmacopoeia it was known as the "liberator of sin." The Chinese believed that the legendary Shen Nung first taught the cultivation of hemp in the twenty-eighth century B.C. Shen Nung is credited with developing the sciences of medicine from the curative power of plants. So highly regarded was Shen Nung that he was deified and today he is regarded as the Father of Chinese medicine. Shen Nung was also regarded as the Lord of Fire. He sacrificed on T'ai Shan, a mountain of hoary antiquity.

A statement in the Pen-ts'ao Ching of some significance is that cannabis "grows along rivers and valleys at T'ai-shan, but it is now common everywhere." Mount T'ai is in Shangtung Province, where the cultivation of the hemp plant is still intensive to this day. Whether or not this early attribution indicates the actual geographic origin of the cultivation of the cannabis plant remains to be seen

A Chinese Taoist priest wrote in the fifth century B.C. that cannabis was used in combination with Ginseng to set forward time in order to reveal future events. It is recorded that the Taoist recommended the addition of cannabis to their incense burners in the first century A.D. and that the effects thus produced were highly regarded as a means of achieving immortality. In the early Chinese Taoist ritual the fumes and odors of incense burners were said to have produced a mystic exaltation and contribution to well-being.

Like the practice of medicine around the world, early Chinese doctoring was based on the concept of demons. The only way to cure the sick was to drive out the demons. The early priest doctors used marijuana stalks into which snake-like figures were carved. Standing over the body of the stricken patient, his cannabis stalk poised to strike, the priest pounded the bed and commanded the demon to be gone. The cannabis stalk with the snake carved on it was the forerunner to the sign of modern medicine (the staff with the entwined serpents).

Marijuana in Japan

Hemp was used in ancient Japan in ceremonial purification rites and for driving away evil spirits. Shinto priests used a gohei, a short stick with undyed hemp fibers (for purity) attached to one end. According to Shinto beliefs, evil and purity cannot exist alongside one another, and so by waving the gohei (purity) above someone's head the evil spirit inside him would be driven away. Clothes made of hemp were especially worn during formal and religious ceremonies because of hemp's traditional association with purity.

Marijuana in Ancient Iran

Ancient Iran was the source for the great Persian Empire; Iran is located slightly to the northeast of the ancient kingdoms of Sumeria, Babylonia, and Assyria. According to Mircea Eliade, "Shamanistic ecstasy induced by hemp smoke was known in ancient Iran." Professor Eliade has suggested that Zoroaster, the Persian prophet, said to have written the Zend-Avesta, was a user of hemp. In the Zend-Avesta hemp occupies the first place in a list of 10,000 medicinal plants.

One of the few surviving books of the Zend-Avesta, called the Venidad, "The Law Against Demons," calls bhanga (marijuana) Zoroaster's "good narcotic," and tells of two mortals who were transported in soul to the heavens where, upon drinking from a cup of bhang, they had the highest mysteries revealed to them. Professor Eliade has theorized that Zoroaster may have used hemp to bridge the metaphysical gap between heaven and earth.

Marijuana in Ancient Egypt

In *Plants of the Gods: Origin of Hallucinogenic Use* by Richard E. Schultes and Albert Hofman, (p. 72), it is stated that specimens of marijuana nearly 4,000 years old have turned up in an Egyptian site and that in ancient Thebes the plant was made into a drink.

Marijuana in Europe

According to Nikolaas J. van der Merwe in the Department of Archaeology at the University of Cape Town, South Africa, the peasants of Europe have been using cannabis as medicine, ritual material, and to smoke or chew as far back as oral traditions go.

Marijuana was an integral part of the Scythian cult of the dead wherein homage was paid to the memory of their departed leaders. As mentioned earlier in chapter 2, evidence of this use of cannabis was found in frozen Scythian tombs dated from 500 to 300 B.C. Along with the cannabis a miniature tripod-like tent over a copper censer was found in which the sacred plant was burned.

It is interesting to note that two extraordinary rugs were also found in the frozen Scythian tombs. One rug had a border frieze with a repeated image of a horseman approaching the Great Goddess who holds the "Tree of Life" in one hand and raises the other hand in welcome.

Marijuana in Africa

The African continent is probably the zone showing the widest prevalence of hemp usage. When white men first went to Africa, marijuana was part of the native way of life. Africa was a continent of marijuana cultures where marijuana was an integral part of religious ceremony. The Africans were observed inhaling the smoke from piles of smoldering hemp. Some of these piles had been placed upon altars. The Africans also utilized pipes. The African Dagga (marijuana) cults believed that Holy Cannabis was brought to earth by the gods. (Throughout the ancient world Ethiopia was considered the home of the gods.)

In south central Africa, marijuana is held to be sacred and is connected with many religious and social customs. Marijuana is regarded by some sects as a magic plant possessing the power of universal protection against all injury to life, and is symbolic of peace and friendship. Certain tribes consider hemp use a duty.

The earliest evidence for cannabis smoking in Africa outside of Egypt comes from fourteenth-century Ethiopia, where two ceramic smoking-pipe bowls containing traces of cannabis were excavated. In many parts of East Africa, especially near Lake Victoria (the source for the Nile), hemp smoking and hashish snuffing cults still exist.

Marijuana in the New World

According to Richard L. Lingeman in his book *Drugs from A to Z* (p. 146), "Marijuana smoking was known by the Indians before Columbus." After the Spanish conquest in 1521 the Spaniards recorded that the Aztecs used marijuana.

The present day Cuna Indians of Panama use marijuana as a sacred herb and the Cora Indians of the Sierra Madre Occidental of Mexico smoke marijuana in the course of their sacred ceremonies.

In *Ritual Use of Cannabis Sativa L* by William A Emboden, Jr., (pp. 229, 231), we find the following:

A particularly interesting account of a Tepehua (no relationship to "Tepecana") Indian ceremony with cannabis was published in 1963 by the Mexican ethnologist Roberto William Garcia of the University of Veracruz, northernmost branch of the Maya language family. In his account of Teehua religion and ritual, William Garcia describes in some detail a communal curing ceremony focused on a plant called santa rose, "The Herb Which Makes One Speak," which he identified botanically as Cannabis Sativa: According to Garcia it is worshipped as an earth deity and is thought to be alive and comparable to a piece of the heart of God.

Marijuana Use by Muslims

It is interesting to note that the use of hemp was not prohibited by Mohammed (570–632 A.D.) while the use of alcohol was. Muslims considered hemp as a "Holy Plant" and medieval Arab doctors considered hemp as a sacred medicine which they called, among other names, kannab. The Sufis, a Muslim sect originating in eighth-century Persia, used hashish as a means of stimulating mystical consciousness and appreciation of the nature of Allah. To the Sufis, eating hashish was "an act of worship." They maintained that hashish gave them otherwise unattainable insights into themselves and a deeper understanding, and that it made them feel witty. They also claimed that it gave happiness, reduced anxiety and worry, and increased music appreciation.

According to one Arab legend Haydar, the Persian founder of the religious order of Sufi, came across the cannabis plant while wandering in the Persian mountains. Usually a reserved and silent man, when he returned to his monastery after eating some cannabis leaves, his disciples were amazed at how talkative and animated (full of spirit) he seemed. After cajoling Haydar into telling them what he had done to make him feel so happy, his disciples went out into the mountains and tried the cannabis themselves. So it was, according to the legend, that the Sufis came to know the pleasures of hashish. (Introduction, *A Comprehensive Guide to Cannabis Literature* by Earnest Abel)

Summary

Due to the prosecution of God's church from the beginning of the Christian era and due to the persecution against marijuana, the true understanding of the Eucharist has remained hidden from Christendom and the world, only to be revealed in these times, the culmination of all human history.

We of the Ethiopian Zion Coptic Church declare marijuana for the communion of saints, the forgiveness of sins, and for the resurrection of mankind. The fruits of the mystery are remembrance of the passions and death of Christ, propitiation for sins, defense against temptation, and the indwelling of Christ in the faithful.

Preparations for communion consist of confession of sins, fasting from sin, and reconciliation with all mankind. As such the participant in the Eucharist will be in a condition in which prayer and meditation are easy and fruitful. He will find his emotion purified and stimulated, his spirituality quickened and his heart filled with love.

What the Bible Says

The following interpretations are not necessarily the views of either the author or the publisher. They are chosen to provoke thought and discussion and were the subject of a Christian fellowship debate. They are shown here to allow equal representation of views and exercise the freedom of opinion.

No prohibitions of cannabis or any other drug is made in the Ten Command-ments. (Exodus 20:1-17)

Cannabis is mentioned in Exodus 30-23 but, as we saw earlier in this chapter, *King James* mistranslated it as "sweet calamus."

Moreover, the Lord spake unto Moses saying, Take thou also unto thee principal spices of pure myrrh five hundred shekels, and of sweet cinnamon half so much, even 250 shekels, and of the qaneh-bosm [Cannabis] 250 shekels, and of cassia 500 shekels, after the shekel of the sanctuary, and pour of oil olive on him and thou shalt make it an oil of holy anointment, an ointment compound after the art of the apothecary: It shall be a holy anointing oil and thou shalt anoint a tabernacle of the congregation therewith, and the ark of the testimony and the table and all the vessels, and the candlestick with all vessels, and the alter of incense, and the altar of burnt offerings with all his vessels, and the laver and his foot. And thou shalt sanctify them, that they may be most holy; whatsoever toucheth them shall be holy — (Exodus 30:22-29)

NOTE: As one shekel equals approximately 0.5 oz. (16.4 g), this means that the THC from over nine pounds of flowering cannabis tops were extracted into hind, about 15. gal. (6.5 L) of oil. The entheogenic effects of such solution, even when applied topically, would have been intense.

The Lord said unto me, "I will take my rest and I will consider in my dwelling place like a clear heat upon the herbs and like a cloud of dew in the heat of the harvest. For afore the harvest, when the bud is perfect and the sour grape is ripening in the flower, he shall cut off the sprigs with pruning hooks and take away and cut down the branches.' — (Isaih 18:4–5)

Jesus began his public life by miraculously turning water into wine at the wedding of *Cana* (John 2:1–10). when the reception ran out. The Bible distinguished then between use and misuse of substance. It says:

Give strong drink unto him that is ready to perish and wine unto those that be of heavy hearts. (Proverbs 31:6–7) but Woe unto them that...follow strong drink; that continue until night, till wine inflame them! — (Isiah 5:10)

Yet the simple joys of drinking were also sung:

He causeth the grass to grow for the cattle, and the herb for the service of man: that he may bring forth food out of the earth; And wine that maketh glad heart of man and oil to make his face to shineth. — (Psalm 104:14–15)

Jesus Speaks of Choices

He said not to criticize other people for their habits. "Not that which goeth into the mouth defileth a man; that which come out of the mouth defileth a man." (Mathew 15:11) The apostle Paul wrote, "I know, and am persuaded by the Lord Jesus that there is nothing unclean of itself: but to him that esteemeth anything to be unclean to him it is unclean. For the Kingdom of God is not meat and drink; but righteousness, and peace, and joy in the Holy Ghost." (Romans 14:14, 17)

Can this Reference Support the Fight to Decriminalize Cannabis Use?

Blessed are the peacemakers. (Matthew 5:9) Believers must concede that God created all things and told mankind to use "Every Green Herb on Earth." The Bible speaks of mercy, healing and a persecution of God's children. "They persecute me wrongfully; help thou me." (Psalms 119:86) Prisons and drug wars do not save souls. "The Lord hath sent me to bind up the broken hearted to proclaim liberty to the captive and the opening of the prison to them that are bound." (Isiah 61:1)

The Need to Search for Truth and Knowledge

The world needs to learn more about cannabis before it can be judged faithfully. This includes those that proclaim laws against its use and those who condone it. Should the Church support the use of cannabis? "My people are destroyed for lack of knowledge; because you have rejected knowledge, I will also eject you, that you'll be no priest to Me, for I desired mercy and not sacrifice." (Hosea 4:6, 6:6) "Remember: Every creature of God is good, and nothing to be refused if it be received with thanksgiving. If thou put the brethren in remembrance of these things, thou shalt be a good minister of Jesus Christ, nourished up in the words of faith and of good doctrine." (1 Timothy 4:4–6)

What Is the Word of God on the Cannabis Plant?

Consider the foregoing; do you think that the Bible might be saying that God created hemp for people to use as "meat" (i.e., to consume), that its seed oil be used as an ointment and that cannabis is "to be received with thanksgiving of them which believe and know the truth"? Paul has also warned that "some people would speak lies in hypocrisy" and prohibit us from using it. The Bible might suggest also that we "shall not bear false witness" about people who use cannabis nor judge them because that judgement is reserved for the Lord. The Lord hates those who speak lies and sow discord among brethren. For those people harassed and imprisoned for using cannabis rightfully, Jesus offers those words of comfort, "Blessed are those persecuted for righteousness' sake: For theirs is the Kingdom of Heaven."

Jesus chose to break the law of the land to heal the sick; should we then break our laws to give our sick the benefits gained from Marijuana?

At that time Jesus went on the Sabbath day through the corn, and his disciples were hungered, and began to pluck the ears of corn, and to eat. But when the Pharisees saw it they said unto him, Behold thy disciples do that which is not lawful to do upon the Sabbath day. But he said unto them. Have ye not read what David did, when he was hungered, and thy, that were with him? And behold there was a man which had his hand withered, and they ask him, is it lawful to heal on the Sabbath days? That they might accuse him, and he said unto them "what man shall there be among you who shall have but one sheep, and if it falls into a pit on Sabbath day will he not lay hold on it and lift it out? How much then is a man better than a sheep? Wherefore it is lawful to do well on the Sabbath days. Then saith He to the man, Stretch forth thine hand, and he stretched it forth: and it was restored whole, like as the other. Then the Pharisees went out, and he held a council against him, how they might destroy him. But when Jesus knew it, he withdrew himself from thence, and great multitudes followed him, and he healed them all and charged them that they should not maketh him known. — (Matthew 12:1-2, 10-16. See also Mark 3, Luke 13 and John 9).

Was the Following a Valid Reference to Cannabis and Genetic Crops?

Then came to Jesus scribes and Pharisees, whom were of Jerusalem saying. "Why do thy disciples transgress the tradition of the elders? For they wash not their hands when they eat bread." But He answered and said unto them "Why do ye also transgress the commandments of God by your tradition? Ye Hypocrites." Then came his disciples and said unto Him "Knowest thou that the Pharisees were offended after they heard this saying." But he answered and said "Every plant which my Heavenly Father hath not planted, shall be rooted up. Let them alone: they be blind leaders of the blind and if the blind lead the blind, both shall fall into the ditch." (Matthew 15:1-3, 7, 12-14)

Passages from the King James Bible that may be relevant to the legal and moral status of Cannabis Sativa L.

And the earth brought forth grass and herb yielding seed after its own kind, and the tree yielding fruit, whose seed was in itself, after its kind: and God saw that it was good. — (Genesis 1:12)

God said "Behold I have given you every herb bearing seed which is upon the face of the earth, and in every tree is the fruit of a tree yielding seed; to you it shall be meat, and to every beast of the earth, and to every fowl of the air, and to everything that creepeth upon the earth, wherein there's life, I have given every green herb for meat and it is so' and God saw everything that he had made, and behold, it was very good. And the evening and the morning were the sixth day. — (Genesis 1:29-31)

The Bible predicts some herbs' prohibition:

Now the Spirit speaketh expressly, that in the latter times, some shall...speak lies in hypocrisy...commanding to abstain from meats which God hath created to be received with thanksgiving of them which believe and know the truth. — (1 Timothy 4:1-3)

The Bible speaks of a special plant:

I will raise up for them a plant of renown, and they shall be no more consumed with hunger in the land, neither bear the shame of the heathen any more. — (Ezekiel 34:29)

On either side of the river, was there the tree of life, which bare 12 manner of fruits, and yielding her fruit every month; and the leaves of the tree were for the healing of the nations. — (Revelations 22:1-2)

What about Cannabis Today?

Hemp today has thousands of uses. Modern technology has devised many new uses for the hemp plant, like biomass energy, building materials, fuel, plastic and so on. Hemp is ecological and its seed is among the best food crops on Earth. Selected varieties produce flowers that provide an herbal relaxant and a spiritual tool. Its herb is used globally as medicine.

On the Ruling of the People

Jesus said to keep church and state apart. "Render therefore unto Caesar the things which be Caesar's and unto God the things which be God's." (Luke 20:25) As we have seen, it was God, not government, who gave man the herbs to use. And it was government that put Jesus to death.

Remember: Every creature of God is good, and nothing to be refused if it be received with thanksgiving.... If thou put the brethren in remembrance of these things, thou shalt be a good minister of Jesus Christ, nourished up in the words of faith and of good doctrine. (1 Timothy 4:4-6). As a result, people at various locations across the United States have had to risk and suffer years in prison for providing medical marijuana to patients as an act of compassion and personal conscience.

What would Jesus do? He chose to break the law in order to heal the sick.

Should People Give Blind Obedience to Government?

See Matthew 15:1-3, 7, 12-14, and Psalm 104:14-15, above

> Now the Spirit speaketh expressly, that in the latter times, some shall depart from the faith, giving heed to seducing spirits, and doctrines of devils; Speaking lies in hypocrisy; having their conscience seared with a hot iron; Forbidding to marry, and commanding to abstain from meats which God hath created to be received with thanksgiving of them which believe and know the truth. For every creature of God is good, and nothing to be refused if it be received with thanksgiving: For it is sanctified by the word of God and prayer. If thou put the brethren in remembrance of these things, thou shalt be a good minister of Jesus Christ, nourished up in the words of faith and of good doctrine, whereupon thou hast attained. — (1 Timothy 4:1-6)

21

Salvia: The Legal Drug

I felt I should include the following information on the drug Salvia, which is a drug progressively being used worldwide. At the current time THIS DRUG IS COMPLETELY LEGAL ALL OVER the world with the exception of Australia. When you read about the effects of the drug and the warnings given by experienced users, you'll sit and scratch your head wondering why Salvia is legal and marijuana is not. Let me make it quite clear that the following information is included in the book as a comparison and not to encourage its use, although you should be aware of much of the information given here if you are going to try the drug. Possibly the information and experiences I describe may dissuade you from experimenting with Salvia, as the experience can be disturbing. Knowledge of drugs and their affect allows you to make an informed decision.

The following information was provided by Daniel Siebert and it's passed on to you freely to share.

The Salvia Divinorum User's Guide

Perhaps a friend gave you a *Salvia divinorum* cutting, or maybe you bought dried leaves, an extract, or a living plant. If so, you need to read this guide. It was written to teach you how to work with this herb in a way that is personally rewarding, and how to do so as safely as possible. It will also teach you how to grow and care for your own *Salvia divinorum* plants. Many more people are trying *Salvia divinorum* now than were doing so several years ago. It is becoming both popular and controversial. *Salvia divinorum* is a powerful visionary herb—it is no placebo. But Salvia is unique. It is not "legal acid." It is not "legal pot." It is not a substitute for any other drug. It is not an analogue of any other drug. It is extremely important that you know about its effects, its possible dangers, and how to avoid the dangers before trying it. Do **NOT** use Salvia until you have read through this guide. NO MATTER WHAT OTHER DRUGS YOU MAY HAVE EVER USED, THEY DO NOT PREPARE YOU FOR SALVIA. SALVIA IS UNIQUE. Salvia has much to offer: fascinating psychoactive effects, sensual enhancement, magical journeys, enchantment, apparent time travel, philosophical insights, spiritual experiences, and perhaps even healing and divination—but Salvia is intolerant of ignorance. If it is used stupidly it can turn on you. By learning what is written here you can avoid serious trouble.

Salvia Divinorum Basics

Salvia divinorum is a species of sage (the genus *Salvia*). There are approximately 1,000 species of sage worldwide, but *Salvia divinorum* is the only vision-inducing species known. Salvia is a member of a very large family of plants known as the Labiatae. Because mint is a well-known member of this family, it is sometimes referred to as the mint family. *Salvia divinorum* makes a beautiful house plant, and it can be grown just for that reason, but most people who grow this plant are interested in its fascinating psychoactive effects.

The botanical name *Salvia divinorum* means "Sage of the Diviners." Under the right conditions, taken in the right way, Salvia produces a unique state of "divine inebriation." For hundreds of years, it has been used in religious and healing ceremonies by the Mazatec Indians, who live in the province of Oaxaca, in Mexico.

The effects of Salvia are very different from those of alcohol; but like alcohol, it impairs coordination. **NEVER, EVER, ATTEMPT TO DRIVE UNDER THE INFLUENCE OF SALVIA—DOING SO COULD PROVE FATAL!**

In many ways *Salvia divinorum* is in a class by itself. No other herb or drug is really very much like it. It is misleading to compare it to other psychoactive substances. It is a truly unique visionary herb.

Salvia contains a chemical substance called Salvinorin-A (often referred to just as Salvinorin). Salvinorin is responsible for Salvia's mind-altering effects. It is not chemically related to any other psychoactive drug. Unlike most visionary compounds, it is not an alkaloid. Although it is not habit forming, pure Salvinorin is extremely strong. Doses of only several hundred micrograms (millionths of a gram) will have an effect, and doses above 1 milligram (1/1000 of a gram) are too much for most people to handle comfortably. Because of its extreme potency, Salvinorin should never be used unless the dosage has been precisely measured with extremely accurate chemist's scales. Fortunately, Salvia leaf is hundreds of times weaker than pure Salvinorin; therefore, Salvia leaf can be used much more safely than pure Salvinorin.

Salvia leaf is physically quite safe. It is very gentle on the body. No one has ever died from a Salvia overdose. Salvia is not a stimulant, it is not a sedative, it is not a narcotic, and it is not a tranquillizer. Like many entheogens, it can induce visions, yet it is quite different from other entheogens. Dale Pendell, in his book *Pharmako/Poeia,* assigns *Salvia divinorum* to a unique pharmacological class, which he calls "existentia." This term alludes to the philosophical illumination salvia seems to shine on the nature of existence itself. Daniel Siebert has proposed the term *enchantogen*—a neologism meaning "a substance that produces enchantment."

Salvia Is Not a Party Drug

It is important to understand the fact that Salvia is NOT a party drug. Salvia is not "fun" in the way that alcohol or cannabis can be. If you try to party with Salvia you probably will not have a good experience.

Salvia is a consciousness-changing herb that can be used in a vision quest, or in a healing ritual. In the right setting, Salvia makes it possible to see visions. It is an herb with a long tradition of sacred use. It is useful for deep meditation. It is best taken in a quiet, nearly dark room; either alone (if a sitter will not be used—see below for discussion of sitters), or with one or two good friends present. It should be taken either in silence or (sometimes) with soft pleasant music playing.

Current Legal Status (as of January, 2006)

Salvia divinorum and its active principal Salvinorin-A are legal substances in the United States, Europe, and most other countries. To the best of my knowledge, Australia is the only country that has passed legislation making S. divinorum and Salvinorin-A illegal. This Australian law goes into effect June 1, 2002. Anyone living in Australia or its territories who is considering being involved with this plant or its products in any fashion after May 31, 2002 is urged to first obtain professional legal advice. Readers are urged NOT to ship *Salvia divinorum,* or products made from it, to Australia or its territories because the person who receives the shipment could face severe criminal penalties.

Throughout the United States and Europe, *Salvia divinorum* remains entirely legal to grow and posses, and there are no restrictions on buying, selling, or ingesting the plant or extracts produced from it.

Salvia Trips: What to Expect

Salvia trips range in intensity from subtle to extremely powerful. This holds true for chewed leaves and smoked leaves, and for oral tinctures, such as Sage Goddess Emerald Essence®. The strength of the trip will depend on how much you take, the way you take it, and your individual body chemistry.

Salvia trips differ from those produced by other visionary drugs or herbs, and Salvia has many advantages:

• You cannot take a fatal overdose of Salvia leaves.

• Salvia is not habit forming.

• Salvia is legal in most countries.

• Its effects are brief in duration, so you quickly return to normal.

• Salvia seldom produces adverse side-effects or hangover.

Noise and distraction will interfere with the trip. When on Salvia, watching TV is nothing but annoying; sitting around a campfire in the woods at night is wonderful.

Because *Salvia divinorum* can alter perception and behavior, it must never be used in a public environment—doing so would draw unwelcome attention.

Especially if you are not used to it, or are taking a potent preparation like an extract, you should have a sober babysitter there to make sure that you don't do something dangerous, like knocking over lit candles, or walking out a window.

When Salvia is smoked the effects come on very quickly: in less than a minute. When it is chewed the first effects come on at about 15 minutes, with full effects at about 30 minutes. If taken as a tincture held in your mouth, the effects come on in 15 minutes or less. Usually a Salvia trip lasts from 15 minutes to an hour. Occasionally trips may last up to 2 hours. To be on the safe side, it is important not to drive or use machinery for several hours after the trip appears to have ended.

Most people have no hangover from Salvia; however, some people sometimes report a mild headache. If Salvia is smoked the smoke may irritate your lungs.

Salvia trips seem to occur in levels. The so-called S-A-L-V-I-A scale has been constructed to rate trips. Each letter of the word *SALVIA* stands for another level of tripping. The scale describes six different levels of intoxication, each one more intense than the previous. The overall intensity of Salvia trips is scored according to the highest scale level attained during the course of the trip.

S-A-L-V-I-A Trip Rating Scale

Level 1—S stands for SUBTLE effects. A feeling that "something" is happening, although it is difficult to say just what. Relaxation and increased sensual appreciation may be noted. This mild level is useful for meditation and may facilitate sexual pleasure.

Level 2—A stands for ALTERED perception. Colors and textures are more pronounced. Appreciation of music may be enhanced. Space may appear of greater or lesser depth than usual, but visions do not occur at this level. Thinking becomes less logical, and more playful; short-term memory difficulties may be noted.

Level 3—L stands for LIGHT visionary state. Closed-eye visuals (clear imagery with eyes closed: fractal patterns, vine-like and geometric patterns, visions of objects and designs). The imagery is often two dimensional. If open-eyed visual effects occur, these are usually vague and fleeting. At this level, phenomena similar to the hypnagogic phenomena that some people experience at sleep onset occur. At this level, visions are experienced as "eye candy" but are not confused with reality.

Level 4—V stands for VIVID visionary state. Complex, three-dimensional, realistic-appearing scenes occur. Sometimes voices may be heard. With eyes open, contact with consensual reality will not be entirely lost, but when you close your eyes you may forget about consensus reality and enter completely into a dreamlike scene. Shamanistic journeying to other lands—foreign or imaginary; encounters with beings (entities, spirits) or travels to other ages may occur. You may even live the life of another person. At this level you have entered the shaman's world. Or if you prefer: you are in "dreamtime." With eyes closed, you experience fantasies (dreamlike happenings with a story line to them). So long as your eyes are closed you may believe they are really occurring. This differs from the "eye candy" closed-eye imagery, of level 3.

Level 5—I stands for IMMATERIAL existence. At this level one may no longer be aware of having a body. Consciousness remains and some thought processes are still lucid, but one becomes completely involved in inner experience and loses all contact with consensual reality. Individuality may be lost; one experiences merging with God/dess, mind, universal consciousness, or bizarre fusions with other objects—real or imagined (e.g., experiences such as merging with a wall or piece of furniture). At this level it is impossible to function in consensual reality, but unfortunately some people do not remain still but move around in this befuddled state. For this reason a sitter is essential to ensure the safety of someone voyaging to these deep levels. To the person experiencing this, the phenomenon may be terrifying or exceedingly pleasant; but to an outside observer the individual may appear confused or disoriented.

Level 6—A stands for AMNESIC effects. At this stage, either consciousness is lost, or at least one is unable to later recall what one experienced. The individual may fall, or remain immobile or thrash around; somnambulistic behavior may occur. Injuries can be sustained without pain being felt; on awakening, the individual will have no recollection of what he/she did, experienced, or said in level 6. People cannot recall what they experience in this very deep trance state. This is not a desirable level, because nothing can latter be recalled of the experience.

Methods of Use
Salvia is never taken by injection. There are many different methods of use. Several will be discussed here.

Traditional Mazatec Methods
The two traditional Mazatec methods are quite inefficient in that they require many more leaves than do the other methods. But they are very safe. Traditionally the leaves are taken in a semi-darkened room as part of a healing or religious ceremony. At least one sober person is present to watch over the people who have taken Salvia. A water-based drink made from ground-up fresh leaves is one of the traditional Mazatec ways of using this herb. It requires a lot of leaves and tastes somewhat unpleasant, so this method is seldom used by non-Mazatecs. Salvinorin is very poorly absorbed from the stomach so it requires enormous amounts of leaves to make the drink effective. But it does work, and trips from the drink last longer than from any other method. Chewing and swallowing a large number of fresh leaves is the other Mazatec method. When this is done the leaves

are nibbled slowly for about half an hour. Although the chewed-up leaves are swallowed, most of the effect is due to Salvinorin that is absorbed through the tissues of the mouth during the chewing. This is a less efficient way of chewing Salvia than the quid method (see below). Most people find chewing and swallowing fresh leaves to be unpleasantly bitter, and for some, it causes gagging.

Modern Methods: The Quid Method

A ball or cylinder of rolled-up leaves is made. This is called a quid. It is to be chewed. The leaves are chewed slowly—about one chew every ten seconds. They are kept under your tongue between chews. For half an hour keep the quid that is being chewed, and the juice that forms, in your mouth. If you can, hold it in your mouth without spitting or swallowing. Then, after the half-hour chewing time is over, spit it all out. Have a bowl to spit into, and a towel handy. Salvia juice stains carpets and other fabrics, so be sure the bowl won't tip over.

Quids can be made from either fresh leaves or dried leaves. Those made from dry leaves are less bitter. To make a quid from dried leaves, weigh out 0.07–0.3 oz. (2–8 g) of dried leaves. A gram scale accurate enough for this can be purchased for under US $50(£25). If you have no scale, count out 8–28 large whole dried leaves. Place the leaves in a small bowl of cool water. Once the leaves are wet and have been soaking for about 10 minutes, remove the leaves from the water, squeeze the excess water out of them, and ball them up into a quid. Some people skip this soaking step when they are in a hurry, but chewing on brittle dry leaves may be unpleasant. If you wish, you can sweeten the quid with sugar, honey, Stevia extract or an artificial sweetener like Equal®. This will make it less bitter and more pleasant to chew.

If fresh leaves are used instead of dry ones, you'll need from 8–28 large fresh leaves.

The effect of Salvia quids can probably be increased by first treating your mouth in a special way to increase its ability to absorb Salvinorin. To do this you'll need a toothbrush and an alcohol/menthol-containing mouthwash such as Cool Mint Listerine®, (or any other brand that contains alcohol and menthol). Gently brush the lining of your mouth, including the tissue under your tongue, and the top surface of your tongue. This removes layers of dead cells normally present. Do not brush hard enough to cause bleeding. Then rinse with the mouthwash for at least 30 seconds. Be sure to get mouthwash everywhere in your mouth, including under your tongue. Then spit out the mouthwash and rinse once with water.

You will experience very little in the first 12–15 minutes of chewing, but don't be misled by this. Full effects are usually felt by 30 minutes (the time you spit out the quid). They remain on this level for about 20 minutes more, then start to decrease. The whole trip seldom lasts much longer than an hour and a quarter, but this varies.

Smoking

Dried leaves can be smoked in a pipe. They need to be smoked hot and the smoke must be inhaled deeply and quickly to have an effect. Because Salvinorin requires high temperatures to vaporize, it is best to hold a flame immediately above the leaves, drawing it down into the leaves the whole time you inhale. The leaves can be smoked in a short-stemmed tobacco pipe, in a bong, or in a "steamroller" pipe. Fill up a medium size bowl with leaves. Use a handheld butane lighter that will go out when you are no longer pressing it, not a match. Have a large ashtray or tip-proof bowl to set the pipe in when you feel you've had enough. Remember that when tripping you may forget you are holding a lit pipe. You could drop it, causing a burn or a fire; therefore, it is best to have a sitter present when smoking. First effects will be noticed within a minute of inhaling. After 5–6 minutes the effects will gradually begin to subside. The total duration of the trip may be less than 30 minutes or as long as an hour.

Extract-enhanced leaves can also be smoked. Extract-enhanced leaves can be very strong and should only be smoked when a sitter is present. It is possible to vaporize leaves or extract in a special vaporizer that heats up material without burning it. Vaporization can be deceiving. Because very little smoke is produced, it is possible to inhale a very large dose without realizing it. Anyone trying vaporization absolutely MUST have a sitter present. Many commercial vaporizers made for cannabis will not work for Salvia. Special Salvia vaporizers can be built easily, but vaporization is not for those new to Salvia.

Vaporization of pure Salvinorin is also possible. It is definitely not for beginners! Unless the dose has been measured very precisely, this is extremely dangerous, as it's very easy to vaporize too large a dose. To be done safely, vaporization of Salvinorin requires weighing the dose on a very precise chemical balance capable of weighing Salvinorin in micrograms (millionths of a gram). These analytical balances cost well over $1000 but there are now available standardized doses of Salvinorin on leaves. Using such preparations enables one to inhale a known, precisely measured dose of Salvinorin. This allows someone to experiment with Salvinorin without having to buy an analytical balance, and greatly reduces the risk of overdose.

There is now a commercially available Salvia tincture. It is marketed by Daniel Siebert as "Sage Goddess Emerald Essence®." This fluid extract of *Salvia divinorum* is intended to be kept in one's mouth until its Salvinorin content has been absorbed. While it can be taken undiluted, it is quite irritating to the mouth if taken in this way. The irritation is due to its high alcohol content. It is better to take it diluted with hot water. The amount of alcohol taken even in a large dose of the extract is not sufficient to produce alcohol intoxication. The effect of the tincture is that of Salvia, not that of whiskey. The alcohol is in the tincture solely as a solvent. The tincture comes with two droppers, one for the tincture, and a different one for the hot water. It also comes with detailed instructions regarding its use and appropriate dosage. A simple method of using the extract is to dispense the measured dose into a small glass such as a shot glass and then add an approximately equal volume of water that has been heated to the temperature at which one drinks coffee. Immediately after mixing the two, sip the contents of the shot glass, and hold it in your mouth without swallowing. Keep your tongue elevated above the floor of your mouth to allow the sublingual tissues (those under the tongue) to absorb the Salvinorin. This means keeping the liquid in your mouth until either the desired effect has been reached or half an hour has passed. Then swallow it or spit it out, whichever you wish.

Which Method Is Best?

There are pros and cons to each method. Some people report that a quid gives a stronger, deeper, more visionary trip than smoking. Others report that chewing doesn't work for them at all, but smoking does. For those who get little effect from either method, the two methods can be combined. First chew a quid, and then, after spitting it out, light up. If you already smoke tobacco or cannabis you'll probably be comfortable with smoking Salvia. If you are a nonsmoker you'll probably prefer the quid method. Bear in mind that smoking anything, even Salvia, can't be good for your lungs. Unlike smoke, orally consumed Salvia does not irritate your lungs.

It requires quite a bit more dried leaf for a quid trip than for a smoke trip. If you have very little leaf material available, smoking is the way to get a trip out of the little you have.

Quid trips come on slowly but last longer. They are better for exploring Salvia's world. They are better for deep meditation.

Salvia tincture (e.g. "Sage Goddess Emerald Essence®") has the same effects as a quid trip, however the dosage can be adjusted more precisely, the effects come on somewhat faster, and holding the not unpleasant tasting tincture in one's mouth is much nicer than holding chewed-up leaves in your mouth. The only side effects reported that are unique to the tincture have been "burning" of the lining of one's mouth. This occurs if the alcohol in the tincture has not been sufficiently diluted. It may leave one's mouth mildly sore the next day, in much the way that it would be if you drank soup that was scalding hot. This problem can be prevented by diluting the tincture with enough water.

Until you know how sensitive to Salvia you are, do not experiment with extracts, vaporizers, or Salvinorin. Chewing quid, using tincture, or smoking leaves will take many people all the way to level five. There is no need for these people to experiment with stronger and more dangerous ways of taking Salvia.

There are some people—albeit a minority—who, even after many experiments, find they remain "Salvia-hardheads." They never experience more than a slight Salvia effect from smoking, or from a quid. Some of these hardheads will get satisfactory results if they chew a quid, and then immediately smoke after spitting out the quid. Others will find even this ineffective. For them, extract-enhanced leaves are necessary to produce effects. See how sensitive you are before experimenting with stronger forms of Salvia. With a little practice, quid chewing, or smoking, or combining the two ("boosting"), works quite well for most people. Many people find it takes several meetings with Salvia before a "breakthrough" experience occurs. So don't label yourself a "Salvia-hardhead" too soon.

Sitters and Safety
When Do You Need a Sitter?
A sitter is absolutely essential if you are taking doses on which you may freak out, become confused, injure yourself, fall, set your house on fire, or do anything that might harm others. Have a sitter present if you are new to Salvia, are experimenting with a stronger form than you have used before, or are using a more powerful way of taking it.

An experienced Salvia user who is chewing a quid may often choose to do it alone, and may be quite safe in doing so. But having a pleasant, sensible, sober sitter is an absolute must if you are trying vaporization, smoking extract-enhanced leaves, or using pure Salvinorin. Smoking leaves usually falls in between in terms of risk. Many people do so without a sitter, but a sitter is never a bad idea. Use sound judgment.

What a Sitter Should Know and Do

The sitter must remember that no matter how crazy the tripper acts, Salvia trips are short lived. Don't take the tripper to the emergency room (unless, of course, there is a true medical emergency). Keep the person safe and wait it out. If you can't keep the person safe, get help. Otherwise keep the matter private. Within an hour or so (usually much less) the tripper will be back to normal. It's very reassuring to hold on to this knowledge if things get messy. It helps to have experienced Salvia yourself before babysitting another person. Experience with other visionary materials may be only partially helpful. The sitter should know that Salvia is different from these. Touching to "ground the tripper" works for some trippers on some entheogens, but may be very threatening for someone on Salvia. If you plan on touching, clear it with the tripper BEFORE the trip starts.

The Roles of the Sitter

The sitter has three essential jobs. The most important of these is to keep the tripper, and others who may be present, safe. This comes before all else. The main danger is accidental injury. Your job is to be a gentle guardian. Be as unobtrusive as possible, but remain alert in case the tripper should suddenly start moving about recklessly. Do not use physical force unless nothing else will do. Use of physical force may result in the tripper or you getting hurt. It could be misinterpreted as an assault. NEVER LET SALVIA BE USED WHERE FIREARMS, KNIVES, OR OTHER DANGEROUS OBJECTS ARE PRESENT. Take the tripper's car keys for safe keeping before the trip starts. Keep the tripper safe from falls, head banging, sharp objects, walking into walls, walking into furniture, walking through windows, wandering out into the street or other public areas, open flames, hot surfaces, and breakable objects. But let the tripper move about in a safe area. Do not grab or try to physically restrain him/her, unless absolutely necessary. Redirect, speak softly, gently take dangerous objects away. Use the minimum touching necessary (the confused tripper may think your touching is an assault or rape and react to the imagined danger). You may have to handle unexpected intrusions of strangers and other awkward social situations.

The second job of the sitter is to reassure. Often, simple repeated explanations may help a frightened tripper, e.g., "You're safe, I won't let anything harm you." "You're just having a bad trip, you'll feel better in a few minutes." "Your name is..." "I'm your friend..." If speech is not called for, be silent. Silence is often less threatening to the confused tripper than trying to decipher what a sitter is saying.

The third job of the sitter is to help the tripper later recall the trip. There are several ways. Use a notebook and record all of the tripper's odd doings and sayings. Later you can ask about these. This may help jog the person's memory about what was experienced. Another technique, if the tripper is not too far gone to talk during the trip, is to ask repeatedly "What are you experiencing now?" A notebook, or a tape recorder, can be used to record responses. Since some trippers will prefer that you remain silent and don't record, clear it with the tripper in advance.

Interactions between Salvia and Other Drugs

One should be particularly cautious about combining Salvia with other drugs. As is the case with most drugs, some combinations may interact in unexpected and possibly negative ways.

Many people who are taking regular medications do use Salvia with no adverse effects. Although Salvia appears to be relatively safe when combined with many medications, there probably are some drugs that it should not be combined with. It is important to remember that each individual is unique. The fact that some people do not experience problems with a particular combination does not guarantee that that combination is safe for everyone.

If you must combine Salvia with another drug, you should always do so cautiously. Start with an extremely conservative dose so as to reduce the risk, should a negative reaction occur. If no negative reaction occurs, you can try increasing the dosage slightly on subsequent attempts. Provided that no adverse effects are experienced, you can increase the dose until you obtain the desired level of effects. One should always have an alert, responsible sitter present when experimenting with new combinations. It is important to have someone on hand who can help you, should the need arise.

We are aware of one individual who reported that his breathing became somewhat constricted and labored for several minutes when he smoked Salvia following a high dose of GABA. While it is not certain that this reaction was due to an interaction of the two drugs, it would be prudent to avoid this combination.

The Neurological Mechanism of Action for Salvinorin-A

Salvinorin-A has been identified as a potent, highly selective kappa opioid receptor agonist. Experimental evidence indicates that the psychoactive effects of Salvinorin-A result from its activity at these receptors.

Guidelines for Using Salvia Intelligently and Safely

Salvia divinorum is a remarkably safe herb, provided that it is used in a safe manner. It can produce fascinating experiences that are deeply enriching, provided that it is used intelligently. Please pay careful attention to the following basic safety guidelines:

NEVER USE SALVIA IF GUNS, KNIVES, OR OTHER DANGEROUS OBJECTS ARE WITHIN EASY REACH. NEVER DRIVE WHEN TAKING SALVIA.

Choose the time and place of your trip carefully. Privacy and safety are essential. Be very careful about heights, and open flames such as candles. Do not take Salvia when you may be interrupted by phone calls, visits, pets, children, etc. Turn off your telephone and set your answering machine to silently record incoming calls. You can return the calls in a couple of hours once you are sober.

Give careful thought to how much you'll take, and how you take it.

After all smoking material is safely out, lie down in bed, on a couch, or on a carpet. You are much safer lying down than you would be stumbling around. Stay put for the rest of the trip. You can trip best with your eyes closed.

Have a sitter (this is especially important if you are new to Salvia, taking a high dose, smoking extract, or using a very strong delivery system such as vaporization). Volunteer to be a sitter for others.

If you have mental health problems, don't take Salvia without first discussing it with your therapist, or doctor.

Practice and encourage responsible use. Don't give Salvia to minors, or to violent or unstable people. Don't share it with strangers. Know who you are giving it to and know why they want to use it. Why ask for trouble?

Never take Salvia while at work or in public. Keep it private. It's not for concerts. It is not for raves. It's not for large noisy parties. Better to use it in a quiet safe private place in the company of a few good friends.

Mixing Salvia with other drugs or large amounts of alcohol may cause out-of-control behavior, or terrifying trips. While experienced Salvia users have experimented with combinations, these are not for Salvia beginners, and are certainly riskier than just using Salvia by itself. While there are no known toxic drug-drug interactions between Salvia and anything else, this has not been studied scientifically (see above for a discussion of a possible toxic drug-drug interaction of salvia with GABA).

Be extra careful of flames (candles, lighters, fire, etc.) when using Salvia.

Be very careful about using vaporized extracts, vaporized leaves, or smoking extract enhanced leaves. These require a sitter to be present. Chewing quid or smoking leaves is much less likely to produce out-of-control behavior than these are.

Never use pure Salvinorin unless the dose you are taking has been weighed with an ultra-accurate balance that can weigh out doses in micrograms, and you know exactly how much you can safely take. Even if you do meet these requirements, you still should have a sitter present.

The Plant and Its Care

If you'll be growing your own Salvia, you should read this. If you'll not be growing your own, you may wish to skip this section.

Salvia divinorum is a semitropical perennial. That means that it can grow year after year, but only if it is not exposed to freezing temperatures. It is a green plant with large leaves and a distinctive thick, hollow, square green stem. It can grow several meters (yards) high if conditions are favorable. When it grows high enough, the branches will bend, or break, and may root if they come in contact with moist earth. Although *Salvia divinorum* can flower under natural lighting conditions, it almost never sets seed that will sprout. So the plant is almost always propagated by cuttings. The leaves are oval, weakly notched (serrated) and can be quite large (up to nine inches in length). They are usually emerald green, but under some conditions, may be yellow-green or even yellow. They are covered with a fine coating of extremely short hairs (trichomes), giving the leaves a satin-like velvety appearance in certain lights. The plants grow best in partial shade, in well-watered but well-drained soil. The roots must not be kept constantly soaked, or root-rot will set in and kill the plant.

Salvia divinorum can be grown indoors in any climate. It makes a beautiful houseplant.

You can grow *Salvia divinorum* outdoors all year round if you live in a humid semitropical climate, with soil that is well watered but well drained and high in humus content. If you live in a colder or drier climate, you can still grow Salvia outdoors, weather permitting. But you may have to do it with some care, making sure it is protected from frost, watered frequently, and misted when humidity is low. Salvia will not live through freezing or drought. It can be grown outdoors in pots which can be brought indoors when it is cold (below 40°F or 5°C). That way it can be grown outdoors in summer and indoors in winter.

Salvia will tell you when it is getting too dry: its leaves will droop. Be sure to water it at the first sign of mild drooping—do not let the plant become limp. If planting Salvia in pots, make sure the pot is large enough to allow the plant to grow well. Although your available space will limit possible pot size, use the biggest pot that is practical. It must have drainage holes. Placing gravel (or broken up pieces of crockery) in the bottom of the pot will help promote drainage and thus discourage root-rot. Most commercial potting soil will work well. Adding Vermiculite® or Perlite® to the potting soil is helpful but not essential.

Salvia will need fertilizer. Any good general-purpose fertilizer will work. Fish emulsion is a good organic fertilizer choice, but because it has a very unpleasant odor, it is suitable only for outdoor use. Satisfactory results can be achieved with chemical fertilizer products. Some of them are: Scott's® All-Purpose Plant Food (18-13-13) lightly sprinkled on the soil about once every six weeks; Miracle-Grow® (15-30-15) or MirAcid® (30-10-10) added to the water once a week, 1/4 teaspoons per gallon; Peter's® Professional Soluble Plant Food (15-30-15) 1/4 teaspoons per gallon of water, once per week.

If growing indoors, take the plants outdoors when it is warm enough, and let rain fall on them. This will prevent mineral salts from building up in the soil and killing your plant.

Salvia divinorum can do well in a variety of different lighting conditions. It does best with a few hours of partial sunlight a day. It can do well when grown indoors near a window. It can handle more sun if kept well watered and misted frequently. It can also handle moderately deep shade. When changing the lighting conditions or the humidity conditions your plants are exposed to, do so gradually. Given enough time, Salvia is very adaptable, but it may take weeks to get used to a new environment.

Many pests can attack Salvia. Whitefly is a big problem for greenhouse-grown plants. Aphids, slugs, caterpillars, thrips, spider mites, and scale insects can also damage your plants. Root-rot and stem-rot can be problems. Fungal spots can appear on leaves. It is not known which plant viruses attack *Salvia divinorum*, but probably some do, as many attack other sages.

Aphids and scale insects can be removed with a cotton swab dipped in isopropyl (rubbing) alcohol.

Slug damage can be reduced by growing Salvia in pots on a raised deck or pallet. Some may still get by and attack your plants. Keep an eye out for these slimy pests. One slug can eat an awful lot of Salvia! Beer can be used to attract and drown slugs.

Set a saucer of beer in a slight depression in the ground; the surface of the saucer should be flush with the soil, so slugs can get in, get drunk, and drown.

Spider mites can be controlled by dissolving Castile soap in water and spraying the leaves, including the underside. Repeat at two-week intervals for three applications. Caution: there have been some reports of soap damaging leaves, so don't use too much.

Your garden hose is your best friend in fighting most outdoor pests. Spray the leaves hard enough to blow the pests away, but not hard enough to damage the leaves. Don't forget to spray the underside of the leaves too. A fine mist nozzle works best for this.

Salvia divinorum is usually propagated by cuttings, not by seed. Cuttings may be rooted either in water or directly in soil. For how to do both, see below.

Rooting in Water

Cut off a branch (4–8" or 10–20 cm long)) bearing some leaves. Cut off the leaves that are attached to the lowest node on your cutting, then immediately place it in about 1.5" (4 cm) of water in a small water glass. Only one cutting is to be put in each glass, so if rot develops in one cutting it cannot spread to another.

It is best if the cutting is cut back to just below a node, since nodes are the places from which new roots are most likely to develop. While it is not necessary to make the cut here, doing so has the advantage that there will be no stem material dangling in the water below the node. This is important as the cut stem end is more likely to start to rot than is a node.

Make sure the cutting is made with clean shears, or a knife, so the cut stem does not get attacked by germs and fungi that could cause stem rot. Place it where it'll get some filtered sunlight. Change the water daily. It may be a good idea to use cooled boiled water. If your water is chlorinated, boiling will drive off chlorine. Non-chlorinated water may be contaminated with plant disease germs, but boiling should kill these. Rooting in water is successful about 75% of the time (the rest of the time stem rot occurs and kills the cutting).

In two weeks roots will start to develop. When they are about one-half–one inch long, transplant to potting soil in a well-drained pot. Cover with a clear glass jar or clear plastic bag to serve as a humidity tent until the plant establishes its roots in the soil and appears vigorous (usually one–two weeks). Then gradually wean the plant from dependence on the humidity tent.

Some growers report that Salvia branches that break off spontaneously in summer are more likely to root successfully than those deliberately cut. Rooting in water outdoors may decrease the chance of stem rot occurring—apparently the UV light in unfiltered sunlight acts to kill germs or fungi in the water.

Rooting in Soil

Salvia can be rooted directly in soil. Materials needed:

- potting soil
- two disposable plastic cups
- some Rootone® powder (this is a rooting hormone mixture that also contains a fungicide) available at most nurseries in the United States
- a 1-gal., thin, transparent, polyethylene food storage bag
- a rubber band
- water

Method

Punch some small holes in one of the cups for drainage. Fill the cup two-thirds of the way up with potting soil. Using a pencil or a finger make a hole in the soil about two inches deep. The soil is now ready for your cutting. You must now prepare the cutting. With clean shears, cut off a length of stem from a healthy plant. Leave a few leaves (small ones) on top. Harvest the larger leaves from the cut-off stem. Immediately after cutting the stem, place it in clean water. Cut it back to just below a node, as roots will develop from the node. Keep the cut surface wet. Place the cut surface, and the stem for about one inch above the cut, into the rooting powder. Shake off the excess. Rooting powder is somewhat toxic, so wash your hands after handling it. Place the powder-coated cutting in the hole in the soil. Gently push the soil around the cutting, holding it in place while filling in the hole. Water the planted cutting until some water runs out the drainage holes. Place the cup with the plant in it into the second plastic cup (which is there to catch any runoff water). You may want to put a small piece of wood or plastic in the bottom of the outer cup to act as a spacer. This allows enough space for excess water to drain. Place a 1-gal. clear plastic bag over the rooted cutting, using a rubber band to hold it in place. The rubber band should be outside the bag and the bag outside both cups. The rubber band holds the bag against the cups. As the plastic bag acts to conserve moisture, frequent watering is not required. After several weeks you can transplant the now rooted plant to a larger pot.

Processing Plant Material

Dried *Salvia divinorum* leaves should be stored in sealed containers away from light. Stored this way, the leaves will retain their potency for many, many years, perhaps indefinitely (nobody knows just how long). If you are growing your own, you'll probably want to dry leaves for future use. There are several ways to do this.

Method 1: Nature's Bounty

Wait until the leaves die or are shed. Gather them. Place them on a plate in a room with low humidity. Turn often. Wait until they are dry, then store. It is not known if naturally shed leaves are stronger or weaker than picked leaves.

Advantage: you won't be depriving your plants of leaves it needs.

Disadvantage: you'll have to wait until the plant is ready to make a donation to your cause. Leaves may not be in prime condition.

Method 2: Salvia "Tobacco"

Take big, freshly picked leaves and place one atop another (like stacking sheets of paper). Then cut through the pile, making 1/4" (1/2 cm) strips. Pile these on a plate into a heap. Turn them twice daily until they are dry but not crispy.

Advantage: The resulting "tobacco" is said to give a smoother smoke than thoroughly dried leaves.

Disadvantage: It is possible that this slow partial drying results in weaker leaves that may not keep as long as thoroughly dried (crispy) leaves.

Method 3: Food Dehydrator

Dry in a food dehydrator. These are available where small kitchen appliances are sold. Drying is very fast and thorough. Dry until the leaves, including the leaf stems, are crispy. Touch the leaves with your fingers to see if they are thoroughly dried. If they are, the leaf stems should snap if pressure is applied.

Advantages: Speed, thorough drying, and convenience.

Disadvantage: Cost of buying a dehydrator.

Method 4: Oven-Dried Salvia

Place on an oven-proof dish. Oven dry in an oven set at no more than 175°F (72.5°C).

Advantage: Speed, thorough drying, and convenience.

Disadvantages: Somewhat less convenient than using a food dehydrator. It may be hard to keep oven temperature at an optimal range.

Method 5: Calcium Chloride (CaCl$_2$) Drying

Calcium chloride is available from chemical supply houses, or, as "Damp-Rid" refills, from most hardware stores. Place a sufficient amount of calcium chloride in the bottom of a polyethylene container. Place a piece of aluminum foil over but not touching the CaCl$_2$, and place the leaves to be dried on top of foil. Curling up the edges of the foil should prevent the leaves from touching the CaCl$_2$. Then seal the container. The leaves should be dry in about two days.

Advantage: Very thorough drying.

Disadvantages: Less convenient than other methods. Slow. However you dry the leaves, store them in a sealed jar away from light. A clean glass canning or Mason jar works very well. Storing the jar inside a kitchen cabinet or medicine chest will keep it away from light. Stored this way, leaves will retain their potency for many, many years.

How to Achieve Effects from Smoked Salvia Divinorum

Many people find it difficult to achieve a satisfactory level of effects from the leaf in its natural state.

Here's why: The active principal of *Salvia divinorum* is a diterpenoid compound called Salvinorin-A. The average concentration of Salvinorin-A in *Salvia divinorum* leaves is 2.5 mg/g. A moderate smoked dose of Salvinorin-A for a person of average sensitivity is 0.5 mg. Therefore, in theory 200mg (1/5 of a gram) of *Salvia divinorum* leaves contains enough Salvinorin-A to produce moderate effects. In practice however, one should assume about twice this dose (i.e., 400mg, or 2/5 of a gram), because some Salvinorin-A is probably decomposed during burning, some is lost in smoke that escapes during smoking, and some is not fully absorbed in the lungs and is thus lost upon exhaling.

A 400mg amount of *Salvia divinorum* leaves produces a fair amount of smoke, and it takes several large lungfulls to inhale it all. Because Salvinorin-A is rapidly metabolized in the body, it is essential that the full dose be ingested within a two–three minute period. It is also essential that the smoke is absorbed as efficiently as possible, otherwise much of it will be wasted. People vary in their ability to inhale and retain large amounts of smoke. Some people have no trouble achieving strong effects smoking ordinary leaves; others find it very difficult.

The potency of *Salvia divinorum* leaves is somewhat variable. So far, no one has identified the specific environmental factors responsible for this. Obviously, it is easier to achieve effects when using leaves of higher potency.

People vary in their sensitivity to Salvinorin-A. Some people are highly sensitive and have no difficulty achieving a profound level of effects; others are extremely insensitive and require a dose two–three times higher than average.

Advice

(1) Use a water-cooled smoking device (a water pipe, or bong). This makes it much easier to inhale large quantities of smoke. Because the smoke is cooled, it can be inhaled more comfortably without coughing.

(2) Try to inhale the full dose in three lungfulls. Each one should be inhaled slowly and deeply then held for 20–30 seconds before exhaling. It is very important to retain each inhalation of smoke deeply in the lungs long enough for it to be absorbed efficiently. Do not pause between each lungful (except for a short breath of fresh air if necessary). This insures that the whole dose will be consumed within the two–three minute period required. If the dose is smoked too slowly, it'll be metabolized faster than it is ingested.

(3) Use a "micro-torch" type lighter. Many people report better results when using this type of lighter. These produce a very hot torch-like flame that causes rapid combustion of the smoking material and hence produces more concentrated smoke. Because of the extra heat generated by these devices, it is important to use them in conjunction with a water-cooled smoking device.

(4) Use extract-enhanced leaves (fortified leaves). These products are concentrated, so that the entire dose can be more easily consumed. Some of these products are so refined and concentrated that a full dose produces no more than a tiny wisp of smoke. These products also have a health advantage, since they reduce the amount of smoke that must be ingested to achieve the desired level of effects. One must keep in mind however, that fortified leaves must be used more carefully because of their greater potency. These products do not need to be smoked in a water-cooled pipe.

Some Useful Contacts

IACM (International Association for Cannabis as Medicine)
Telephone: +49-2952-9708571
Website: *www.acmed.org*
Address: Am Mildenweg 6, 59602 Ruethen, Germany

Yahooka www.yahooka.com

NORML (International Organization for the Reform of Marijuana Laws)
Telephone: (202) 483-5500
Website: *www.norml.org*
Address: 1600 K Street, NW Suite 501, Washington DC 20006-2832

MPP (Marijuana Policy Project) www.mpp.org
Incorporated as a nonprofit organization in 1995, MPP works to minimize the harm associated with marijuana — both the consumption of marijuana and the laws that are intended to prohibit such use. MPP focuses on removing criminal penalties for marijuana use, with a particular emphasis on making marijuana medically available to seriously ill people who have the approval of their doctors.

RELEASE (incorporating INCLUSION)
Telephone: 020 7729 9904 (24 hour help line)
Website: *www.release.org.uk*
Address: 388 Old Street, London, England EC1V 9LT

IDMU (Independent Drug Monitoring Unit) www.idmu.co.uk
The main service provided by I.D.M.U. is *expert evidence* to the criminal courts on most aspects of drug misuse, including comment on consumption patterns, valuations, effects, paraphernalia and yields of cannabis cultivation systems. This is based on existing published studies and our own independent research projects

Families anonymous

Telephone: 0845 1200 660 Facsimile: 020 7498 1990

Drug addiction and the family

Address: Doddington & Rollo Community Association, Charlotte Despard Avenue, Battersea, London, England SW11 5HD

DRUGSCOPE

Telephone: 020 7928 1211 Facsimile: 020 7928 1771
Website: *www.drugscope.org.uk*
Address: 32–36 Loman Street, London, England SE1 0EE

THC4MS *www.thc4ms.org.uk*
A volunteer organization for MS sufferers advising and assisting with access to cannabis products to help.

Index

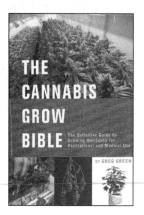